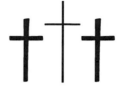

Time and the Biblical Bang

The One Biblical Story from Perspectives
of God's Eternal Nowness

CHARLES ALEXANDER

WESTBOW
PRESS
A DIVISION OF THOMAS NELSON

All Scripture quotations, unless otherwise indicated, are taken from the Holy Bible, The
New Revised Standard Version, NRSV. Published by Thomas Nelson Inc., Nashville,
Tennessee 37214. Copyright © 1989, by the Division of Christian Education of the
National Council of the Churches of Christ in the United States of America.

WestBow Press books may be ordered through booksellers or by contacting:

WestBow Press
A Division of Thomas Nelson
1663 Liberty Drive
Bloomington, IN 47403
www.westbowpress.com
1-(866) 928-1240

Because of the dynamic nature of the Internet, any web addresses or links contained in
this book may have changed since publication and may no longer be valid. The views
expressed in this work are solely those of the author and do not necessarily reflect the
views of the publisher, and the publisher hereby disclaims any responsibility for them.

Any people depicted in stock imagery provided by Thinkstock are models,
and such images are being used for illustrative purposes only.

Certain stock imagery © Thinkstock.

ISBN: 978-1-4497-9490-3 (sc)
ISBN: 978-1-4497-9489-7 (hc)
ISBN: 978-1-4497-9491-0 (e)

Library of Congress Control Number: 2013908524

Printed in the United States of America.

WestBow Press rev. date: 06/03/2013

Dedicated to Mum and
Mom for many years of love and encouragement.

Contents

ACKNOWLEDGMENTS

*I*n thanksgiving to God for Canon Dr. Michael Green, who has inspired me as a friend and in his gifts as a theologian-practitioner.

Ralph Carter, who introduced me to the writings of Dr. Hugh Ross; and Dr. Titus Matthews, former head of physics at the University of Calgary, who gently helped me stay on a track that honored the integrity of both faith and science in their own rights.

Dr. George Egerton, University of British Columbia, who is a great encourager to me and who offered me perceptive advice in preparing the manuscript for this book.

My clergy brothers, John Briscall and John Torley, for many years of unconditional support. Also to the people of St. James's,' Calgary, and The Open Gate Church (formerly St. Mary's), Metchosin, Victoria, who in a variety of ways helped me consider deeper perspectives of the one story of the Bible; and

For my beautiful wife, Verna, who is a wonderful and patient partner in our shared ministry for the gospel of Jesus.

All of these superb people, in their own way, have motivated me to view the biblical story from twenty-first-century perspectives.

Finally, to our glorious Lord God, who woke me on many occasions with insights I didn't understand!

INTRODUCTION

*E*den's joyous dance is an amazing story, and is often not well understood as being one chronicle. From a panoramic perspective, this biblical story often features very ordinary people: they experience moments of ecstatic embrace, they dance the wrong steps, they invent their own steps, they arrogantly ignore the Leader, they despair, they reach great heights, and they plummet to the lowest depths. Their most significant ego-struggles lie in allowing God to take the lead. Nothing has changed very much!

Ultimately, this dance is the story of God's absolute sovereignty. The Lord of the Dance once more leads the right steps while embracing His adoring bride in the arms of His engaging love. In the story of Israel, we will see some astounding conclusions arising from a view of the Bible through a new set of lenses. Instead of looking at the Bible in the light of two covenants, one old and one new, we shall look at the Scripture from the perspective of *three theological seasons.* Coupled with a view that attempts to observe biblical time from the perspective of God's eternal nowness, plus a fresh look at creation theology, the Bible reveals some startling perspectives on some very old questions. Questions of free will, our eternal destiny, natural immortality, the resurrection of Jesus, current issues, and last things may never be observed in the same way again!

Possibly, today is a time closely akin to the days of the building the tower of Babel. No one can stand eyeball to eyeball with God and engage in dialogue with Him on an equal level. We have built enormous towers of knowledge. For some, such attempts symbolize the desire to meet almighty God on their own terms. Paradoxically, we see clearly that the people who may embrace the dance of Eden are those who are willing to bow the knee in worship. We now know that the rate of increase in knowledge is much more than doubling every year. The question is one concerning how well we may use such knowledge. The authentic biblical scholar is intimately acquainted with the one story of the Bible, while enjoying the personal relationship with God of which it speaks. And the world of science is also moving in a much friendlier manner.

Somehow, it would appear that twenty-first-century people are more sophisticated and knowledgeable than were their forebears. Hugh Ross, a Christian astrophysicist, tells us how much the world of physics has changed since the 1990s. Consequently, "the community of scientists now considers the idea that God created the universe a more respectable hypothesis today than at any time in the last hundred years. Denial of theism among astronomers is now rare, and even the few dissenters hint at the strength of the evidence."[1]

My good friend and former parishioner, Dr. Titus Mathews, who is a previous head of physics at the University of Calgary, hastens to remind me that physics and faith are both disciplines in their own right. God cannot be proven through scientific tools. Or, as Mark Worthing also puts it, "neither do I wish to imply that science can 'find' God, that is, conclusively verify either God's existence or nonexistence."[2] However, he does go on to say that the two disciplines need not be entirely divorced from each other. "therefore, any attempt to explicate knowledge of God apart from the structure of space-time that God created is inevitably irrational."[3]

In this book, I will not attempt to violate the tools with which both science and faith operate, but simply help one discipline glean a better understanding from the other. We may well ask, "Is science the only legitimate way to address questions of progress? Is there a credible place for the entire area of biblical revelation?"

In the mid-1960's, Michael Cain starred in a troublesome movie entitled, *What's It All About, Alfie?* It's not simply that Alfie reminds us of the egotistical selfishness within ourselves, but that the story reminds us of certain common failings persisting throughout the entire human story. Reflecting on this thought, I began to wonder if the Bible in some way did the same thing.

Rather than there being two stories, an old and a new, I want to suggest that the Bible is really telling us one story: a story of humanity's response to God's loving initiatives. The story seems to be disjointed at times; nevertheless it is one story.

For example, in the famous "servant" passages of Isaiah 42-53, the suffering servant is identified by the Jewish people as the remnant nation of Israel. A cursory look at such verses as Isaiah 37:31-32, 41:8-9, and 43:1-3, 10 all appear to make Israel's claim that the Old Testament stands alone a credible one.

But is there something much deeper to ponder? We are aware that Matthew directly quotes one famous passage (Isa. 42:1-4) in order to make the point that Jesus Christ really is the unique and prophetic remnant fulfilling the purpose of the entire biblical story (including the New Testament: Matt. 12:17-21). Is it possible that the covenant promises are fully fulfilled in one remnant person? Maybe that one person really is representative of the suffering servant of Isaiah? If the Bible actually speaks of one story, then surely the entire book would begin and end with Jesus as the prime subject.

In order to glean a clearer picture of this proposal, we shall have to view it in the light of God's relation to time itself. We will also need to pursue a basic view of time, particularly as we understand it today. How does God connect Himself with time? What does it mean for God to exist in the eternal present? Our basic questions in this regard, almost incidentally, draw us into some very fascinating areas of questioning.

What about free will and predestination? Is the question really one concerning individual salvation? Is God really a sovereign God? Does He change His nature because of humanity's ever-changing search for meaning in culture? How does our contemporary view of time affect our view of biblical revelation? How does it affect the meaning of the cross and resurrection? Can there really be a place called hell? What is the relation of time to spiritual gifting? How does the meltdown in all of creation's interrelationships affect the way we must think of latter days? Can there be a tangible connection between "It is very good" (Gen. 1: 31) and the biblical view of new creation? (Rev. 21:1-3). It is almost impossible to hold together the idea of there being one story in the Bible without noticing how naturally these questions appear in both parts of the one story.

We will be pursuing the meaning of biblical time by exploring a paradigm. I call it *moments of light*. It will certainly force us to look at the questions mentioned, but many other questions will also emerge.

Physicists persist in their search for a "theory of all things."[4] Similarly, we may ask if it is a futile search when trying to find ultimate meaning in one story of the Bible. Quite possibly, a single theory may be found in this simpler paradigm; this single theory may occur by applying it to the breakdown of creation's relationships. If so, then we ask: What is the place of humans in this primary meltdown? Must we now discard the Bible's basic tenets? And will our exploration of its one story show that the Bible can continue to hold the exalted position it once held?

I will tell the story as one who has been profoundly affected by the discovery of its meaning. But in order to maintain my own credibility, does this mean that I have to admit to a loss of credibility for the Bible? Sometimes the God of fundamentalism holds great difficulty for me.

However, in the writing of this book, I am persuaded more than ever that the Bible holds supreme authority in all matters pertaining to the fundamental claims of the Christian faith. Unlike an Agatha Christie novel, I have decided to lay my cards down at the beginning of the story.

CHAPTER I

Getting on the Same Page

*I*n order to avoid confusion in communication, we will need to have a common understanding of certain terms and concepts. I used to be a journeyman electrician. As in most trades and disciplines, electricians had to learn a common, basic terminology, and also the common purpose associated with a particular task. We had to have an agreed-upon understanding of the words we used and the principles those words conveyed. When things weren't going the way they were intended, and when troubleshooting, electricians usually reverted to an examination of first principles.

For example, if all the lights went off in a large factory room (with the switches on) we didn't examine every individual light bulb. We checked the source first. It was only when we were satisfied that the primary source was intact that we proceeded with an isolation process that would reveal where the problem lay within the system.

Nothing may operate as designed if the parts are not properly connected to the source and to one another. Getting to the root for the analysis and solving of difficulties will be a primary theme throughout this book. In other words, what do we learn from creation principles?

Unfortunately, as Christians, we often focus our thinking upon secondary issues; and often to the detriment of examining our source relationships. Indeed, I suggest that the ignoring of creation's principles is a major problem today.

When expressing divergent views, we must ask: Are we all speaking from the same understanding of gospel principles? (Gal. 1:6-7). It's a very important question for today. To continue with our electrical example, we could say that no matter how much electrical energy we think should be applied to a cooking stove, the conclusion would be quite meaningless if the apparatus in question were really a gas stove! That matter would be a question for people of another field.

If we are speaking about one story in the Bible, not two, we are dealing with unique parameters to the exclusion of others. Let's look at some of the terminology employed in this book.

Moment of Light

The moment of light will figure prominently throughout this book. It's all about what was revealed through certain historical events in the story of Israel and of the new Israel that followed. The term may be likened to the day in the Genesis account of creation.

A moment of light speaks of a datable period (or event) in history at a time of God's appointment. In it, God reveals that the meaning of the event has profound theological significance for the entire story.

It is not so much a matter of the amount of time involved but of the meaning of the event itself. Always in these moments of light, God reveals something of His nature and of His purpose for creation. For example, the incarnation of Jesus Christ may be described as a moment of light. Somewhere back then (at whatever point it was in the process of creation), God said, "Let there be light." We need to know what that event means in terms of God's revelation to us.

Chronos may be defined as the succession of time from one datable point to another. *Kairos* may be defined as a time of God's appointment. For example, chronos is used to identify the specific point in time noted by Matthew for the birth of Jesus (Matt. 2:1). In Galatians 4:4, on the other hand, the apostle Paul tells us that "when the fullness of time had come" i.e., when the time was right (kairos), "God sent His Son into the world."

Both chronos and kairos are very important for our consideration of the term moment of light. But they are not enough to offer the full depth of its meaning. In a wider sense, we are saying that the very structure of this book addresses the idea of theological time from the perspective of three seasons we call creation, redemption, and restoration. In the process, numerous questions will arise. But when our unique term is applied to the entire biblical story, some very exciting perspectives emerge.

Miracle

A miracle may be described as divine involvement during the normal course of nature. God's involvement may not completely conform to the laws of science, knowledge, and reason as we know them. By its very nature, a miracle is always an act "from above" (*anothen* in Greek).

The twenty-five to thirty "fine tunings" physicists identify in the creation process of the earth, or the raising of Jairus's daughter from the dead, are good examples of the miraculous (Mark 5:21-23, 41-42). However, on the one hand, much too much is sloppily attributed to the concept of the miraculous. "Miracle" and "mystery" are not the same word. Sometimes the word "miracle" is assigned to situations that are just simply, extraordinary. On the other hand, both fact and miracle are absolute necessities in the understanding of the gospel story.

We can't appreciate the significant depth of the meaning of miracle unless we ponder why biblical writers insist that miraculous events took place at some points in history. God doesn't play dice with the lives of people. Did He decide who would survive the disastrous earthquake in Haiti, or the sinking of the *Titanic*? Does the answer to such questions satiate the mental pain of those relatives who didn't survive?

Without dismissing the subject, the need for relationships, faith, reason, and fact are all elements that are necessary to understand the gospel story. At least, that's the case if we want to approach the subject with a modicum of integrity. The question of miracle is a pivotal dividing point separating conservative and revisionist thinking today. Indeed, for many revisionists, the acceptance of the very idea of miracle equates with the abdication of independent thought.

Apostolic

We are not limiting the word "apostolic" to a particular order of ministry. For example, long after the death of Jesus, the apostle Paul speaks of ordinary, anointed people being involved in apostolic ministry (Eph. 4:11). The word "apostle" is simply a Greek word (*apostello*) meaning "to send." In that sense, God is apostolic: He is a sending God by reason of His sending His Son into the world (John 3:16). Similarly, Jesus sent His community into the world with an apostolic and universal commission (Matt. 28:19-20). But we read that the sending God had already given an apostolic commission to His children in Eden during the very early days of their creation (Gen. 1:28).

The authority to carry out such an astounding commission would not have been possible unless the Adam-Eve community had also been given the power to perform their task (Gen. 2:7). Similarly, the community of Jesus could not have exercised the necessary power to mission without the personal, charismatic experience of a Pentecost (Luke 24:49).

Sign

The word "sign" refers to an observable substance revealing a reality that it conveys. In the big picture of the gospel, a sign is an act or a situation demonstrating something of the very nature of God and of His kingdom. Whenever we read of signs and wonders in the Bible, we are thinking not only of the nature of life in Eden, but what was once possible to those embracing its ecstatic dance. Wedding rings may well be a visible sign that a man and a woman are committed to a lifelong and exclusive relationship. However, the ring does not convey anything in itself. So if my wife, Verna, lost her wedding ring, she would still be married to me; whether she liked it or not!

If we think of creation as a sign, we see that creation actually conveys that which it promises. For the Christian, Jesus is most certainly not simply a symbol of life and truth. He *is* the Life and the Truth (John 14:6). He conveys all that He signifies by word and action.

So what is the reality we want to signify in this book? The reality is all about the character and life of the kingdom of God, as expressed in essential relationships. What we are to realize throughout the pages of this book is that signs may also appear as moments of light.

Revelation in the context of time

At first sight, the meaning of this word "revelation" seems to be obvious. Its roots are found in the word "apocalypse" (*apokalupto*), which means (according to Moulton's Analytical Greek Lexicon) to reveal or to uncover. (It's the same word used in the name of the last book in the Bible). But the most important consideration in our biblical journey is the question: Where does its revelation originate?

Judeo-Christian revelation is all about how God took the initiative to reveal Himself, and how He has shown something of His own nature in the process.

You may notice that I use the masculine gender to describe God. It's not because God is a man any more than He is a woman! Jesus told us that God is Spirit (John 4:24). Masculine language is often employed for the purpose of making a clear distinction between natural religion and revealed faith. (Nature is thought of in the feminine terms of birthing life). In other words, God is totally independent of the nature He created. Yet Jesus told us to address God as Father (Matt. 6:9). God is not an impersonal force out of *Star Wars*. We don't say "Daddy" to George Lucas's universal "Force."

It's not for us to project our psychological needs onto God. Often, we do so in order to conform Him to our own image (Ps. 115:8). However, we do have to struggle with our understanding of the God who reveals and names Himself. How are we able to name anything that is higher than ourselves? God doesn't have to because there is nothing higher than Himself. (Isa. 45:23). This means we are called to worship Him, as He is, not how we think He ought to be.

We've discovered that such an idea is one of the marks of natural religion, and that is why, all too often, when we begin our thinking from natural bases, truth (or God) becomes whatever a particular culture or individual desires it to be. That kind of thinking sits well with the postmodern mind.

It's important, right from the beginning, to make a distinction between a view of revelation emanating from natural thought (good old Mother Nature) and the revelation that reveals something of the nature of our eternal God. Also, we consider how the revelation is made manifest by *God's own initiative*. Distinctions may not always appear to be simple because God created good old Mother Nature anyway. For example, if I made a robot which looked like me, it would let an observer see something of who I am, but, fortunately, not a great deal. Creation does tell us something about God, but the very nature and character of God requires significantly more tested inspiration than watching stars on a clear night.

The Bible does admit to the fact that something of God's nature can be seen in His creation. For example, the psalmist said, "The heavens are telling the glory of God; and the firmament proclaims his handiwork" (Ps. 19:1)

Elsewhere, King David ponders the thought:

> O Lord, our Sovereign,
>> how majestic is your name in all the earth!
>
> ... [W]hat are human beings that you are mindful of
>> them, mortals that you care for them?
>
> Yet you have made them a little lower than God,
>> and crowned them with glory and honor.
> You have given them dominion over the works of your
>> hands; you have put all things under their feet.
>> (Ps. 8:1, 4-6)

God's wonderful mountain-cathedrals, or the verdant streams meandering through rolling pasturelands, are clearly not sufficient to reveal to us all that God wants us to know of His nature and character. And it is that knowledge that guides us into a deeper relationship with Him.

However, nature does tell us something of God, and also His love for beauty and order.

Natural religion

From the very beginnings of civilization, humans have needed to grapple with forces they didn't understand or control. People figured that some sort of force was responsible for the activity experienced in nature, whether good or bad. Every force, like lightning for instance, was associated with a particular deity.

In other words, nothing happened unless some god made it possible. So the Anglo-Saxons said that the deity Thor (the name from which we get "Thursday") was responsible for the lightning bolts that zapped their turkeys. Fear gets into the picture quite quickly. This vast multitude of natural deities falls under the category of polytheism.

Natural religion must be raised once more when we consider methods whereby we interpret God's revelation today. What we see in natural religion is that humans not only fear unknown forces, but they tend to produce gods that look, feel, act, or smell like something they know from nature, including themselves. One example is the incident in which God is credited with using a utilitarian and deceitful method to secure His purposes (1 Kings 22:19-23). This literal interpretation may well conform to the anthropomorphic character of natural deities. (The process of God's self-revelation was still rolling.)

But is this anthropomorphic deity really consistent with the nature of the God whom Jesus revealed?

This is a question we must constantly ask when reading about God in the Old Testament. Clearly, there are instances when the God whom Jesus reveals is *not* consistent with some earlier biblical views. For example, rather than following a deity who calls us to annihilate our enemies (Josh. 10:40), Jesus tells us to love our enemies (Matt. 5:44). The Bible records a gradual progression of how God reveals His own nature. This revelation is made complete in the Word become flesh (John 1:14). We will also see that Jesus really shakes people up when they can't get past nature, or even their own aspirations, in trying to explain the character of God.

Because there were so many unmanageable forces, natural religion was polytheistic. The rather sophisticated Roman authorities persecuted

Jews and Christians because the Romans said they were *atheists*. They weren't, of course, but it's true that they didn't believe in the many Roman gods, only one God—making them monotheists.

Natural Religion and Manipulation

Natural religion wasn't about submission to whatever the deities wanted; it was about getting them to do what you wanted. How did their believers do that? By bribing the gods! It was all *manipulation*. Tickle the gods and they will oblige.

So from the very beginning, we see the use of two forms of sacrifice. Both were designed to create appeasement. One was the offering of nature's produce, such as fruit and vegetables. The other was the offering of a life, like Mama's clucking chicken or Mike's yapping billy goat.

Of course, good old Mother Nature represented new life, fertility, reproduction, a good harvest this fall, and a cute baby next spring. After all, in a simple agricultural society such as early polytheists knew, that was what life was all about. There was a simple and natural dimension to natural religions. Everything was cyclical. The seasons came and went in predictable order, and the sun came up every morning. Birthing, new life, harvesting, maturity, and the cycles of nature often took on a feminine dimension. Natural religion, therefore, usually possessed an inherently feminine characteristic.

Revealed faith

Not surprisingly, when culture or natural religion is the source and determiner of truth, we are led to believe that the truth concerning the nature of deity is naturally related to contemporary situations and community needs. Everything becomes relative to something else.

In the world of ideas, the same principle is in vogue. There are no absolutes. (Does that sound familiar?) By their very nature, absolutes cannot be defined; hence there is a need for revelation, not natural aspiration. Determining the nature of these deities becomes a little complicated, and also contradictory. That's especially true when we realize that cultural values change about every eighteen to twenty years in the Western world.

In the West, we loudly herald those relative principles to decry the possibility that there may be absolute truths or values. This denial may be aided by the moguls of the media, who promote a globalized set of individual values over social values. Such globalized values offer no barriers to the moguls' singular goal of international trade. Political values (i.e., "political correctness") rather than religious absolutes serve to put every value on the same level of truth.

If we are to avoid the temptation to make God in our own image, we have to struggle with an integrity that desires to pursue the way in which God chooses to reveal Himself. We need to know something of the *manner* in which He decides to name Himself (Gen. 22:16; Ex. 3:14). To name a deity gives the worshipper some degree of control over the deity. How are we thinking if we believe we can name God?

Recognizing such problems in the bases of natural religions, Judeo-Christian writers put forward a number of reasons why God is described in the masculine. Masculine language is employed for the purpose of making a clear distinction between natural religion and revealed faith.

In other words, God is totally independent of the nature He has created. God eternally transcends nature. He does not reflect the nature of creation; it is creation that may or may not reflect God's nature. Biblical literature shows us that God acts in both masculine and feminine ways. Clearly, we can't just label God with a characteristic or gender that suits us at any particular point in a constantly evolving culture.

The Self-naming God reveals His own requirements to be consistent with His nature; they are designed to keep us in relationship with Him and with others.

This concept of the morality of personal relationships is a huge dividing point between natural religion and revealed faith. Not surprisingly, the apostle Paul shows us how faith, based in nature, may easily lead mortals in exactly the wrong direction:

> For the wrath of God is revealed from heaven against
> all ungodliness and wickedness of those who by their

wickedness suppress the truth. For what can be known about God is plain to them, because God has shown it to them. Ever since the creation of the world his eternal power and divine nature, invisible though they are, have been understood and seen through the things he has made. So they are without excuse . . . Claiming to be wise, they became fools; and they exchanged the glory of the immortal God for images resembling a mortal human being or birds or four-footed animals or reptiles. (Rom. 1:18-21, 22-23)

The Bible as revelation

When trying to put together crucial elements that provide a big picture of the biblical story, some aspects of this story will not receive a lot of attention. For example, there may well be two different traditions that speak about the creation. Many scholars are of the opinion that, roughly, chapters 1 and 2 of Genesis have different sources. They were written at separate times in history by people desiring to express a particular aspect of God's revelation. Therefore, priests would emphasize something about the importance of sacrifice, while prophets would stress something of God's revealed Word to His people.

In this vein, the writer of Genesis 1 records what God actually *did* in creation; then the book proceeds to introduce the human factor into the harmonious equation. The second chapter, probably written by another person, is much more about relations with God and with others.

In terms of our present purpose in outlining the one story, I don't think that anything of significance is lost by not addressing questions concerning who wrote what and when. This is a lesser problem when we consider that many of our problems of biblical interpretation lie precisely at the door of ignorance concerning the meaning and claims of the bigger story that unfolds.

It is precisely at this point that we see a strange paradox appearing. It is possible to observe some biblical students who know a great deal about the Bible, but who do not appear to laud the basic experience and relationship with God, through Christ, to be important. After all, the biblical story places such a relationship at its very core!

There are many scholars who suggest Moses could not possibly have written the entire Pentateuch (the first five books of the Bible). They make a good point. For example, how could he have written about his own death, or humbly declared himself to be the greatest prophet of all time? (Deut. 34:10).

Regardless of who wrote or edited these five books, we may well understand why they are attributed to Moses. Scholars are now rethinking the enormous power of the oral tradition of ancient days. This tradition has lost sway for many in our modern, Western culture. Nevertheless, we need to appreciate the care and power of it in another age. AH

A very fine scholar, Peter Craigie, who was a good friend of mine until he went to be with the Lord, offered this simple principle of interpretation. "In such a context, it is necessary to stress that ultimately the authority of the books of the Law is to be found in their source in God-that is, in their character as revelation."[1] Craigie, a brilliant Old Testament professor, was fully aware of, but not overly distracted by questions of authorship.

It is in this vein that we cursorily note apparent contradictions, such as 1 Samuel 31:4-5 when compared with 2 Samuel 1:6-10 (how did Saul die?), or Matthew 27:5 with Acts 1:18 (how did Judas die?). Clearly, a variety of traditions have helped biblical compilers to glean a bigger picture.

Our concern is not so much with various traditions that may or may not have given us the Bible. Our interest is in what the community has received and has recorded as being an important contribution to the whole revelation of the one story.

The church community has accepted a final canon of Scripture that has left us with an impressive, real, and consistent gospel story that is supported by the facts of history.

In terms of the knowledge of God, maybe a good way to explain this process of revelation is by way of an orange simile. It's a good way of reconciling the god of war (who is so apparent in the Old Testament) with the more peace-loving God of Jesus.

If we begin to take off some of an orange's peel, we see a little of the orange underneath. We know something of its texture and character. The more we continue to peel, the more of the orange is revealed. Eventually, all of the orange is exposed. But the orange does not change in the process of peeling.

At some point this simile breaks down. One very important factor is that most of the peeling is done by the Self-revealing God Himself. In His fullness, God can never completely be known. Only God can fully know God. For us, He is ultimately unknowable (1 Cor. 2:10-11). The creature can never aspire to the full knowledge of the Creator.

However, Jesus did say that if you have seen Him, you have seen the Father (John 14:9). In other words, if you want to know God, then you need to know Jesus. It's not the other way around. The Word of God is a Person; and that Word is Christ (John 1:1). In this sense we may say, without equivocation that the Bible records the infallible purposes of the sovereign God in the revelation of His activity through the story of creation, redemption, and restoration. (Isa. 46:10).

How we think of the Bible as revelation

I am not using the word "story" as if it refers to some sort of historical collection of scientific data, but in reference to a continuing saga of a community as they celebrated the meaning of their dance with God. It is a story intended to be passed on.

Peoples of different cultures and times tell of their fundamental beliefs and values in a variety of ways. When we consider this, we must begin to read the Bible from the perspective of a Jewish person desiring to communicate matters of importance. The fact is that the Jewish people believed God revealed certain fundamentals by becoming involved in their history.

In other words, the Bible is really a Jewish story, and is told in a Jewish way.

The Jewish tradition doesn't express itself in the same way as the Greek (or Western) custom. "Specifically, their world was not one dominated by rationalistic philosophy, although the emergence of classical philosophy was taking place in the Greek world in the latter half of the Old Testament period."[2]

At his bar Mitzvah, a contemporary Jewish boy recites a story that begins with the words, "My father was a wandering Aramaean . . ." He knows who he is because he is part of an historical chronicle. The God whom he believes in is active in the Jewish story. There isn't a great deal of philosophy involved here.

A notable exception is Gregory Palamas. He was a fourteenth century pietist engaged in the eremitic tradition of the Byzantine church. Having received a first-class education in classical Greek, nevertheless he preferred the spirituality of Hesychasm. This was an approach of earlier desert fathers who had their origins in the fifth century. It was an *apophatic* tradition (negation). Here, there is a lessening of the positive and exclusive use of sense and reason (*kataphatic*). The silent approach to God was much preferred. This was the favored method of the desert fathers in discerning God's self-revelation. "Palamas refused to give any credence to what the ancient philosophers said of the knowledge of God. He developed a realistic doctrine of supernatural knowledge, independent of any sense experience but granted in Jesus Christ to man."[3]

The Greek or Gentile mind was more likely to articulate essentials of life from a rational perspective. Greco-style writers of today are more likely to lean on their analytical inheritance. It was a tradition begun with people like Aristotle and Plato. In answer to the question, "How do you know that God loves you?" a Jewish boy will tell a story, while his Greek friend may debate the relative merits of love through the reasoning of words such as *agape, philia*, and *eros*.

Let's face it. The Greek response is more likely to be the way we moderns of the Western, technocommunication age prefer to think. It's no wonder, when people of this inherited mind-set look at a controversial passage of Scripture, that they often prefer to view it through rational eyes. God didn't reveal Himself to the Jewish people as if He were addressing the nation of Denmark, or a convention of philosophers. A modern Dane doesn't think in the same way as an ancient Jew.

So it's very important for us to get into the heart and mind of the Jewish believer. The Jewish person is a person of memory. He or she knows the meaning of personal identity because of engagement in a common story, which also requires a high degree of intellect in its life-translation.

Judeo-Christian theology is tied to real events of the one story of the Bible. In other words, the essential belief of these two faith communities is tied to verifiable events made possible in moments of light. The best of Jewish scholarship has rarely been divorced from the story of Israel as a community. This will be an important consideration when we trace the nature of authority in the New Testament.

You may want to check out the different techniques the apostle Paul employs when offering his apologetic of the faith. It's almost possible to see his mind shifting gears from when he speaks to the Athenian debaters on Mars Hill (Acts 17:20-34) to when he makes his defense to a hostile Jewish crowd in Jerusalem (Acts 22:1-20).

In the first instance, Paul makes identification with a crowd by starting his address from the basis of natural religious thought. It's very propositional. In the second instance, he immediately identifies with the common Jewish story, and then enlarges upon that story with a Christian application.

Maybe it isn't coincidental that both Jews and Greeks held one irritation in common: the question of Christ's resurrection. We'll certainly get to that later.

Biblical revelation for today

Present day revisionists, governed by principles of an ever-developing social Darwinism, tend to view faith statements in the Bible as emanating from evolutionary processes inspired and transmitted through the mores of culture. Consequently, the word "miracle" rarely enters their vocabulary.

With such a philosophical basis, it isn't surprising that faith statements may be ignored or resymbolized according to the current understandings and values of the culture. On the other hand, a blanket literalist approach (i.e., every word of the Bible has been dictated by God to scribes, prophets, etc.) is likely to produce a more fundamentalist orientation. Of necessity, this method entails a defense of every biblical word and concept as being equally valid and for all time.

A much more difficult but rewarding approach is an historical one that struggles with the methodology Jesus adopted as a Jewish person speaking to Jews.

Jesus wanted to view all biblical thinking in the light of creation principles—that is, in light of what God intended at the beginning. In that light, He expected us to understand the plain sense of what He was saying.

Clearly, He felt that the revealed principles of creation were valid and necessary for all times and cultures, at least in the light of the kingdom principles that creation represents. When a group of Pharisees criticized Christ's disciples for plucking corn on a Sabbath day, Jesus reminded them, "The Sabbath was made for humankind, and not humankind for the Sabbath"(Mark 2:27). Similarly, when confronted with questions on divorce, He immediately focused His questioners back to creation principles (Mark 10:2-6).

This approach was not a license to interpret Scripture in whatever way was convenient, but to struggle with the meaning of the one story, as God intended in the first place. What did His hearers have in mind when Jesus spoke of Jonah being in the belly of a big fish? Were they hearing it as a literal story or as a theological story? Or was it both? Was the deeper meaning of a mythical story based upon real facts of history? The beginning of Jonah 2 suggests it is.

Of course, we are immediately drawn to questions concerning the closed nature of revelation. Does God still speak today? Scholars of a variety of persuasions speak of God continuing to reveal His will and purposes in the present. Some would say that God is a growing God. He is growing in His own nature because He is influenced by the changing insights and attitudes found in His creation. But what does this say about the Judeo-Christian God who knows the beginning from the end? (Isa. 46:10). He is the sovereign God whose creation purposes will not fail.

In a more liberal view of revelation, we observe a God who continues to speak through the varieties and changes of human culture. In that sense, people accept additions to or revisions of the former revelation. From the charismatic point of view, God continues to speak. He may even use changes in knowledge and culture in order to clarify His will. For the charismatic-minded, the revealed voice of prophecy has not become silent.

The conservative and charismatic nature of the gospel reveals God's will without adding to or negating the former, foundational revelation, particularly as found in Jesus. Yes, Copernicus was right. The earth is round and it orbits around the sun. We didn't know that for sure until long after the canon of the Old and New Testaments was agreed upon. But when we understand God's Self-peeling of the orange (fully revealed in Christ Jesus—see John 14:9), such knowledge is easily translated.

Our conclusion here is really quite simple: all revelation that is truly of God will be consistent with His nature, particularly as we continue to see Jesus at the heart of the one story.

A revelation that is truly of God and of fundamental value to the faith never reveals something that is contrary to the revelation passed down by Christ's apostles. For example, what is truly and uniquely a Christian distinction from other monotheistic faiths is that the Christian nature of the one God is, and always has been, Trinitarian. This was clearly new knowledge revealed in Jesus, not a change in God's nature. It was not culture but the Person, who is the Word, who began to lift this veil. New Testament scholars could not avoid this startling revelation. That is why we are part of the apostolic faith.

The nature of God, the revelation of the faith, and the way the faith is relationally acted upon are all intrinsically connected.

Revelation and other religions

Do other faiths claim to possess a book based in revelation? Yes, they do. Furthermore, some of these religions claim that the words of their books were given by direct revelation from God, or by someone very close to Him.

Now, I don't want to get into a harangue about comparisons here; I simply want to raise a point that will be relevant for our purposes. I haven't the slightest intention of demeaning any other book or religion. Let freedom of choice remain. But also let truth prevail.

I'll mention two books here. One is the Qur'an and the other is the Book of Mormon. There are two things common to the understanding of both books:

1. The writer (note, *one* writer in each case) claimed to receive his particular revelation from a messenger of God at a particular time (or period) and in a specific place.
2. Both religions claim that their books represent the final revelation of God and are therefore superior to all older or subsequent religions.

In the first instance, Mohammed, while sitting under a tree (or, some say, in a cave), claimed that he received a visitation or a number of visitations from the angel Gabriel. The period in question was the seventh century AD; it was near a place called Mecca. (The fact that this was but the first of 114 visitations subsequently claimed in Islam does not alter the point.[4])

In the case of the Book of Mormon, Joseph Smith—again, one man in the early nineteenth century—claimed to have received the words from golden plates that were delivered to him by an angelic figure named Moroni. Smith said there were two witnesses, and also that the translation of the mysterious language on the plates took place over three years. The rendition was supposedly made possible by special glasses provided for him. The golden plates and the glasses were then taken back to heaven. It is claimed that these visitations began around the year 1804 in the United States.[5]

The Greek word for "angel" literally means "messenger." However, the seventh-century apparition of Gabriel and the nineteenth-century apparition of Moroni are recorded as angelic figures spending several years *teaching new revelations of new faiths.*

In contrast, the (wingless) first-century spirit figure of Gabriel simply *announces* the forthcoming birth of Jesus (Luke 1:26-38). Similarly, one of the angels appearing to the shepherds *announces* that the baby Jesus will become the universal, messianic Savior (Luke 2:11). Announcing is the job of a messenger relaying the message of his master.

We also note that the Bible is actually a library consisting of sixty-six books (the total of canonical Old and New Testament literature). There are probably at least fifty authors of these books. Also, their writing took place over a period of more than twelve hundred years.

The Bible, as we assert here, is really one story. We are truly amazed by the consistency of the one story that is a revelation of God's workings in creation, redemption, and restoration. No other book in the entire world has received such a measure of scrutiny and criticism. Much of the Bible's documentary evidence is closer to recorded events than that of other reputable books, such as Plato's *Republic*. The Bible's many factual claims are truly amazing and are more easily datable.

A process of revelation

At this point I dare to suggest a simple way of considering what may be a credible process of biblical revelation.

1. The true revelation of God's nature is always revealed by the initiative of God.
Clearly, the parameters of theological thought may be stretched but not broken. However, it is imperative in these days of theological confusion to discern where the boundaries of revealed faith end and where the aspirations of evolving culture begin. There are absolutes in the Christian faith that are not dependent upon cultural processes. Most often, though, God reveals Himself in a particular context and culture.

As such, cultural considerations are not totally divorced from the revelation process. If they were, then what would be the context for the revelation? Often, God speaks through His prophets about real-life situations; in turn, they predict or interpret the events in the light of God's revealed will and purposes. (See Amos 3:7; Heb. 1:1.)

2. The agreed-upon revelation is received as the common experience of the community through which God reveals Himself. As in the beginning, the experience of God was graced into a community. And it was a community that was called to live out its implications. As Christians, we do relate to a book: the Bible. However, the Christian community was not initially founded on the basis of a book. It was a community following a Person (Acts 1:21-23).

Of course, the Person is Jesus. "In the beginning was the Word" (John 1:1). I know from my own personal experience that I was not converted to the relative merits of Christianity, but to Jesus. We read in the first chapter of Acts that when an apostle was chosen to replace Judas, the community's conditions were that he be chosen from among those who had a personal history with Jesus and who had been an eyewitness to His resurrection.

The most essential reality of the faith was given credibility by the factual experience common to its founding community. Without this common experience of an historically understood truth, there would have been a danger of cultic individualism being the major determiner of the faith. (Jesus, as both God and Man and as the subject of the resurrection, stands apart as the focus of the historical faith). The requirements of factual and common experience are good reasons why individually subjective thoughts of poets and mystics have not contributed to the creedal statements of the Christian faith. All revelation is tested in the community according to a common, revealed understanding of the nature of God (2 Pet. 1:20-21).

In the Old Testament, it isn't uncommon for God to reveal Himself to an individual such as the patriarch Abraham or the prophet Jeremiah. But that revelation always is intended to be addressed, tested, and lived out within the life of the community. We observe similar constraints in the New Testament (e.g., 1 Thess. 5:20-21).

Therefore, in the New Testament, it is very difficult, if not impossible, to discern any place where a revelation intended for God's community was exclusively claimed and accepted by one individual. That principle is very important when we consider doctrines that have been added to the first-century church.

In the New Testament, no one is granted exclusive and monarchical authority. Jesus never granted it to one individual. Such authority would fly in the face of the very nature of God existing in the community of the Trinity.

One questionable claim is made of Peter on the basis of Matthew 16:18. However, the similar accounts in Luke 9 and Mark 8 do not make mention of Peter's exclusive authority. Indeed, a careful exegesis of the verse from Matthew attributes monarchical authority to Jesus alone. According to John 20:21-23, it was given to all the apostles equally. Clearly, in that inbreathing of authority, no one is singled out above the other apostles. In refusing to accept lesser apostolic authority than the "super-apostles" (2 Cor. 12:11), Paul refers to the ancient rock (*petros*) of Moses (Ex. 17:6) as being Christ Himself (1 Cor. 10:4). We note that the very same confession was also made by Martha before Jesus raised her brother from the dead (John 11:27). The historical accounts recorded in Mark 8:27-30 and Luke 9:18-20 also make no mention of monarchical authority being granted to Peter.

As in the nature of the Godhead, Jesus did not give superior authority to one person alone, but to *one community*. The Greek word *poreuthentes*, "to go," is a plural word, so the authority to be apostolic was given to Christ's apostles assembled on the mountain (Matt. 28:19-20). And that authority was intrinsically manifested in the character of agape-love that we see enveloped in the words of John 3:16.

3. *The assimilation of written records are discerned in the community; they are recorded, are approved or rejected, on the basis of the authenticity of the community's common experience and revelation of the knowledge of God.*

It was up to the community, not to an individual to discern, gather, and interpret the written record of the historical revelation. The church as a community, particularly in the second century, struggled very hard to discern whether writings claiming to have apostolic authority were genuinely of that period. Many of those writings were Gnostic. The famous criterion for discernment (2 Tim. 3:16-17) was written when the New Testament had not been completed or formally acknowledged. However, Christian "sacred writings" (which were considered to be God breathed in the manner of Gen.2:7) were already being recognized as writings possessing godly authority (e.g., 2 Tim. 2:15; 2 Tim. 3:15-16)

As noted, the written record is not a private revelation given to one person. Recorded revelation has become the common experience of revelation over time. By the end of the first century, there was significant recognition of the documents that later became the canon of the New Testament. That's also a reason why individual Christian mystics and poets have not figured largely in the transmission of basic and essential revelation. In the transmission of the Judeo—Christian faith tradition, individual prophets are subject to tests (1 Thess. 5:20-21).

In some other religious situations, we see that "the book" comes first. For example, in Islam, the Qur'an was given to one man, not to a community. Subsequently, it continues to guide individual adherents of its authority into a common experience.

In the Christian revelation, the Word comes first. It is the Word (the Person of Christ) who reveals *His* words and life to the community. A subsequent, individual forming of the Holy Spirit in revealing the Person and nature of Jesus Christ comes after. All those people who come after the record was produced therefore share personal experience of the resurrected Christ, which parallels and conforms to the experience of the earlier community.

This is what comes first; it is the personal experience of the Person of Jesus Christ. It's all about relationships—that's the gospel. Processes of discipleship are meaningless unless that common experience of the Person of Jesus is a daily experience. "Jesus Christ is Lord, to the glory of the Father" is common experience to the entire historical community. We cannot place the written word above the experience of the community or vice versa. The church cannot be divorced from its belief or its belief from the community. The community of God exists in the playing out of God's revelation.

The Bible and theological language

There are a variety of literary forms used in the biblical story. These forms are often found in the major segments of the Old Testament: the Law, the Prophets, and the Writings. However, literary devices are employed throughout the entire Bible. Usually it is easy to discern literary devices, such as the poetic, apocalyptic, allegorical, analogical, metaphorical, and mythological. Many Westerners are afraid to use the word "mythological" of any biblical content, because they understand its use differently than did those ancient writers. Because of such fear and confusion, I often prefer the term "theological story."

John Stott warns about literary devices when he pleads that readers of the Bible should always look for the natural meaning of a passage. That is, we should seek to discern the meaning that the writer wanted to communicate. "For sometimes the natural meaning is figurative rather than literal."[6] Stott also asks that we try to understand that classical Greek and Hebrew thought forms are expressed in the secular language of the day.

The Bible wasn't written specifically to be a scientific or historical book. However, it's also clear that, whenever a chronology is presented, we are intended to take *time* seriously. The Bible speaks primarily about God, and the fact that language is employed to speak about Him means we are reading language that conveys theology, i.e., reasoning or explanation that attempts to describe something of the nature of God. So all the literary devices the Bible employs are intended to be conveyors of theological truth. Wonderful examples of how this approach more naturally occurs may best be found in the parables of Jesus. He never spoke of His impending death and resurrection as things that were other than factual.

Clearly, the Bible does not specifically answer questions that could not have been posed in the past (e.g., matters of overpopulation or medical ethics). But it does furnish us with sufficient evidence of the nature of God to help the church struggle with how the God of Jesus may want us to deal with such issues.

Concerning authority, some ask the question, "Which has more authority, the Bible or the church?" There is no need to take sides in answering this question. The fact is that the Bible is in the church, and the church is in the Bible. You can't have one without the other.

Some may also ask the question, "Why do Christians need a New Testament?" The answer may be summed up in one simple sentence: if the revelation of God's nature and purposes were complete in the Old Testament, then there would be no need for another.

We will encounter more and similar questions on this biblical journey. Augustine once said that the new is in the old concealed, and the old is in the new revealed. We will have to agree with Augustine if we are able to demonstrate that the Bible is really one story. We are soon to discover how fascinating and exciting God's purposes for creation are, as interlaced throughout the Bible. Quite possibly some considerable new light will be shed on Scripture as we apply our unique paradigm of moments of light.

CHAPTER TWO

It's About Time

Time as the Fourth Dimension

Albert Einstein referred to time as the fourth dimension because of the ways it is related to the three physical dimensions of height, breadth, and width. We're not getting into scientific theories of the bending of space-time, the consistency of the speed of light, or the effects on matter when approaching the speed of light; for our purposes, we don't need to. But we do need to have some appreciation of the nature of time, particularly as it relates to us. Stephen Hawking asks us to remember that "In the theory of relativity there is no unique absolute time, but instead each individual has his own personal measure of time that depends on where he is and how he is moving."[1]

Another way of saying this is that it might take me eight hours to fly to London, but from where you live and at the same speed, you may do it in an hour. On the other hand, if I could travel a hundred times faster than you, then I would be the first to arrive.

Speaking in more absolute terms, Hawking goes on, "The situation, however, is quite different in the general theory of relativity. Space and time are now dynamic quantities: when a body moves, or a force acts, it affects the curvature of space and time, and in turn the structure of space-time affects the way in which bodies move and forces act."[2]

For the purposes of the one story of the Bible and in the world in which we live, there is no need to include this abstract view of time. Nevertheless, we can't achieve our purposes if we are clearly violating basic rules of science—at least, as we know them.

For example, we do know that light travels at the rate of 186,000 miles per second. So if we look at the nearest star through a telescope, we are actually looking at Sirius the way it emitted light four years ago. It takes that long for the star's light to reach us. Imagine looking at a star a million light years away. It may not even exist anymore!

If it were possible for us to arrive at Sirius in just an instant, and if we dragged a big telescope with us, we could look back at the Earth and see what we were doing four years ago. God can do that because He is not constrained by time. He created it!

Einstein's special theory of relativity shows that, if we attempt to travel into space at the speed of light, our bodies are going to change. The faster we go, the quicker our teeth will ache, the sooner our eyes will pop, and the more quickly our faces will look like melting marshmallows. If we could go fast enough, time itself would seem distorted. It would slow down for us. We could actually come back to earth looking younger than our grandchildren! But in our four-dimensional universe, we could never travel at the speed of light. (That is, unless we are on the starship Enterprise and traveling at warp speed.)

We certainly can't say the same thing about God. After all, "God is spirit" (John 4:24). He is not subject to any of the dimensions related to time. If all creation exists in Him, then He doesn't change. He knows perfectly well what has happened, or what will happen four thousand or four million years from the present. That's because God does not exist in time, but time exists in God (Col. 1:17),

God, as time's Creator, isn't subject to time at all. In the instant that space and matter began, time also began. But we humans are still subject to time because, as physical beings, we are part and parcel of the basic laws of nature. We exist in the dimensions of height, width, and depth and are, therefore, subject to the fourth dimension of time. Maybe this would be news to Isaiah, but he did pen that remarkable revelation that states God is able to declare the beginning from the end, and His purposes will not fail (Isa. 46:9-10). God really does know the future, including ours.

Science knew very little beyond the four-dimensional universe until quite recently. Mathematicians, applying their skills to something called the string theory of basic particles, discovered that "in the attempt to quantify the theory it proved that a consistent mathematical description of these strings is difficult; scientists arrived at eleven or more space-time dimensions and a thousand different possible universes, without being able to explain why it was our universe in particular that became reality."[3]

What this quotation speaks about may be mathematically understandable, but in practice it is very, very difficult. Consider (somewhat lightheartedly) how a spirit-filled Adam and Eve community effectively could have become stewards of God's earth. Would they have possessed the ability to explore more than four dimensions? Would this have been essential for them to exercise global authority? How could they possibly have taken charge of what was going on in South America or Tibet when they were limited to a four-dimensional world around the Euphrates? Is it possible that Adam and Eve *needed* such an ability in order to accomplish God's commission to them?

By spelling out some of the essential relationships that signaled the creational harmony existing under Adam and Eve, we shall have a clearer understanding of what has gone wrong.

Does God Exist *in* Time?

The answer to the question, "Does God exist in time?" is yes and no.

The "no" answer would seem to be obvious. If God created the physical elements that allow the dimension of time to exist, then God must have preceded time. Gregory Ganssle, editor of a book dealing with God and time states, "God is atemporal. He experiences all of his life at once in the eternal present. Nothing of his life is past, and nothing of it is future. God possesses his life 'all at once.'"[4] My biblical view of time comes very close to this one. It will be interesting to see how God acts when He already knows what is going to happen. King David once alluded to this possibility. (Psa.139:16) Certainly, this view of God's nature in relation to time is more apparent in the New Testament. God is never surprised!

However, this does not mean that God does not delight in, or is not pained by, "the moment." To God, past, present, and future all exist in the same moment. In other words, everything exists in the eternal nowness of God. God, in an eternal moment, sees the finished biblical story, even though, through the limited eyes of chronological time, it has not yet been played out.

God is Spirit, and therefore He is not restricted by the dimension of time. God is pained by Hitler's Holocaust while simultaneously viewing the demise of the dinosaurs and the landing of the first person on Mars.

John Polkinghorne, a renowned Christian physicist, notes the aforementioned classical view before offering his own insight on a nonstatic perspective. He is considering the question of how God relates to time. "God relates to the whole of cosmic history 'at once.' . . . A God incapable of exercising a timeless free response to a multitude of temporal free actions is just a God condemned to react to things as they happen, doing the best he can but continually having to revise his plans in the light of changing circumstances. Only God who sees all that was, and is, and is to come, 'at once,' is able to produce the best for his creation."[5]

However, a little later in his book, while recognizing that God continues His involvement in the creation process, Polkinghorne also sees God limiting Himself to the unfolding natural processes He initiated. The question of whether God can see the future is very important to our understanding of the one biblical story. Nevertheless, we must allow that some, even Polkinghorne, continue to allow for God's self-restriction of abilities in time. By disagreeing, I believe that God is thoroughly consistent in how He relates to time. It is only in this way that he can declare:

> "I am God, and there is no other; I am God, and there
> is no one like me, declaring the end from the beginning
> and from ancient times things not yet done, saying,
> "My purpose shall stand and I will fulfill my intention."
> (Isa.46:9-10)

Polkinghorne, a convinced Christian, has to deal with such a biblical view when saying: "I also believe that by endowing his creation with the power of true becoming, God has permitted a kenosis of his omniscience, parallel to the kenosis of his omnipotence. Even he does not know the unformed future, and that is no imperfection in the divine nature, for that future is not yet there to be known."[6]

Admittedly, Jesus in His humanity did not wrestle with something like Heisenberg's uncertainty principle. But through the inspiration of God's eternal nowness, something of the future was known to Him. It was the omniscient God who revealed to Jesus all He needed to know concerning his work and destiny in God's kingdom. Therefore, the man Jesus was able to perform everything God wanted Him to do and to say concerning the kingdom of God. "Very truly, I tell you, the Son can do nothing on His own, but only what he sees the Father doing; for whatever the Father does, the Son does likewise. The Father loves the Son and shows him all that he himself is doing"(John 5:19-20).

That is how Christ's predictive prophecy was made possible. God is never surprised; as such, he does not predict the future; he sees it! And so, the delay of Jesus in reaching the tomb of Lazarus is understood in this way (John 11:17). Indeed, we realize that all biblical prediction must be tested against the prophetic words of Jesus. This principle will become very important when we place latter-day teaching alongside that of Jesus.

This supposed "limiting" of God's ability to know the future allows for the incorrect teaching that God possess a changeable nature (James 1:17). The Spirit-God is not limited to His creation's dimensional characteristics. And it is in this vein that we may understand how God communicates something of His knowledge to us by means of what we call predictive revelation. How else could the prophets speak about the future? (Amos 3:7).

As far as our universe is concerned, all history, all that is present, and all that is future already exist in God. In God's eternal nowness, all time exists, all grief exists, all joy exists, and all knowledge exists.

Let me employ a contrast with the human, limited, experience of time. My elderly friend, Anne, used to be the secretary of a church in which I pastored. Later, she became a pivotal part of our healing ministry at St. James's Church, Calgary. Some years later, Anne suffered from Alzheimer's disease. Eventually, it was the cause of her death. In my frequent visits to her at a nursing home, we arrived at a point where we no longer had common ground for sharing memories of life. No longer did we have a common past. Anne was no longer able to project what our common story meant for the future. She was no longer capable of planning an event for tomorrow. No longer did we share a common story or a hope.

All Anne knew was that a friend, no longer associated with a memory of her past, came to visit. Our time together seemed to bring life to her day. However, in a matter of minutes after I left, she had forgotten our visit. Anne lived totally and absolutely in the now. Of course, her now held little or no memory. For her, the present had no connection to the past or the future. We did hold a common story, but in reality, it meant very little to her because our story no longer was connected by a common memory.

The human experience of time is always in connection with someone else, some other event, or some common place. It is always relative to something else.

In contrast, God doesn't have Alzheimer's. As Spirit, He is not constrained by the physical dimensions of time which he created. Therefore, His eternal now encompasses all time for all ages. And it isn't relative to anything. However, Jesus, in His humanity, experienced the kenosis of the glory He shared in Trinitarian life. And so His knowledge of Real Adam abilities was totally dependent upon the anointing and revelation He received from the divine Father through the Spirit. The fullness of the human story always exists *in* Him. When we look at the elements required for time to exist, we realize that it cannot be any other way.

The amazing thing is, without an understanding of time, ancient prophets of God understood the experience of this truth.

Let's jump right in here with a quotation from the apostle Paul when writing to Colossae. Talk about revelation! Like all other prophets, Paul probably knew little or nothing of the science of time, yet this text may give us some idea of how God's present is everlasting: "He himself is before all things, and in him all things hold together" (Col. 1:17).

Of course, Paul is speaking here of Jesus Christ through whom everything has been created. If everything holds together in Christ, and if everything has meaning in Christ, then we may say something that sounds like the very opposite of an earlier question. All creation is in God; therefore all time is in God.

Obviously, Paul is not speaking here of anything resembling panentheism, which is the belief that at least something of matter is and always was a part of God. That would make matter and time both inseparable from God, and therefore immortal. (That is precisely a belief found in some eastern religions). For example, (Bernard Haisch, an astrophysicist and believer in a creative deity—and, on occasion, one who seems not to be well versed in the teachings of Jesus—falls into this trap of not observing a clear distinction of God from His creation.[7]

If all things hold together in God, the logical next step is to ask: if there is a Designer of the universe who is ontologically distinct from His creation, must not the Designer also have a *purpose* for His creation? Did the prophets succeed in relaying God's purpose? (Isa. 46:10).

The elements of faith and empirical data, plus the initiative of God revealing Himself in the human story, are all needed to discover the meaning of the human story. Placing God at the center of all things, the apostle Paul gives us a theological perspective. For him, God is the pre-existent One who exists in perfection before creation, and therefore before time began. Without God's sustaining power and purpose, nothing can hold together. What we may say is that God gives meaning, and He continually gives meaning to everything that exists. (Rom. 8:29, Col. 1:15-17)

In this eternal sense, the pre-existent Jesus is truly the cosmic Christ. He straddles the pages of all time. He, alone, draws all time into Himself. As the Creator of time and the focus of all meaning, nothing can be hidden from God, because it is all *in Him*. God is, now and always, fullness and perfection; therefore His nature cannot be changed by the changes and variations of time.

It is very important to say this because it's fashionable today, in one view of time, to speak of the "growing God." In this line of thought, God is changed by external pressure and circumstance. He learns something from His own creation. Such an idea presumes that God has no awareness of future, chronological time, and, in some sense, ties God's very existence to the creation itself. Roots of this thinking may be found in a type of process theology that had beginnings in nineteenth-century British idealism. "God is the world-process . . . He is no static perfection . . . we are to think of God as the perfect in process, as a dynamic progress from perfection to perfection . . ."[8]

Somehow, that statement by itself is self-contradictory. How is it possible to move from perfection to perfection? How can He be the perfect in process? Of necessity, it would mean that God evolved into a further stage of so-called perfection, being influenced by the next stage of creation's evolution. Doesn't this also make the Creator somehow dependent upon and tied to His own creation? Hugh Ross offers a twenty-first-century perspective: "The remarkable advance of research reveals a God who lives and operates in the equivalent of eleven dimensions of space and time. Such extra-dimensional capacities are more than adequate to resolve the doctrinal conflicts and paradoxical issues that have divided the church and perplexed both believers and unbelievers for centuries."[9] 9

Obviously, the above view of a growing God is not going to be advocated in this book. I feel that an understanding of God's unfolding revelation in the context of the one story doesn't reveal this kind of God at all. A growing God only finds perfection in relation to His creation. Isn't that the very basis of primitive, natural religion? This is surely a notion which divorces God from each successive stage of his creation!

I should add, however, that some people now take a slightly modified view. The idea of change in God is being described by Clark Pinnock as the "open view." This idea continues to assume a God who can be surprised by a future He does not know. Pinnock speaks of God as "a most moved, not unmoved, Mover."[10] God can have passions and feelings that are influenced by the people He has made.

Clearly, the Christian experience of revelation cannot allow for conclusions such as this. How can God be angry, jealous, or destructive when He knew everything before time existed? (1 Peter 1:20-21).

Let me illustrate with one more of Pinnock's quotations. "Though God knows all there is to know about the world, there are aspects of the future God does not know. Though unchangeable with respect to his character and the steadfastness of his purposes, God changes in the light of what happens by interacting with the world."[11]

For Pinnock, the movement of change within God is possible because the future hasn't happened. And God doesn't know what it is. Of course, this would mean that, in some sense, God's so-called changeable nature is somehow dependent upon movement in His creation. Then how could God exist in absolute perfection prior to His work of creation? Supposedly, God's perfection only exists in relation to the processes of change within His creation. How absurd!

I'm not interested in attacking Pinnock. In fact, I admire the fact that he is forcing evangelicals to reexamine their thinking, even if his postulations don't work. But I do identify two glaring problems that force me to conclude there is a major inadequacy in his train of thought. First, I need to be convinced that he has grappled with the scientific nature of time at much broader levels than he demonstrates in his book. Second, I wish he had produced more biblical data for his premise. Let me simply give two examples that Pinnock's ideas do not address.

(1) The God who is revealed in Isaiah knows the "end from the beginning, and from ancient times things not yet done" (Isa. 46:10) Isaiah also records that God is answering even before we call. (Isa. 65:24). In other words, *there is nothing yet to come that is not in the knowledge of God*.

(2) Much of the prophetic literature in the Bible is not simply of a forthtelling nature, but of a foretelling and predictive nature. For example, after eighteen hundred years of diaspora, the nation of Israel was reestablished in the Middle East. This was the result of a massive return of Jews from many nations of the world. It had been prophesied in Jeremiah 29:14. Wasn't God the source of this prophecy, as well as many other predictive utterances?

Hugh Ross reminds us, "It is reasonable to conclude that the universe must have been caused by an ENTITY who transcends matter, energy, and all the space-time dimensions associated with matter and energy."[12] Ross goes on to say, "In Hawking's words, time itself must have a beginning. Proof of the beginning of time may rank as the most theologically significant theorem of all time, assuming validity of the theory of general relativity."[13] Ross devotes the rest of his chapter to postulating how Einstein was right.

I am laboring this point from biblical and scientific perspectives in order to debunk the idea of God's changing nature moving from perfection to perfection. It is a sentimentalist notion. The entire postulation is circumscribed by our limited view of what I call moments of light. As we consider the nature of time, we will see that the idea of God's changing nature just doesn't work.

Pursuing the one story, and in the light of God's unfolding revelation, a different perspective on time will emerge. We are going to see that, in order for God to grant freedom of choice, He doesn't have to sacrifice His knowledge of future events.

How will this view affect the varying opinions about predestination? Will God's chosen vulnerability to human decisions mean that His original and sovereign purposes will become modified or defeated? Can He still be sovereign if those sovereign purposes are changed?

God may possibly exhibit sadness at the effects of human decisions, but His sovereign purposes and His ontological nature do not change, no matter how created beings respond.

"For the sake of the faith of God's elect and the knowledge of the truth that is in accordance with godliness, in the hope of eternal life that God, who never lies, promised before the ages began" (Titus 1:1-2).

Clearly this God, the Alpha and Omega of life, really does know the beginning from the end (Isa.46:9-10). God may well be moved. (Jesus invites us to pray in order to cooperate with God). He can exhibit passion of His own free choice. But it is totally absurd to assume that He has to forfeit or limit His eternal knowledge or His unchangeable nature in the process. After all, creation is a reflection of the nature of God, not the reverse. God is the One who exists throughout all eternity. The universe, and therefore time, was a creation of the God who eternally exists. God is and always was complete in the perfection of His Trinitarian nature.

Contrary to the light of Christian revelation, we are often coaxed to a view of time that diminishes the essential revelation and biblical paradigm of the one story. Nor is it feasible to subscribe to a view that contravenes demonstrable, empirical laws of material science. Apart from charismatic infusion, given in the will of the Spirit (1 Cor. 12:4-6), we are subject to these laws. Indeed, in His humanity, Jesus demonstrates this point in the miracles made possible by God.

In His eternal and ontological nature, God does not have to bend to limitations prescribed by time. God is truth, and He delights in our discovery of its realities. The exploration of this one story and its purpose is consistent with most modern views of time, and will also speak for itself.

Additionally, we don't use Old Testament literature as if it were a complete revelation of God's nature. Many do, including some who participate in debates concerning matters of time and of God's individual election. That's why they can't get around problems of their own making. However, there are many Old Testament passages that are perfectly consistent with revelation in the New Testament. If we are to pursue this one story, then we need to follow both Old and New Testaments with great care.

The Bible does speak about time extensively. The fact is that we cannot possibly understand the meaning of creation, redemption, and restoration, the essential components of the one story, without an understanding of time. Otherwise, we are going to find ourselves enmeshed in a spiritual fairyland of sentimentalism.

Time and Natural Thought

Questions regarding the meaning of time have long existed among thoughtful proponents of natural religion. It is important to raise this matter because, in holding this theistic view of time, there really is a relationship between the nature of time in the universe and fundamental principles of belief.

The major question concerns the point at which time began. A cyclic and naturalistic view of the universe would assert that the planet Earth, in particular, has always existed and will continue to exist forever. It is immortal. "Instead of having a beginning, time was thought to consist of endless eras, repeated over and over again for eternity."[14] In other words, as in the patterns of nature, all things exist in cyclic fashion. The static universe, as Einstein once thought, was either expanding or contracting. A repetitive and cyclic view of time may easily become a natural corollary and, indeed, continues to remain an intrinsic and basic principle for eastern religions such as Hinduism and Buddhism. The belief in reincarnation is a good example.

There is no doubt that both of these ancient religions had a profound effect upon the later sophistication of Gnostic thinkers. For example, Plato believed in a static universe, and he taught his students that everything was destined to repetition in cyclic fashion. Much later, Augustine, bishop of Hippo in North Africa (AD 354-430), expressed his disapproval of this repetitive and predestined view of life. It denied the uniqueness of Jesus Christ and implied that subsequent, predestined actions would negate the need or ability to choose Jesus Christ. For Augustine, time began at the moment of creation.[15] But when was that?

In the mid-seventeenth century, James Usher, the learned archbishop of Armagh, began his very lengthy work of determining this date on the basis of biblical manuscripts. Eventually, he believed he had found a fixed and indisputable point to refine his chronological scheme, namely the date of Nebuchadnezzar's death, BC 562. Usher's date for the beginning of time was October 22, 4004 BC, at 6:00 p.m.[16]

However, though Oxford and Cambridge presses were producing Bibles and still inserting this date alongside Genesis 1 until the very beginning of the twentieth century, science had not yet discarded the belief in a static universe. In many disciplines, such as geology, archeology, and biology, new questions and time frames were unfolding. But space was to become the major frontier upon which questions of time were to be played out.

In order to fix a date for the beginning of time, and by accepting that the universe had been in a condition of expansion or subsequent contraction from the very beginning, Albert Einstein produced a formula that he felt would still preserve the notion of a static universe. Mark Worthing makes note of comments relating to Einstein's own comment, in 1915, that the Cosmological Constant was his "biggest blunder." (Mark.W. Worthing, God, Creation, and Physics, Fortress Press, Minneapolis, 1996, page 214).

And so, in 1917, Einstein produced this formula designed to explain a constant rate at which the universe would expand until something, like a weakened force of gravity, reversed the process.

Einstein later came to believe that the age of the universe was considerably less than the 13.7 billion years consistently accepted by most natural disciplines.[17]

Much earlier, at the time of his death in 1882, Charles Darwin had not settled on the static universe theory. Nor had he accepted a proposed younger date of the universe, the estimate then being just a hundred million years old.

Although the Bible was never intended to be a book of science, the astounding power of biblical revelation made known a Creator who exists before time began. The apostle Peter (quoting Psalm 90:4 was surely correct in asserting that a thousand years is as one day in God's view (2 Pet. 3:8). What does 13.7 billion years mean to God? If it is true that the history of humanity occupies only about two seconds on the twenty-four-hour clock of the universe to date, so what? The expanding universe is precisely what God intended. God will accomplish His purposes for humanity in His own way, and in His own kairos time. God is Spirit. He is not subject to the factors of time that He brought into being.

Time: A Layperson's View

For our biblical and gospel purposes, by accepting the concept of time as part of our four-dimensional universe, we need not go beyond the fact that God reveals His purposes to us in the context of time as it is played out in this universe. We also see that time is contingent upon other factors.

From the four-dimensional perspective in which we quite narrowly think of our lives, purpose, and existence, time is not an abstract notion.

Why does it take me eight hours to fly from Calgary to London? The reason is obvious. There's a lot of space between Calgary and London. But if there's no such place as the planet Earth, then neither Calgary nor London could exist as distinct entities. If there were no space between Calgary and London, then there would be no distinction between them—that is, no distinction of place, and hence no need for distinctive identities.

There must be measurable space in order to define distinct dimensions and places in relation to one another. A very tiny blob of matter that once was caused to explode in all directions was the reason for the beginning of time. Space between any two points of matter, or places, introduced the reality of time.

In order for me to get to one place from another, I have to pass through space (or distance). No matter how fast I travel, it will take a certain amount of time, which is also relative to space and speed of travel. Even if I walk just one step, I have crossed space, and it has taken a measurable time to do it. There's a very simple principle here: it really doesn't matter what the distance is between two points, it still takes time to cross space.

In other words, because there is place and space, there is also time, no matter how fast space is traveled (except at the speed of light).

There is a measurable distance around the circumference of the Sun. There is time involved between any two points on that circumference. As the Earth spins around the Sun's circumference, time is involved. In chronological terms, we call that measure of time "one year."

For our purpose, and in simple terms, it's now possible for us to articulate a simple principle: time is related to space and place.

This principle will be of the utmost importance when we consider the dimensions involved in discovering the meaning of a place called hell.

We humans live in a material, four-dimensional universe, and so, in these natural terms, we are subject to an equation such as the one proposed. Imagine if Calgary didn't exist, or never had. It would be meaningless to postulate how much time it would take to travel from London to this nonexistent place. If we take either place or space from the equation, then the dimension of time also becomes nonexistent. The consideration of time requires the dimensions of both place and space.

The point I am getting at, with regard to this book at least, is that, as far back as we may think of life existing on this planet, all parts of that description were in place: space, place, and time. There was no such thing as time until God caused space and place to exist. "Let there be . . ." At that inexplicable moment, by the power of the Word, there was a mighty explosion. From that millisecond on, there was a continuing separation of place and space. So time began—but only after God created place and space. So it would be more accurate to say that time exists in God, rather than to say that God exists in time.

In all our thinking about existence, we cannot think of time without relating it to place and space. Nor can we think of place and space without including time.

A Theological Way to View Biblical Time

We have already alluded to a connection between creation, redemption, and restoration. The Bible story may be best understood by viewing it through the paradigm of those three theological time frames. This paradigm has its meaning in a story. God has entered into and thus become involved in this living story. Using the broad brush of our creation principles, we may see that the simple use of the word "creation" means that we are gleaning its primary principles from a particular point in history.

Creation

There is a definite point at which God says, "It is very good." He is satisfied that all that has emerged at this one particular point is exactly what He intended. There are no surprises! The beginning of the biblical story is when He spoke into His creation. "Creation" is a word that summarizes all that God purposed when He decided to make the world. The key to our thinking here will center around the power of the Word of God. What is the connection between the Word of God and His activity in creation?

We may start from a particular point at which creation stands as a sign. In itself, it is a sign pointing toward God's purposes for the world. Many of these purposes and principles are signed in the story of a place called Eden. The story of Eden therefore provides much of the beginning and substance for all good theological thinking. How often did Jesus remind us to go back to creation stories? (Mark 10:5-6).

If we don't know what the original purposes of creation were, then how may we possibly understand the ramifications of what has gone wrong? Is it possible that many conservative evangelicals begin their thinking in the wrong place? Is it also possible that liberal thinkers begin in the wrong place? For many, and most often, the gospel story has its genesis from redemption principles onward. Do modern revisionists make a similar mistake when their thinking begins with principles of restoration and how, through their particular view of justice, it may be achieved? Could it be that the starting point for Jesus is often the very point that makes religious people angry?

As a starting point for our exploration of theological principles, we will certainly ask such questions as: In what way does Paradise relate to "Let there be . . ."? What practical implications are there in relating creation to restoration? How do the latter days relate to creation's principles? I am suggesting that the words, "creation, redemption, and restoration" may admirably sum up a theological view of time, enabling us to peer, ever so tentatively and awesomely, into the mind of God. They help us to see the Bible as one big package.

In summary, creation is all about what God intended in the beginning of time.

Redemption

In God's omniscience, from before the foundation of the world, Peter records that God knew there had to be a redemption story as part of His purposes for creation (1 Pet. 1:20). The word "redemption" is often used to mean "to buy back or to rescue." It's a word that will need some explanation.

The redemption story is a chronicle of how God set about the task of rescuing the purposes He intended in the beginning. "Rescue" is a good word. The whole point of redemption "is our rescue from a perilous predicament through the very costly self-giving of Jesus. Rescue and costliness are the point."[18] Redemption speaks equally about a salvation extended to humankind so that, in some measure, humanity's stewardship of all creation can still be a signature of what God designed. How may we know the meaning of salvation unless we can see how far we have moved from God's creation purposes?

Of course, alongside salvation is the word "deliverance." This word speaks of being delivered from the ultimate consequences of a creation moving in the wrong directions.

The much longer story of redemption has its climax in the very costly offering of Christ's death on the cross. It is here we will be drawn into addressing questions such as: Was He really dead for nearly three days? How is it that God can offer redemption to those who died before His awesome sacrifice took place? How could redemption be offered to all those who died after Christ? How may redemption be offered to those who have died without ever having heard the gospel? How does the power of the cross radically affect our lifestyles, motivations, the meaning of justice in our time, and the meaning of life beyond death?

Restoration

The concept of restoration opens wide questions concerning human freedom, particularly as it relates to the sovereignty of God. It's all about how God has brought about the restoration of all He intended in creation's beginning. The climax to this story is the resurrection of Jesus Christ from the dead. God revealed to the prophet Isaiah that He does know the beginning from the end; His purposes for creation will not fail (Isa. 46:10). Surely, if everything were left to the behavior and thinking of God's created, human image, then His purposes would not be accomplished! In that case, God would have a contingency plan even before the foundation of the world. (1Pet.1:20) With our modern understanding of time, we marvel at how the writer of this passage (apart from God's revelation) could possibly understand what he was writing. How does this verse affect certain contemporary thinking that limits God's ability to view the future?

By taking this three word perspective of a theological process, some firm-standing positions of both conservatives and revisionists are called into question. For example, is the strictly legal and precise method of justification, employed by some conservative evangelicals, adequate for finding a central focus for the faith? Indeed, is the centrality of the cross the most important tenet of the faith?

We are proposing that the major creation principles are really all about relationships. So we will look carefully at what those relationships are and how they are played out, even during latter days.

The reason why relationships are a primary principle of creation is very simple: God is a relational being.

Then does God intend relationships to be at the very heart of all He has created? Or is He telling us that some sort of legal standing is of the utmost importance? This question of legal preciseness is truly imperative today when we consider that modern revisionists gravitate to a position where a legal piece of paper (such as one denoting that a baptism has taken place) is sufficient for full entry and position within the Christian community. In itself, that position may not be totally rejected, but can it possibly be acceptable to God when there is not an equal commitment to walk in the revealed pathways of His holiness? Most certainly, in the Bible, moral standards of behavior and certain abilities are required for those in leadership (1Tim. 3:1-13). This question is particularly poignant when essential principles of revelation are ignored.

We read of behavior that the Bible shows us to be threatening to the maintenance of God's essential relationships. Deviation from the behavioral path is seen to be highly offensive to the awesome holiness of God. Is it ever stated as a biblical principle that we may come to God on our terms? Is it a godly way of thinking to focus on the meaning of restoration being simply the pursuit of justice? How can our present, multitudinous, and individualistic views of justice possibly be valid when God's revelation for personal transformation has been ignored? What is the real nature of justice?

I want to suggest that, by focusing our thinking on one or other of these two words (i.e., redemption or restoration), the meaning of the one story of the Bible (creation, redemption, and restoration) is seriously diminished. The gospel as a whole must include the meaning and exploration of *all three words*.

But what does all of the above mean in relation to God's purposes for creation? Let's look at some of those purposes.

CREATION

CHAPTER 3

When Time Was a Friend

And God Created

*I*n the beginning God. When was that? We know it started with a bang! Through careful language, it's actually the writer's way of saying, "There was a beginning to creation; God existed eternally, before creation came into being; the transcendent God was complete in His nature before He began the work of creation; time began when the power of the Word caused creation to come into being; from the substance of energy-matter (which God had caused to exist), time began but as yet was not completely ordered."

Time, signified by the word "day," represents distinctions within the order in which God did His creative work. These distinctions may well be considered to be moments of light. In other words, like my use of the word "moment," the word "day" in the creation story does not represent a chronological measurement, but a recognition of what God has done.

Having grown up in Liverpool, England, I personally appreciate this little story: Tom Maloney, a Liverpool comedian and school teacher, tells of a boy in class who was once asked the meaning of God's ontological nature. In superb theological fashion, and as only a child can answer, he replied, "God always was, is, and always will be, was." (At least, that's the way it sounded in an old LP of Tom Maloney's recording, A Load of Maloney)

Similarly, in the Gospel of John, the writer does not attempt to define the word "beginning" in relation to the nature of the Word. "In the beginning was the Word, and the Word was with God, and the Word was God. All things came into being through him, and without him not one thing came into being" (John 1:1-3).

John doesn't use the word "was" as a simple past-tense verb. Rather, he employs the imperfect tense. It's his way of saying that it's impossible to determine a beginning for the Person of the Word. He always was, is! He is the living Word whom John is to declare as being the incarnate Christ. There is no doubt that the writer is clearly identifying the Word with the Genesis God of creation.

In 2 Peter, the writer expresses the power of God's revelation. "By the word of God heavens existed long ago and an earth was formed out of water" (2 Pet. 3:5). As far as we know, Peter knew next to nothing about science. What an astounding revelation is carried in this statement!

How did the Genesis writer know that water came first? In other words, God's existence and activity cannot be restricted to our human concepts of time. For creatures, time has its essential nature connected to a four-dimensional universe. But before there was space and place, there was God. He is the self-existent God whose identity and nature is complete. And God remains complete, entirely apart from His creation. The God of Judeo—Christian thinking exists eternally, before (if we can employ the word) anything else.

Ancient religions usually speak of their deities being connected to some form of material that existed somewhere in space. It's a little like some scientists who are looking for new ways to begin again, or who are answering one problem by creating another, and are desperately looking for basic answers about Earth on other planets. For example, some are looking for life in outer space to explain where life on Earth has its origin. Won't the same questions emerge again?

In ancient Babylonian thinking, the gods took hold of existent chaotic stuff in space. and reshaped it the way they wanted it. "Marduk divided the dead body of Tiamat into two parts. 'Half of her he set in place and formed the sky therewith as a roof.' Next he established the earth, the residences of the gods, and the constellations."[1] These deities really didn't have any meaning or existence apart from nature. Such thinking may also provide a basis for pantheistic belief. (*Pan* means "all," while *theos* means "deity" or "god.") In pantheism, everything is god, and is therefore immortal.

Here, in my understanding of the word, deity and creation are intrinsically connected; one cannot exist apart from the other. It is creation that is eternal, and always will be, was! Consistent with the cycles of nature, time goes round and round in circles. That's why reincarnation is at the heart of many natural religions. This natural view is becoming more popular in the western world. As we shall see, with a right understanding of the words, it will be impossible to believe in reincarnation and the resurrection at the same time.

The ultimate goal in pantheistic belief is to lose one's sense of personal identity in order to become absorbed into *pan*, or into the all of everything. In some Hindu thought, everything material is an illusion anyway; nothing is real. The force that gives this illusion is called "Maya."[2]

Physics and Ancient Spirituality

Strange though it may seem, thinking similar to pantheism exists today, but with major roots in early twentieth-century thought. However, there's been a brand of humility that has worked its way into the scientific world ever since the advent of quantum physics. Scientists, who always disassociated themselves from the word "magic," now often engage with the word "mystery." For them, there will never be an answer to all the emerging questions. And so in recent years we have heard such language reaching far beyond Enlightenment thought. It speaks of scientists never even hoping to answer the exponentially growing questions they discover.

In today's world of science, the more predictable, macroscopic laws of physics about big, cosmic things, such as Newton's laws, can no longer be considered to have sole or primary sway. In the micro world of particle behavior, many of the givens have similarly been found to be unpredictable. In the mid-1920s, Werner Heisenberg's uncertainty principle helped us to appreciate the unpredictability of some particle behavior.

Physicists generally agree that Newtonian and quantum physics are both important; they need each other. (As a physicist friend once told me, "Both disciplines were needed to put a man on the moon.") Those who exalt micro over macro science tend to downplay the notion of a transcendent God, especially as the Creator of all things. However, many micro enthusiasts do think there may be an existential force, like a universal mind.[3]

Some in this vein may more easily and naturally gravitate to a monistic spirituality usually associated with Buddhism. It speaks of the "oneness" of all things. Like a *Star Wars* belief, it looks to some kind of natural force. This has paved the way for many Westerners to adopt principles of Buddhism into their spirituality.

In the West, efforts to unite all religions on the basis of this oneness will ultimately fail. There may be a modicum of institutional success; however, Christian integrity alone can do no other than maintain the Christian view that holds all things together in the deity of the Trinitarian God.

Since the 1990s, physicists who, in natural form, maintain a belief in an ever-circular, directed universe have become a rarity. The big bang appears to be a demonstrable fact. Thus, as a growing number of physicists now concede, there must also have been a Beginner or a Causer.[4] Francis Collins, the head of the International Human Genome Project, laments the fact that many North American Christians tend to divide people into believers in God *or* believers in evolution.[5] Clearly, most deeply committed physicists, who believe in God, cannot accept this simple polarization; they believe God was present and involved in all the stages of creation.

Natural views concerning an ever-repeating, cyclical universe are in sharp contrast to the Judeo-Christian revelation of a linear, nonstatic universe. In Judeo—Christian thought, there is a beginning leading to an end. As the Bible reminds us, God knows the beginning and the end.

He is the Alpha and Omega. God is the Creator of everything and yet absolutely distinct from everything He has made.

Can the Trinity Be Explained?

God exists eternally. He has no need for anything at all. God doesn't have to create in order to be God. He is complete in His triune-oneness.

The New Testament is even clearer about the reason why God has no need for anything else in order to be complete in Himself. God exists in the complete and perfect relationship of love expressed as one God in three Persons: Father, Son, and Holy Spirit. Both in ontological (three Persons, but one in eternal being) and in economic terms (how the Persons relate to each other and the world), Trinitarian views of God in Christian thinking have always been in sharp contrast to the views of other monotheistic religions.

Trinitarian thought is very clearly a dividing point in the understanding of God's essential nature. Without entering into this very long debate (and, because no one can explain God, anyway), let us say something very quickly and simply. If God's *very nature* is that of love (1 John 5:8), not simply that God performs acts of love, then there has to be an *object* of that love. Love must also be received if it is to exist in perfection.

Otherness is therefore an essential ingredient of perfection in the nature of love. The distinctiveness of Persons within the Trinity is seen with the Father as focus (Matt. 6:9) loving the Son and the Spirit; the Son loving the Father and the Spirit; and the Spirit loving the Father and the Son. Each of the Persons receives love as well as gives love to the others. It's like a circle of love with the arrows going in both directions. It is completeness and equality in a focus of otherness, with the Father being the source of focus.

If this were not true, then the monotheistic God may well have an egocentric nature. Or, as Kallistos Ware says, "Egocentricity is the death of true personhood. Each becomes a real person only through entering into a relation with other persons, through living for them and in them."[6] The one God exists in three Persons. God is not one Person;

that would mean God is an egocentric deity. Nor is God a duality, a mutual admiration society. Actually, New Testament writers never try to explain the "how" of God living in a Trinity of Persons. They avoided trying to explain what has always been and always will be an incomprehensible mystery.

The religious view of a monotheistic God existing in one personage, and aided by a few anthropomorphic brushstrokes, would give rise to a possessive deity with a jealousy that is directed toward His creation. There are also a lot of other things, such as going to war against those who don't believe in your god.

Eternally, God exists in the perfection of oneness in community, one God in three Persons existing in the relational perfection of love, will, and action. There are no arguments or secrets within the Godhead.

God didn't need anything. Creation was a choice, not a necessity. Many years ago, I heard an evangelist attempt to answer the question, "Why did God make the world?" He replied, "God did it because He was lonely." Not a good answer at all! Certainly God doesn't need us. A reply such as this means that God needed to create, that He had a need beyond Himself, that He would not be fulfilled apart from creation. The God of the Bible is completely self-existent. "Creation is therefore a free act, a gratuitous act of God. It does not respond to any necessity of divine being whatever. Even moral motivations which are sometimes attributed to it are platitudes without importance."[7] God didn't *have* to do anything. He *decided* to create. Why He made this decision, God only knows.

In the process of creating, God was not diminished in any way. A little bit of Him did not become intrinsically and forever connected to nature. God is always complete; He exists eternally, apart from nature. This means that when God creates, it doesn't mean that a little part of Him is lost in the thing He created.

God is the eternal, self-generating energy of love.

Frank Wilczek, the 2004 Nobel Prize winner in physics, shows us that the idea of self-generation is not a concept unique to the world of theology. Electric and magnetic fields, filling what was once thought of as empty space, "can animate one another in turn, giving birth to self-reproducing disturbances that travel at the speed of light. Ever since Maxwell, we understand that these disturbances are what light *is*."[8]

Of course, Frank Wilczek and Stephen Hawking also need to wrestle with the question of how electric and magnetic fields got there in the beginning. I don't believe they have been successful in that area. How did these fields appear from nothing?

If God decided to create a hundred universes—a growing possibility in modern thought—His self-generating energy means that He is always complete. He doesn't need to be in, around, outside, or on top of what He created. When some think that a little bit of Him is lost in there somewhere, they are thinking in terms of panentheism.

Another way of saying this is to suggest that, even if the universe does lose its thrust from the big bang and begins a reverse fall, it won't come back to God. It will come back to nothing. If it came back to God, then the constituents of time would be insinuated into His nature—elements that were not there in the first instance. God is spirit! However, many in the scientific community now agree that the universe will not come back on itself. It continues to move outward at an ever-increasing rate at its outer edges, and will continue expanding forever.[9]

Some scientists suggest there may be limits to this expansion. Denyse O'Leary, a science journalist, summarizing the conclusions and implications of the big bang, records her own findings in this statement: "The universe will continue to expand because it does not have enough gravity to contract. The expansion may even be speeding up because of an antigravity force."[10] In our twenty-first-century appreciation of physics, it may well be this mysterious "antigravity force" is what physicists are calling "dark energy" or "dark matter." Possibly this force will never allow gravity to slow down the ever-increasing speed of the ever-expanding universe.

Interestingly, the biblical and theological perspective is one of creation being forever sustained by the power of God's Word alone (2 Pet. 3:5). God is still active in His universe. He is not a deistic god who does a job and then whisks away on some kind of cosmic excursion.

When the New Testament speaks of God creating through the power of the Word, it is spelling out what is already implied in the Old

Testament. If God existed before anything else, then He must have created by the power of His will and word alone. In the Trinitarian nature of God, word, will, and action are one moment. To a physicist, matter and energy are interchangeable, and therefore the same thing. The writers of Genesis and 2 Peter didn't know that. The explanation, for some scientific believers in God, is that, by the power of His will creating energy, a very highly compressed amount of matter came into being. This matter, containing an enormously large amount of energy, would at God's command soon burst to begin the process of a physical universe. God's love, will, and actions are consistently the same.

It's often put this way: God created ex nihilo—out of nothing!

Basil the Great, a fourth-century Byzantine bishop and theologian, says, "He calls all things from non-existence into being; once things are created He keeps them in existence."[11] In other words, God is the sustainer of all things.

As an astronomer/astrophysicist, Hugh Ross not only speaks about God's sustaining power in His universe, but about how His creativity is observable by the fact that He was consistently fine-tuned every facet of His creation. He did this in order to make creation habitable for humanity. "Recent research shows that at least twenty-five different characteristics of the universe must be exquisitely fine-tuned for life's essential building blocks to exist . . . We can conclude only that the Cause of the building blocks of life is unimaginably intelligent, creative, capable, and caring."[12]

If physicists are correct in asserting that there have been something like twenty-five to thirty "fine-tunings," then we may venture a theological statement: in the process of creation's stages, God continued to speak into the development of earth's formation.

Austin Farrer, an early twentieth-century theologian, adds to this thought: "God makes the world make itself . . . and this in spite of the fact that the constituents are not for the most part intelligent. They cannot see beyond the tip of their noses, they have, indeed, no noses to see beyond, nor any eyes with which to fail in the attempt. All they can do is blind away at being themselves, and fulfill the repetitive pattern of their existence."[13]

The Knowledge TV Network began a series on January 31, 2008. It was simply called *Time*. In the second episode, aired on February 6, the program asserted that, 570 million years ago, an explosion of life forms suddenly appeared in the oceans.

If we assume, as Christians, that this was also a point at which God was speaking into His creation, then He must have had a plan for this process. Would this mean God planned for humanity to suffer the same fate as all other species—namely, that it would also become obsolete? If that is true, then surely God is also responsible for the horrible processes and events that terminate and ravage life.

In the Genesis story, we see that humanity did die, but outside of Eden. It was not in God's purpose for humans to die. The Genesis 3 narratives make that clear. Isn't that an amazing assertion the writer makes? It goes against all that he has experienced of life. Death proved to be a matter of choice by those passing on their DNA to subsequent generations.

In the very substance of His Trinitarian being and nature, God is a relational God.

Because creation's essential meaning is *in God*, then we understand why creation itself will be called into a primary condition of relationships. That is its very nature, and yet it reflects something of God's own nature. Therefore, the gospel itself will have a particular and primary focus in what I am calling "essential relationships." However, the creation story by itself doesn't say a lot about *why* God chose to create the universe.

Maybe it was for the unbridled joy of sharing the wonder of creation with the creatures that would inhabit it. The KJV offers an interesting reason. "for thy pleasure they are and were created." (Rev. 4:11) Even though God is omniscient, quite possibly it really was (as the KJV notes) for the sheer pleasure of watching life grow, change, and realize its potential. Parents enjoy watching their children grow, even though they know they will become adults. Maybe it was to enable a created being to enjoy and utilize the utter delights of His creative genius. Maybe it's because He just loves to share good things. Maybe it's because He loves variety. After all, He had already created a heavenly and spiritual host, but that was an immaterial creation that wasn't subject to the time constraints of a four-dimensional world.

One thing is certain. An intelligent Creator would not have created without a purpose in mind.

Surely, if all time exists in the Spirit-God, then He knew everything that was to happen with this new enterprise. If so, then why did God create the world at all? A simple Old Testament view is not helpful. Here, God caused a flood to wipe out rebellion (Gen.9) Er was wicked so "the Lord put him to death."(Gen.38:7) Similarly, Onan received the same fate, (v.10) If this principle were to be extended beyond the Bible, then we should ask why God, knowing the future, didn't wipe out Hitler before World War 2.Why did He create a world that would also produce the Holocaust, in which six million Jews were exterminated? (That was six million members of a small nation in whom He had invested most of His purposes).Why did He create a world in which thousands of Ethiopian children died of starvation? Why did I have to bury two-year-old Tommy, who died of cancer and blood disorders directly inherited from his alcohol—and drug-captive parents? Was it because freedom and love would have to be taken out of the equation if such things were not allowed?

Unfortunately, some of our recent popular books on Christian life are not helpful to me in the struggle to know the God who elicits so many questions. For example, one Christian writer says, "God prescribed every single detail of your body ... Because God made you for a reason, he also decided *when* you would be born and *how long* you would live ... choosing the exact time of your birth and death ... God also planned *where* you'd be born ... Most amazing, God decided *how* you would be born ... It doesn't matter that your parents were good, bad or indifferent. God knew that those two individuals possessed *exactly* the right genetic makeup to create the custom 'you' he had in mind."[14] *Rick Warren*

How may I possibly use those primitive and fatalistic statements in response to the inquiries of Tommy's adoptive relatives, or the friend who asks why he was born blind, or to another suffering the horrid effects of brain malnutrition, or the parents of a dead child who was killed on the sidewalk by a drunken driver? My question to God is, "I know that

You were not the cause of all this suffering, but why did You bother creating a world, especially when you knew of the immense pain that was to follow?"

That will be my big question when I meet the Lord one bright day. I'm sure this book won't answer the question. Maybe we have to continue with *what* He did in order to glean some understanding of the *why*. Like Job, I feel that the awesome encounter with our holy God will, undoubtedly, leave me bereft of all speech and anger.

As we look at the life and message of Old Testament prophets, we are going to see why such questions are very important. They battled hard and long with questions concerning the effects of natural religions. The same problem most certainly exists in mainline Christian churches of today. A dominant philosophy of natural religion is reappearing. Although we know considerably more of the science of genetics, of DNA composition, and so one in a different way, the response must be this: the only time we should begin to take natural religion seriously is when scientists can create human genes out of a lump of clay. Even better, out of nothing. Of course, this means that they would have to create that lump of clay. Only then may humans think of deifying themselves. Or, in the feminine character of natural religion, of addressing themselves in terms of female deity, the matrix of a cyclical universe.

It is hardly likely that questions of purpose and values for living will be resolved by scientific inquiry. Yet the human quest for meaning and truth will never be extinguished. The created will always long for identification with the Creator. Maybe it is not too preposterous to suggest that, in our post-Enlightenment era, we no longer need to give much credence to the blanket and "feely" prognostications of certain types of philosophy. For example, the nineteenth-century philosopher Ludwig Feuerbach believed that God is an outward projection of people's inner nature.[15] The deities that emerge from this approach are likely to appear as reflections of our own wants and needs—anthropomorphic. However, the integrity and meaning of this very complex being we call "human" must be maintained. We maintain integrity while moving along a rugged pathway that explores truth.

Truth is truth no matter where it leads. Christians should never be afraid of what is empirically true.

For our theological purpose of discerning the nature of our Creator-God, we must admit, once again, that science will not and cannot, by itself, lead us to God. Science will never be able to describe the ineffable nature of the Creator. At some point, beyond the basics of scientific endeavor, we will, paradoxically, be forced to tread *two* parallel pathways. One will be the quest for scientific certitudes, and the other will inevitably be the pathway of revealed faith.

Maybe that's the reason why the priests of mystery today are more likely to be found among scientists than among our revisionist clergy. It will be the latter pathway that will force us to consider, not so much the results of our human search for God, but the historical realities of God's search for us. It is this pathway that will lead us to deeper understanding of the existence and nature of God.

Here, we tread an astounding arena of revelation. We begin to appreciate how the awesome Creator-God has entered into the historical paradigm of the human story. But the primary purpose of this book is to discern *what it is* that God has chosen to reveal to us. It is in this self-revelation that God makes known to us His nature and purposes for creation.

"Let There Be . . ."

Everything begins through the power of God's Word. His will, His actions, and His Word are seen to be consistently the same. As God thinks and speaks, things happen. His Word is living and active (Heb. 4:12). Try to put a time frame to that!

The opening verses of Genesis present an initial picture of apparent disorder and darkness. As God is responsible for the big bang, what is to happen from that point on is connected to what God has already created. In Hebrew texts, the word *ruach*, meaning breath, wind or spirit, is used to describe the Spirit hovering over this as yet unordered state (Gen. 1:2). However, we must never think of this chaos as the story of a creation moving progressively toward a condition God did not intend. The apparent state of erratic randomness had a purpose. According to the Genesis and John writers, the Word comes into action in the creation and ordering of the planet Earth. But this does not mean that God wasn't already speaking into the chaotic process. We must never assume that God was *not* responsible for the creation of this disordered state; He was.

The apparent state of disorder is what is observed before the Light of God shines upon creation. Subsequently, by God's order, the Light of God illuminates the process by which God brings about recognizable order, form, and time. Light and order are synonymous. First-day Light speaks about the order of new beginnings.

The Genesis writer understands the Word of God to be the agent bringing about order and distinction in creation. Throughout the Bible, metaphors of chaos are employed to describe something other than God's completed purpose. For example, the sea is often a metaphor describing chaos or resistance to God's purposes (e.g., Ex. 14:15). The imagery of sea stands in contrast to that of Eden's rivers, denoting God's presence and provision (e.g., Josh. 3:17).

In the process of creation, the Spirit broods over the water to accomplish His purposeful design from the genesis of seemingly unordered beginnings. In many, many, ways, the work of the Holy Spirit continues in the work of bringing order from apparent disorder.

"Let There Be Light."

It was the first day! That is a theological statement. And for our theological purposes, we may just as easily think of "day" as "moment." The creation story is remarkably poetic in character. We should not think of the word "day" in the chronological framework of a twenty-four-hour period. Rather, the word introduces us to four very important theological concepts.

First, this is our introduction to the perception of time as it relates to the successive stages of *what* God has created. Our concept of time and its separation begins here. In a world possessing the dimensions of place and space, time is now present. This is a physical universe, and, as far as we know, unlike anything God had previously created.

Second, the scientific view that only matter-energy and empty space existed at the beginning is now seen to be erroneous. Frank Wilczek tells us that the electromagnetic disturbances existed in the beginning-along with place and space. These manifestations *"are light*. So the equations predicted the existence of new kinds of things, new kinds of matter, if you like, that weren't known at the time."[16] The very nature of God, Light, was impregnated upon creation at the moment of its ordering. Instead of thinking in terms of hours and minutes, the Genesis writer introduces us to certain realities of *what* God has done or revealed. This event is truly the first moment of light.

Third, "Let there be . . ." is a theological statement introducing the revelation that life forms that God calls into being by the power of His Word are now able to exist and be sustained in their environs. Something had to occur in the created world *before* those particular life forms could exist (Gen. 1:20-23). The awesome wonder of divine inspiration is clearly evident. What began on the first day would be sustained and connected to the natural lights of the fourth day.

According to the writer of the Book of Revelation, there is no fourth-day light in the new creation. First-day Light is the everlasting constant of a new order. It represents an eternal discovery of the inexhaustible revelation of God's holy presence upon His creation.

The writer of the Genesis passage knew absolutely nothing of the big bang or the twenty-five to thirty fine tunings that were necessary for life forms to exist and be sustained. He was divinely inspired in stating how, by the power of God's will and Word alone, God was intimately the instigator of every stage in the creation of the universe.

Speaking in theological terms, a Christian physicist may say that God *spoke* at least twenty-five to thirty times in order for the world to come into being as we know it today. Similar thinking is already evident in the New Testament (Titus 1:2; 2 Tim. 1:9). In our description of time, we may consider God's successive commands in His fine-tuning of the earth. They are the successive *moments* of speaking into His creation.

Fourth, here is the first sign that all creation is seen to be a reflection of the very nature of God. And, immediately, we are riveted by the thought that God is light. A New Testament thought is, "God dwells in unapproachable light" (1 Tim. 6:16). He is also the "Father of lights" (James 1:17). In the conversion of the apostle Paul, we see that God is the life-changing power of light (Acts 9:3-5; John 8:12). If meaning is to emerge from this dark and seeming disorder, then it has to be the work of the Spirit. Humanity can never evolve to this exalted state of pure light, but can be supernaturally enlightened and enabled to be a reflection of it. All sense of meaning may then be seen in the light of the very nature of God.

Natural light does not appear until the fourth day. "Fourth-day light" speaks of the reflection of nature's lights (sun and moon) which provide for the distinction of days and seasons. Obviously, it is not the primary light in which God calls His people to walk.

From a theological point of view, we may say that the awesome light that accompanied the initial moments of the big bang is the energy of God's *shekinah* glory. It was that glory that shed light upon the disorder of dark and raw nature (Gen. 1:3). All meaning for creation has to emerge in the awesome light of God alone. The beginning, the heart, and the end of the biblical story *is* the glory of God.

By the power of the Word, all creation is initially baptized in the illuminating light and glory of God's creative and sustaining presence. From the moment of its beginning, the universe became a sacramental sign of God's creative love. It conveyed something of the very nature of the infinite into the creaturely finiteness of the created. It was a moment of awesome presence and glory.

I must confess that I have struggled with the naming of my foundational description of time. In many ways it may have been perfectly appropriate to name it "moment of revelation." The meaning of "first day" is powerful. Hence, the light of this day would have been the illumination of God that revealed *what* He had begun in contrast to the primary stages of creation. However, and upon reflection, I felt that the biblical concept of "day" provides the most lasting and powerfully poetic expression in the word "moment." We cannot gloss over the fact that creation was initially baptized in the light of God's glory.

In this early stage, we have an amazing coincidence or a magnificent stroke of revelation. As we noted, physicists tell us that energy and matter are the same thing. Clearly, the Genesis writer is recording something he cannot possibly understand. The power of God's Word sheds the energy of light upon the first millisecond of creation's exploding matter. But the Source that enabled the existence of this tiny ball of matter was created at the initiative of the Word of God. "All things came into being through him, and without him not one thing came into being" (John 1:3).

It is the Light of God that first illuminates all that becomes possible in the process of creation.

The Light of God exists eternally before the physical order of creation begins to emerge. It is not eternally connected to or dependent upon the substance of creation. God is Light! His Word enabled Light to be reflected upon His creation. It was the first image. God's purposes have begun. In His sovereign nature, they will prevail.

But, in the very moment when God said, "Let there be Light," the entire universe was baptized in the awesome *shekinah* glory of God.

From a theological perspective, it was not a continuous baptism of fiery beginnings, but a sign of assurance that served to further and sustain all of God's purposes for creation. It was a signature event that denoted the primary difference and separation between darkness and light. Genesis 1:2 reveals that, before God's process of order emerged, darkness prevailed. Without this particular, glorious light, creation could have continued in disorderly directions. There is and always will be a distinction between God and creation.

The event provided many concomitant metaphors throughout the entire Bible (e.g., 1 John 1:7). In natural terms, although the brilliance of baptismal Light may possibly have faded, fourth-day light governed the principle of the separation of day from night. Will first-day Light ever appear again? In our quest for the meaning of light, we shall see how the emergence of a new order will answer this question.

John, like a good Jewish writer, presents an astounding thought when likening this principle to Jesus. (It's very difficult to accept that he was really writing for Greek Gnostics.) Speaking of Christ as the living Word, John writes, "The light shines in the darkness, and the darkness did not overcome it." Speaking of John the Baptist as Christ's forerunner, the apostle says, "He himself was not the light, but he came to testify to the light. The true light, which enlightens everyone, was coming into the world" (John 1:5, 8-9).

John is speaking of a brand-new creation (John 1:12-13). He is announcing that in Christ, the light of the world, a new order is being introduced into the existing order. It is a new creation, made possible only by the brilliant energy and Light of the Creator.

What would that mean to a Jewish reader? Similarly, Paul speaks of a people who have been rescued from the powers of darkness in order to receive their inheritance with the saints in light (Col. 1:12-13). The writer to the Ephesians speaks metaphorically of disorderly behavior becoming visible when exposed to light (Eph. 5:1-9). In fact, the Bible often contrasts darkness as a chaotic condition that is concomitant with an unfinished work in God's planned order with light as a state that is consistent with the finished brilliance of God's own nature.

The continuing power of God's light is sustained in the principle of what we are calling "essential relationships." In other words, the entire order of creation is held in equilibrium through the power of God-enabled relationships. These relationships are a reflection of their source, which is the triune relationship eternally existent in the Creator. This principle is at the very heart of the gospel story. In fact, we may say that the gospel story is all about essential relationships of creation.

The writer of Genesis 1 moves through the stages of creation. His use of the word "day" becomes the acknowledgment that time has not only begun, but the process of order in formation has also been given birth. Each so-called "day" was a moment of light.

From the moment of creation, the physical dimensions are present to enable the fourth dimension of time. Indeed, the fourth day indicates that the introduction of physical elements, such as sun and moon, means that time will always be related to an otherness relating to earth's order of being.

Of course, that is not true of the Light, the Creator of the universe. As we move through the stages of creation, each major facet is preceded by the words, "And God said." The power of the Word is responsible for every stage in creation. After each stage, "God saw that it was good."

We are also called to observe how the natural light of the fourth day provides the process by which time, days, and seasons may be measured because they are governed by the changing nature of this light. The writer of this passage had no idea of the scientific implications of "fine-tuning" when creation moves in its rightful order. For him, everything is going according to God's plan. Creation is just the way God originally thought of it. This would certainly also mean that God is involved with the fine-tuning of all creation's stages.

God wasn't simply waiting to see what emerged from His initial command. Nor was He waiting to see what planet would best suit His purposes. "The whole cosmos was assembled step-by-step over billions of years and across billions of trillion of miles just for us!"[17]

Obviously, the Genesis writer describes the earth's shape according to the ancient three-tier view. We would only get upset today if we felt that the writer had been compelled to write in scientific terms, rather than theological and poetic terms. All that he wants us to know is that, however it was done or, in chronological terms, however long it took, creation came into being because God said so. The order emerged precisely according to His design and purpose. God was not surprised by the result.

Finally!

Finally, we come to the words, "Then God said," which mean something is about to happen of an astounding and wondrous nature. For all remaining time, this act of God will change the entire shape of interrelationships within the total schema of His plan for creation. The earth is ready for humanity, and humanity is ready for the earth. The time is now ripe; the conditions are ready for the holy Breath of God to crown His ultimate purposes for His creation (Gen. 2:7).

"Let us make humankind in our image, according to our likeness" (Gen. 1:26).

When I was in theological college, an Old Testament professor explained the use of the plural "us" as being a simple literary device. It was the royal plural, just as the Queen of Britain would use it. In major speeches, she always says "we" instead of "I." This gives the idea that she is representing something bigger than that of her own person.

I'm a lot less convinced of that explanation today. What could God be representing that's bigger than that of His own Person? "By myself I have sworn" (Isa. 45:23). There are no other gods that can claim such a focus of loyalty!

Quite possibly, as monotheism was not clearly articulated by Israel's writers in its early period, the polytheistic concept of the "Most High" or the God above all gods, El Shaddai, was the highest deity on which most primitive seekers focused their sense of awe. In some primitive religions there was often a sense of their being a god above all gods. Possibly, in early Israel this notion may have been present. However, at the time of Isaiah of Jerusalem, monotheism exclusively was beginning to be proclaimed in Israel (Isa. 37:16). From a reading of the very intimate psalms, especially the Twenty-third Psalm, I have yet to be convinced that King David was not a monotheist as well. Is it possible that the Genesis writer was actually inspired to write of God in a magnitude, or character, larger than he could personally imagine? What had he experienced of God's supernatural Light? This foretelling revelation puts the revisionist followers of Enlightenment methodologies somewhere in distant shadows.

When God *decided* to make humanity in His own image, He must have been revealing something of His own nature and of His own power in the process. It is not surprising to believers in the Trinitarian nature of God that the principle of *otherness* is employed in terms of the economy of purpose. Was He saying that He wanted His own nature and His abilities to be reflected upon the face of creation? Was this process to be spearheaded by gifting a creation-authority to humanity? Here was a creature inbreathed, and unlike any other creature in God's creation, equipped to relate to the earth and also the Source of otherness in God. In completeness of body, soul and spirit, humanity had been clothed with a spiritual body. (Just as the Apostle Paul explained in 1Cor.15:44).

There are enormous ramifications here. If God gave to humanity the authority to rule over everything in creation (Gen. 1:28), then humanity must also have been given the ability to do the task. God made creatures uniquely able to focus all things that existed into harmony. This new community would be the primary medium that pointed to God as the very center of harmonious relationships.

All creation was subject to, and came under, the loving care of these unique creatures (Gen. 1:28; Ps. 8:6; Heb. 2:8). The fact that God gave to Adam authority to name the animals signified that Adam was given control of all living creatures. Adam was to be responsible for the inter-connectedness of all things in creation. This authority was for the purpose of keeping all things in harmony with each other and with God. Naming was about living in an order of trustful relationships.

Imagine the astounding possibilities that are at play here. The Spirit who breathed on the disorder of matter also breathed into the human form. Humanity, now breathed upon by the Spirit became a reflection of God's divine life and nature. The Adam community was now enabled to exercise a powerful measure of governance and order within God's creation. This community would now have the power and authority reflecting that of first-day order of Light. There was not a time limit placed on this embryonic community; God's inbreathing of His own life was intended to last forever.

The Genesis 1 account, which records the command to be fruitful and multiply, meant that human offspring would also be privileged with the unique relationship as "sons of God" (Gen. 6:2). Surely, it must also have meant that sex was in the plan of God. How could this small community be fruitful, multiply, and fill the earth without enjoying the gift that makes procreation possible?

This race of Adam was intended to possess the power to hold all things, all places, and all time under their rule. (The command is given in plural terms.) Such an apostolic command would have required that the community have the ability to operate above the level of what we now accept as the natural. Nothing else in all nature received the inbreathing of God, nor was it given the authority for such a universal responsibility. And all without time restraint. What other creature could have received it? So we must consider that this ability had to be of a supernatural nature. It didn't evolve. Maybe God was fine-tuning for the thirty-first time!

Are there certain elements of multidimensional ability here? Maybe it is a far-reaching question, but the thought does raise other questions. Would this inbreathed ability to reflect God be an essential gifting to make possible the performance of a global mission? Does their commission now assume that there are human creatures already existing who have not ever stood in the awesome glory of God's grace? For all the earth to be under the Adam community's control, must this community have been endued with a God-given ability to rise above the time constraints of place and space? Hopefully, the unfolding story will furnish an answer to these questions.

The Adam community, in terms of its unique power over creation, was totally focused on using this inbreathed power to honor and maintain God's kingdom rule. In the process, they would partner with God in the playing out of His purposes for creation. They would be a priesthood, offering all creation in worship to the almighty Creator.

In particular relation to time, we may glean something in the first sign of Jesus (John 2:1-11). When taken as a literal event by the power of the Word alone, the instantaneous changing of water to wine must rank as a natural impossibility. Similarly, in Acts 8 there is that strange story about Philip and the Ethiopian eunuch. After the eunuch's baptism on the roadway, how was Philip suddenly found to be in Azotus? Certainly, in the life of Jesus, we do discern a particular measure of control over time and nature (John 11:6). What other creature could walk on water? Were these incidences signs of what was once possible in Eden?

What would God's commission really mean if the original Adam had indeed been restricted by fourth-dimensional time? How could he rule over all the earth if he had to leg it or jet it from the model garden? After all, at this stage in his existence, and from a theological perspective, time was not considered to harbor any problems. It was certainly not an enemy, nor was it an obstacle to his everlasting purposes.

The Genesis writer certainly didn't think of God in Trinitarian terms, but we have spoken of the perfection of God's love expressed in the three Persons of the Godhead. Although God has no need to express His love by creating a universe, human beings are totally connected to the earth from which they were formed. That's the main theological point the Genesis writer is making by saying that humans were created out of the clay of creation. With all due respect to Origen, humans were not originally spirit-beings sent down to a physical creation. (Origen called this little jaunt of so-called reincarnation "the transmigration of souls."[18])

Recently, I watched an episode of the *Raymond* TV sitcom in which a little girl completely baffled her daddy with the question, "If we are all intended to go to heaven, then why should we start off on earth?" Questions such as this were asked by pioneers of Gnostic philosophy. It was God's plan for every unique, physical person of this inbreathed community to live forever in a material existence.

In this way, and at the right time in the process of humanity's creation, God breathed into this creature. From that time, the nature and creative possibilities of God were reflected upon all creation. The first Genesis account simply declares that God created humankind in His own image. Of course, this does not mean that humanity was made of the so-called "substance" of God, because God is Spirit. Humanity, made from clay, was gifted with reflecting God's nature onto creation. The second account speaks little of the how. In fact, all the biblical accounts of creation are much more concerned with the *why* than the *how*.

One thing stands out with the intensity of a flashing neon sign. When God finished this little job, He said, "It is very good." God was completely satisfied with the product and order that had emerged. It was no random accident. However, we must make note of a particular observation found in the first Genesis narrative: God did not say, "It is very good," until Adam and Eve had been gifted to understand and perform their place and purpose within His schema of creation.

John O'Keefe, a renowned modern astronomer, marvels at the complexity of the universe and arrives at an astounding conclusion. "We are, by astronomical standards, a pampered, closeted, cherished group of creatures; our Darwinian claim to have done it all by ourselves is as ridiculous and as charming as a baby's brave effort to stand on its own feet and refuse his mother's hand. If the universe had not been made with the most exacting precision we could never have come into existence. It is my view that these circumstances indicate the universe was created for man to live in."[19]

Not every believer occupied in the arena of science would totally agree. Some would suggest that Darwin never claimed that human status was self-achieved. However, they may well agree that God intended a special place for His human image. They were a product of the process of first-day Light!

Francis Collins, of the Human Genome Project, is also a committed Christian. He notes, "Evolution, as a mechanism, can be and must be true. But that says nothing about the nature of its author. For those who believe in God, there are reasons now to be more in awe, not less."[20]

Again, I must repeat that the various Christian perspectives on the *how* of creation should not cause us to be angry at or derisive of each other. The truth of these questions and findings brings honor to God, not defensiveness.

In the meantime, we press on further with the questions of *why*. It is the *why* questions that constitute the bulk of biblical literature.

One thing is certain: the Adam community was clearly the most unique creation among all that had ever existed. Here was an inbreathed creature that was both physical and spiritual in nature. In that sense, Adam could truly be the priest for all creation. Standing between the eternal I Am and the time-governed created, in a God-given priesthood, he was uniquely able to offer all creation to God in joyous worship.

This creature, in both genders, was truly the priesthood of creation. But was creation really finished?

CHAPTER 4

First-Day Light on a Glorious Priesthood

*B*efore we begin to describe the peculiar characteristics of the remarkable creature we know as human, there is need to broaden our theological picture a little more. It is very important. As we tread this road, we need to understand that the accounts surrounding humanity's creation are primarily contained in a theological story. In order to walk this road, we need to place the two accounts of creation, not in opposition, but in *apposition* to each other. So I will meld the two stories in order for us to discover the bigger picture of their meaning. It's a bit like a 3-D movie; you can't get the full picture until you look through both lenses of the glasses.

In the Judeo-Christian way of thinking, a question of how is clearly very different from a question of why. People who pursue scientific disciplines help us to appreciate the differences. On the other hand, "if the universe is expanding, there may be physical reasons why there had to be a beginning. One could still imagine that God created the universe at the instant of the Big Bang . . ."[1] Here, a little tongue in cheek, Stephen Hawking is interested in the origin of time. He offers a scientific theory of how it all began, but wisely leaves it to others to suggest why. We can see very quickly that the greater interest of biblical writers is in the question why.

We have seen that God, by His very nature, is a relational God. His Light is pivotal in shaping new directions in the biblical story of creation's relationships. In the perfection of His triune Personhood, He created the universe with the stamp of His own nature upon it.

In other words, the planet Earth and everything in it is intended to exist in a synthesis of interdependent and harmonious relationships. These relations are a reflection arising from the very nature of the Trinitarian God. The Creator is a relational God; He plans all nature to be a reflection of His glory.

Clearly, the motivating force that keeps all things and all relationships of creation in harmonious synthesis is the power of love. Why is that? It's not simply because God does acts of love; it is because God *is* love. His very nature is love. (1John 4:8) Therefore, all creation is intended to harmonize together in a synthesis of loving relationships emanating from God's nature, and as He has revealed Himself.

These relationships are not held together in a sloppy way. They are not brought into effect by our individual perceptions of how a love relationship is carried out. For example, Jesus once said to His disciples, "You are my friends *if you do what I command you*" (John 15:14; italics mine). We are talking about God here. God, who is love, knows more about the how of love than do we. What we may describe as essential relationships are held together by the power of God's love. They may be summarized in four ways.

1. Relationship with God

Humanity is not and cannot be fulfilled until it is in harmony with God, with others, with creation, and with itself. The heart of worship finds sweet fulfillment in these essential relationships of creation.

God is the source and focus of all creation. It's only a matter of good sense that, as the Alpha and Omega of life, all created things must have their meaning and purpose in Him (Col. 1:17). Primarily, we know who we are in relation to Whose we are!

In the first account of creation, we are simply told that God created humankind in his own image. In what is probably a further tradition, a similar thought is posed in this way: "Male and female he created them, and he blessed them and named them 'Humankind' when they were created" (Gen. 5:2).

God created both male and female in His own likeness. In other words, both male and female are created with the ability to reflect the power, the nature, the purpose, and the light of God's glory upon creation. "The glory of God is man fully human, fully alive," said Irenaeus.[2] Humanity could never find fulfillment and meaning apart from an intimate relationship with the Original, the very Source of life.

Questions of humanity's essential connection with matter, or with creation itself, are clarified in Genesis 2:7. Man is fashioned from the very substance of the earth—from dust. That's exactly the way wild animals were created (Gen. 1:24; 2:19). From a genetics point of view, the difference between humans and other creatures (e.g., apes, whales, and dolphins) is quite minimal. However, the most significant difference between animals and humanity is not brainpower, nor the opposable thumb; it's the arrangement of the DNA, plus the all-important, inbreathed life of God.

Nearly all of earth's other creatures are primarily motivated by instinct. Humanity moves in the extraordinary reflected power of a personal relationship with God, and is intended to live in an intimate consistency with His nature. They walked together in the garden (Gen. 3:8). It is a blissful picture of harmonious relationship. The advent of Eden's full humanity was truly a moment of light upon creation.

God's essential purposes for humanity cannot be divorced from creation itself. To be ruled by the Spirit is the only guarantee that humanity may exercise stewardship of creation, which means to maintain and cultivate order in God's creation (Eph. 5:18). Adam and Eve were not environmentalists; they were gifted stewards of God's creation. When God created people, He produced something entirely unique, and people were uniquely gifted to have an intimate relationship with Him. But the human creature was fundamentally connected to the earth, formed from the very stuff of creation. So the inbreathing of the Spirit is *fundamentally connected* to the empowering of universal and essential relationships.

In further passages from Genesis, there is a distinction between the Adam community and other creatures not gifted by God in the same way.

In the early Byzantine church, they used the term *theosis* to describe the Adam community's unique relationship. "God became man in order that man might become god, to use the words of Irenaeus and Athanasius."[3] By this inbreathing, the community of Eden became divine, reflecting the glory of God upon creation. (Gen.2:7) Adam (whose name, for theological purposes, will be used to represent this entire relational and embryonic community) had a personal and intimate relationship with God. But essential roots of his identity and meaning are also expressed in his ability to accomplish God's purposes for the earth.

In Genesis 6:1-2, we see that the direct descendants of the Eden community are described as the sons of God. No other creatures or persons in the first six chapters of the Bible, humanlike or not, are afforded that designation. Adam was not originally a native of Eden; God placed him there (Gen. 2:8). In other words, Eden was not a product of human endeavor, nor could it ever be. Eden was the place where Adam was to live, in signature of the kingdom God entrusted to them. Human beings did not nor ever could have created it, but were called to be partners with God in the playing out of his signatory purposes for Eden. This provision of Eden by God is a very important point for present-day revisionists to observe. No one is capable of working for the completion of God's kingdom, but all persons in Him are called to be partners with Him in His purposes.

God made Eden to be a perfect and idyllic model of His kingdom from which the Adam community could proceed on its apostolic and signatory commission. Humanity can never prepare the way of the kingdom by building another Eden. It couldn't in the beginning, and it cannot now!

The sons of God have a unique connection and relationship with Him. It is the sons of God who inherit the God-given commission to maintain order in God's creation. God does not have grandchildren! He has a distinctive, firsthand, and direct connection to the Adam community. So we see in the Gospel of Luke that the genealogy of Jesus is traced back to Adam, "son of God" (Luke 3:38).

The Genesis writer tells us, "When God created humankind, he made them in the likeness of God . . . When Adam had lived 130 years, he had a son in his own likeness, in his own image" (Gen. 5:1, 3). Later, in his gospel, John picks up on this human distinctiveness that is played out in direct and intimate relationships. "But to all who received him, who believed in his name, he gave power to *become* children of God, who were born, not of blood or the will of the flesh or of the will of man, but of God (John 1:12-13; italics mine).

From the very beginning, that is why there was need for an apostolic mission from the model of Eden.

2. Relationship with God's Community

The Hebrew word *adham* is really a plural noun that is interpreted to mean "mankind." In Genesis 3:20, we read that Eve means "mother of all living." This description of Eve is more likely to be in reference to her being the mother of the children of God. This is a relational distinction. It is logically difficult to see how Eve was the mother of the population residing in the land of Nod or anywhere else. We note that Nod was the place where their son Cain found a wife.

Most scholars would agree that, "Our species of humans first began to evolve nearly 200,000 years ago in association with technologies not unlike those of the early Neanderthals. It is now clear that early Homo sapiens, or modern humans, did not come after the Neanderthals but were their contemporaries. However, it is likely that both modern humans and Neanderthals descended from *Home heidelberensis*."[4]

In Genesis, other people or humanlike creatures did exist at the time of Cain and Abel. Some believe that Neanderthal creatures had very limited cohabitation with humans about forty thousand years ago.[5] Indeed, some geneticists would admit to the notion that a very small percentage of interbreeding did take place, until the demise of the Neanderthal. Nevertheless, despite this fragmentary thread, it's very hard to imagine that the sons of God were normally attracted to female Neanderthals. "Neanderthal man . . . was probably not a direct descendent of *Homo sapiens*, but at any rate a relative."[6] And certainly, we should never assume that Neanderthals and Homo sapiens were ever the same species that branched off in different directions. Rather, a common ancestor seems to be a strong probability which resulted in two subspecies. We may easily presume that the inhabitants of Nod are certainly not connected to a Neanderthal population.

"We should never forget that Aborigines, 'bushmen,' Asians, Europeans and Americans are not different species of human being but form a single human species, the same human race . . . Under our skin we are all Africans."[7]

The apostle Paul appears to believe that all people of the earth were of the line of Adam or, at least, of a common relational nature (Acts 17:26). However, Adam and Eve represent a unique community that lived in a unique relationship with God at a particular time. The children of Eden possessed a special inbreathing that resulted in a unique relationship and responsibility.

From the initial apostolic commission in the Bible (Gen. 1:26-28), we realize that, first, the priestly and apostolic charge given to Adam and Eve to bring the world into essential relationships, beginning with God, is also a commission to bring all people into the community of the sons of God. The entire Adam community was commissioned to be a royal priesthood. They directly related to the King of all creation and were commissioned by Him for an apostolic ministry.

Second, after their fall from grace-filled relationships, Adam and Eve passed on a nature incapable of effectively sustaining this apostolic commission. Some sort of a devolution process set in.

Third, for the purposes of God to be sustained, the inbreathing of the Spirit had to be transmitted to this descendent community again and again. We will never understand the meaning of Pentecost apart from these creation roots.

In Genesis 4:16-17, Cain leaves his homeland and settles in the land of Nod, where he sires Enoch. Enoch is the prototypical figure signifying the promise that human life was originally intended to last forever (Gen. 3:3). Enoch's translation to a permanent home is a new creation. Maybe the terminology "sons of God" can be interpreted to mean "children of an Eden community living in the purposes of God."

The underlying principles of modern Darwinism are moving into more and more disciplines, most of which demand more serious investigation.[8] Indeed, we may do well to consider the reason why, outside of grace, humanity has become a product of some sort of moral and physical devolution.

Denyse O'Leary, who is a strong believer in God, describes some problems of Darwinism's atheist exponents from this perspective. For her, aspects of Darwin's thought have been stretched into arenas beyond the biological intent that Darwin expressed. Indeed, atheists are not shy to use Darwin in order support their own agendas:

> First, there is the problem of their need to see Darwinism as a biological Theory of Everything. Darwinists insist on the implausible origin of life from non-life for the same reason as many of them insist on Social Darwinism. If there were any aspect of life that was not explained by Darwinism or other naturalistic, no-design theories, Darwinism would have to base its claims on evidence. And the state of the evidence is not good.
>
> Then there is the problem of their bad behavior. For example, Richard Dawkins, the world's best-known living Darwinist, claims—on behalf of his Oxford chair as Professor of the Public Understanding of Science- that "if you meet somebody who claims not to believe in evolution, that person is ignorant, stupid or insane (or wicked, but I'd rather not consider that) . . ."
>
> Third, there is the problem of underlying agenda. I have never heard such hardline, aggressive promotion of atheism under the guise of science as I have heard from the Darwinists. It is, at best, amusing to hear Darwinists charge that the creationists have an underlying religious agenda, when the Darwinist's own anti-religious agenda is pretty obvious . . .
>
> Fourth, Social Darwinism (sociobiology, evolutionary psychology, and whatever the next rebrand will be called) is a Bad Idea that should just be abandoned. Every time Social Darwinism rears its ugly head, many people learn about Darwinism for the first time. They discover that

learned professors think that less educated people are inferior ... The chief danger from compulsory teaching of Darwinism is that any dissenting view may begin to sound reasonable by default. However, a view cannot be assumed to have merit simply because it is not Darwinism.[9]

From a theological perspective, (and accepting much of Darwin's thought) I continue to believe that the implications of human devolution merits much more attention than it gets. For the purposes of this book, the goals before us are primarily of a theological nature. We are principally concerned with the God-given nature that makes it possible for humans to live and worship in God's interdependent community. As such, we are not particularly concerned with the evolution versus intelligent design debate, or with the many varieties of Darwinism.

Incidentally, in the world of science, some acknowledge of how the proponents of intelligent design (ID) have shown something of the enormous complexity of the universe, but in itself ID has not produced new discoveries in the field of science. Indeed, Francis Collins declares, "Intelligent Design fails in a fundamental way to qualify as a scientific theory."[10] However, I believe that the proponents of ID have produced much in the area of mathematical probability to present a case for a Creator-God.

I reiterate that our primary purpose is to look to the Self-revealing God who has involved Himself in the one story recorded in the Bible. Further, He has done so by revealing something of His own nature and purposes for creation. In our contemporary world, it is important that we briefly consider some important principles arising from the basics of the first order of creation.

Human Sexuality: Unfortunately, in many mainline church circles today, this subject is rarely debated on the basis of biblical principles, but rather on the basis of sentimentality and cultural pressure.

God, Who is Otherness, never intended humans to discover their identities in the context of sameness.

We see in the Trinitarian nature of God that, when love is genuine, it is not played out in an individualistic fashion. God is absolute completeness and oneness. In His very nature, we see that love always has a focus of otherness. The Father loves the Son, the Son loves the Holy Spirit, and the Spirit loves the Father. God is the perfection of love, equally given and received.

Consequently, we may say that the significance of our identities and lives are determined by the differences that make up the relationship of unity.

There are three Persons in one God, but each Person exhibits difference. Let's face it: we really are people who need people. The extraordinary stress and mental sickness of the modern Western world may show us that we need to relearn the creation principle that we exist in mutually dependent relationships.

Four matters, concerning relationships, point to an action plan devised by God.

First, the work of looking after Eden requires the effort of more than one inbreathed person (Gen. 2:15). The gifts that God gives to people are shared throughout the whole community. In the New Testament, we read that people need each other in order to accomplish God's purposes (1 Cor. 12:7, 14, 18-22).

Thomas Smaille offers one reason why there is also need for difference in gender; it focuses on the primary working out of the family community. "An only son in his mother's house can easily become first and central; in his father's house he is more likely to be kept second and subsidiary. He will not only have a helper behind him, but a norm, a corrective, a protector over him. He will know the safety of being second, of not being the one round whom everything revolves, but of being dependent on somebody else who is 'greater than I.'"[11]

Second, we see that the creation of Eve is not an afterthought; man cannot exist in love and harmony without the otherness of woman. It was God who decided that man could not be alone. (Was Adam operating in self-centered bliss?) Having been taken from out of Adam's side, the woman is also designed to exist in a state of otherness (Gen. 2:18). If God exists in the otherness of three Persons, how can this inbreathed creature exist meaningfully in isolation of personhood?

This is not a cultural fad. In order to accomplish God's purposes for creation, unity is expressed through the honoring of distinction in gender, nature, and function.

Third, the human identity cannot be realized by relating to nature alone. That sort of focus would lead to self-idolatry or to making God into an image reflecting humanity's own perceived needs (Gen. 2:20; Ex. 20:4; Rom. 1:21-25). The apostle Paul introduces the idea of self-idolatry into the homosexual debate. Indeed, the basis of his thinking may easily relate to what he discovers in natural religion. There is a side of us that longs to be fulfilled in the difference provided by the opposite sex.

Completeness and identity are discovered in difference, not sameness. For this reason, a child, in order to express confidence in his or her sexual identity, needs to experience good role modeling by both a male and a female parent. This is clearly a creation principle. A number of my Christian, homosexually oriented friends have told me that this biblical principle has been a major factor in their willingness to live a life of struggle to fulfill the will of God.

Kingdom-focused discipleship means putting the wants of self-centeredness under control. It's a concept hardly understood in our postmodern world. Surely, the mistaken notion that Jesus said nothing about same-sex relationships arises from ignorance of His creation-centered theology. In relation to questions about divorce, Jesus really did speak about homosexuality by outlining God's creation purposes. From this perspective, it is absolutely inconceivable for Him even to countenance an institution of blessing same-sex relations. The physical means by which that relationship is expressed is accomplished between a man and a woman. (Mark 10:6-9). In the very physical intimacy of sexual oneness, how can two people of the same sex become one flesh?

We must not linger in an area often coated in a veneer of sentimentalism. Unfortunately, when same-sex issues are with sentiment or in a political arena, which usually does not countenance creation principles at all, then creation theology is always abandoned.

Speaking of the very low percentage of homosexual leanings in identical twin males, Francis Collins concludes, "Sexual orientation is genetically influenced but not hardwired by DNA, and that whatever genes are involved represent predispositions, not predeterminations."[12] Even if there were genetic "predeterminations," such a discovery would merely prove that, in sin and brokenness, there has been a radical change in certain predispositions of the entire human condition.

That is why all sincere Christians identify with the struggle for holiness in themselves and all others. Heterosexual Christians can do nothing less than sympathize with homosexually oriented people in their own struggles (1 Cor. 6:9-10; Gal. 6:1-3). To identify with one who struggles (as we see the Paraclete doing in John 14:16-17) does not mean that unhealthy behavior is affirmed. It means that, in our arrogant nature, we admit that we are all lepers. All of us need to cry, "Leper!" when approaching the presence of our holy God.

Fourth, we see that throughout creation, except possibly for worms, the different physical makeup of two sexes is required in order to procreate. Obviously, the physical structures of man and woman were designed differently. This physical difference facilitates a physical intimacy leading to procreation and the fulfillment of God's command to fill the earth. Sexual behavior other than this depends on mimicry of God's design. Clearly, in God's design, it was solely in the union of man and woman that two people could become one flesh.

Isn't this the very reason why Jesus said, "For this reason [i.e., two people of distinct genders become one flesh] shall a man shall leave his father and mother and be joined to his wife"? (Matt. 19:5; bracketed material mine). Not surprisingly, there isn't one verse in the entire Bible that supports the idea of God's blessing on same-sex unions. Human beings cannot bless what God has not ordained. Culture may persuade us to bless, but God's very nature and purpose does not honor it.

Men and Women in Priesthood: In the commission given to the royal priesthood of the Eden community, both man and woman are priests. They are both priests because, together, they offer to God the innocent fruits of creation. A blood offering in Eden is meaningless because, in innocence, there is no need to offer a substitutionary offering of blood to God. In Eden, all offerings are the fruits of innocence taken in stewardship from the earth. Generally and historically speaking, the man has become the focus (but not always the sole focus) in offering these sacrifices of apostolic priesthood on behalf of the community.

Usually, there is a difference in focus between a man and a woman. The nature of each sex is a primary motivator for this difference. The woman has a natural (but not exclusive) desire to be nurturing, supportive, enabling, dialogical, and comforting. She is usually the one who becomes primarily and more inwardly focused on caring for the children of a relationship. She is also predisposed to support the emotional and physical needs of the man in their peer relationship and focus.

For many today, traditional relationships and roles between men and women are changing. This is particularly true in the area of who provides for the family. Economics may have a major influence. It is not uncommon to observe a sharing of responsibilities. In these situations, both man and woman play major roles in providing for the family.

However, we still observe that the focus for the woman tends more naturally in an inward and local direction. Historically, these roots probably go back to the hunting and gathering way of life in which the husband possessed a focus extending beyond the home. As the one traditionally equipped to be the provider and protector for the family, he was away from home more often.

Most contemporary women are not ignorant of non-local knowledge, activity, or interest. Nevertheless, for both theological and practical reasons, we must take seriously the differences in the nature of man and woman as designed by God. We do so in order to make possible a primary apostolic focus in both. Now, both the Christian man and the Christian woman see themselves as contributors to a primary purpose of priesthood extending beyond their own home. And, in the sense of mutual purpose, the apostolic focus of both Adam and Eve should be observed to be a shared ministry.

Man and woman need each other in order for the apostolic commission to work. It is most certainly not a question of who exercises most power in the relationship. However, the outward apostolic focus is different from the inner pastoral focus. Normally, the outward focus is demonstrated in the masculine gender.

When the pastoral focus dominates the apostolic focus, the community becomes more inwardly centered, whether that focus is initiated by men or women. We may even say that one of the reasons why Western churches are fast losing membership is precisely because of the dominance of a pastoral focus over a predominantly outward-focused approach to ministry.

A healthy outward focus is often lost in modern relationships. In our postmodern world, it is not unusual to observe a primary focus on the self and its needs. The rise of individual wants over community needs has grown very strongly. And so today, in the life of the church, whenever we see that the apostolic focus has become secondary, numerous problems of identity and purpose arise, and confusion emerges.

However, the outward and apostolic focus will not work without the nurturing and pastoral inner focus. Indeed, we must not make firm rules of order where we note that God has chosen leadership in unusual or a-cultural ways. For example, in the history of Israel, its people would have been in a very sorry state without the leadership of Deborah and Queen Esther. And it was a woman, Rahab, who made it possible for Joshua's army to enter Jericho. In the New Testament, there are also numerous examples of women who provided excellent leadership.

Historically, although under social constraint, women of the past two centuries have also made enormous contributions to the world of science. Given the opportunity to move according to affirmed calling, and in the context that relational order is maintained, we assume that women will more easily take leadership roles today.

Historically, men, in their providing and protective nature, have more naturally taken leadership roles, but not always. Today, gender roles are not quite so static. For example, many couples, convinced that the continuing closeness of a mother is vitally important for the healthy formation of her children, forfeit the material benefits of two incomes for a significant period of time. After that time, the woman often re-embarks or sets out upon her own career. Sometimes, the woman is better equipped to provide the most substantial income for the family. Therefore, the man stays at home with the children for a period.

My point is that, wherever possible, children really do need to have a parent at home. The more natural choice is usually the woman. A babysitter is a poor psychological substitute in providing formation. I would venture to say that the woman is superior to the man in this regard. I recall, as a boy, coming home somewhat distressed, only to realize that my mother was working. It was wartime, and for six years my father was abroad. Nevertheless, I felt robbed of my mother's much-needed consolation at a time of distress.

But from a theological point of view, in historic and post-reformation churches, there is absolutely no theological reason why a woman should not share leadership at the celebration of the Eucharist. Maybe we need the courage to explore the meaning of priesthood in the New Testament church. (That is a major purpose for my book, The Church I Couldn't Find).

Eve is also a priest of creation. Because of the woman's natural disposition, a woman may not always be the best equipped to be *the leader* of a local church community. Questions should also be posed concerning the leadership abilities of a particular man. Yet, despite cultural trends, present experience is also revealing a practical and psychological reality. Generally, men more naturally hold within their make-up a primary outward and apostolic focus.

In mainline churches, we have now had time to observe the results of apostolic life as evidenced by growth in membership. With a primary inward focus, women in church leadership usually are not easily equipped to produce lively and growing congregations. Of course, men possessing a similar focus produce similar results. We should take note of these results, if only to better evaluate factors that make for a more effective and apostolic priesthood. Maybe, in this way, we may also better understand the nature of the relationship existing in the Genesis 2 account. Whatever may be the outcome, it is imperative to heed the biblical proposition that man cannot be alone!

Some years ago, when presenting a paper to my Calgary synod in favor of the ordination of women, I hastened to point out that questions of ordination and leadership were distinct but complementary issues. As such, they should both be considered carefully in relation to matters of function. The motion passed, but criteria for effective leadership were never seriously considered. Unfortunately, political rights and post-second-century tradition became the major criteria for theological discussion. These are not the most effective way in which a Christian community should carry out its primary apostolic commission. The question of the most effective type of leadership must always be paramount in the community's embrace of its apostolic focus.

3. Relationship with God's Creation

The identity of the Adam community is primarily realized in a focus lying beyond itself. Otherness is a primary requirement in the community's understanding of its own purpose and nature. In Genesis 1, we see that this otherness is primarily focused in God, and is expressed in a relationship with creation. Such a co-relationship is like another Trinitarian type of relationship, except God doesn't need creation.

In both accounts of creation (i.e., Genesis 1 and 2), God places the Adam community in a material and physical context for a particular purpose. Fashioned from the stuff of creation, humans are intrinsically connected to the earth. They are designed to be at home in the physical environment that God provided. Humanity needs the earth, but God doesn't.

This is an essential principle of creation, and one that will not fail in the ultimate purposes of God. The purpose God had in mind is very clear. He commanded His children to fill the earth and have dominion over it. This empowered community was to be a sign to all creation of the harmony and focus God had originally designed. It was the beginning of a covenant relationship. Never at any time before or after, has there emerged another creature uniquely equipped by God's Spirit to take responsibility for the stewardship of all creation. Indeed, we may say that the biblical narrative of creation becomes one story when it is connected to the apostolic mission given to the Eden community.

"Be fruitful and multiply, and fill the earth and subdue it; and have dominion over every living thing that moves on the earth" (Gen. 1:28;

see also Ps. 8:6). Some people are very cynical about that passage of Scripture. They think it gives license to plunder and ravage creation. Nothing could be further from the truth.

The Septuagint use of the verb *katakurieuo* strongly suggests the interpretation "to bring under your control." It is very important to note here that the verbal commission to bring the earth under your control is written in the plural; it is given to both the man and the woman. This commission is really quite remarkable. As far as we know or understand, humans are the only creatures who possess an ingrained life mission to preserve other creatures.

Both man and woman are required for the apostolic mission, i.e., a caring and creative mission beyond the signature life of Eden. The commission is, as sons and daughters of God, to raise up a universal race living in an intimate relationship with God and with all creation. Clearly, God designed creation in such a way as to ensure that Adam's apostolic commission could not work unless the functions of both the outward and inward focus worked together in unity.

In this sense, the entire Adam community is engaged in an apostolic mission. As the citizens of Eden, they are to become a prophetic sign to all peoples of the earth.

Genesis 2:15 records, "The Lord God took the man and put him in the Garden of Eden to till it and keep it." Man was not created there, but when he was ready, God provided him with an environment where he could model and live in signature of kingdom life.

God had already created the perfect arena for kingdom life into which humanity was placed. God did so in order for the Adam community to sign and focus the life of worship in a priestly ministry for all creation. Eden, therefore, was initially created and designed by God, not by humanity. The model of what kingdom life is belonged to God, not to humanity.

With Eden as its base, and also its sign to the world, this was to be a community of proclamation; it was called to offer all creation before God in a life of worship. Both male and female shared in this priestly, outward purpose they were given. Later, we see that it is Jesus, the real Adam, who actually succeeds in fulfilling this priestly charge (1 Cor. 15:24). It is the royal priesthood of Jesus that will continue as an everlasting signature.

For the Adam community, their worshipping work is to raise up a universal people to become sons and daughters of God. They offer up all creation to God in a priesthood of worship (John 1:12-13). Theirs is a priesthood of creation; they stand at the pinnacle of all life offering all creation in unified harmony and praise to God.

> Let the peoples praise you, O God;
>> let all the peoples praise you.
>
> Let the nations be glad and sing for joy . . .
>
> The earth has yielded its increase;
>> God, our God, has blessed us. (Ps. 67:3-4, 6)
>
> Let heaven and earth praise him,
>> the seas and everything that moves in them.
>> (Ps. 69:34)

God intended to hang around to help them in their priestly mission and in the enabling of Eden as the primary sign to the world of kingdom life. God doesn't partner a creature who interprets this mission as a charge to plunder His creation. It is very clear that He is most certainly not like the deist god who clocks off work and then moves on to take on an indeterminate vacation. How could a deistic creator maintain the purposes and relationships of creation?

An example of this continuing relationship of Creator to steward, of Lover to the beloved, is highlighted in the picture of God walking in the garden. God, the consummate Lover, is courting the responses of the beloved.

The question asked by God is a matter of checking out their responses to the covenant He had established for them. "Where are you?" (Gen. 3:9). Of course, God knows the answer, but do Adam and Eve? It's a matter of both intimacy and accountability. God is right there, and He wants to stay. But He is doing more than simply helping His new pals with a caretaking job. We may imagine that God had raised that question once before. Maybe it was on an occasion when Satan stopped showing up for morning worship!

We see in God's decision to give authority to his sons that He allows Himself to be vulnerable to the decisions humans make. Adam and Eve possess both the authority and the power for God's commission. Whether or not we can describe this power in contemporary terms, we do know one thing for certain: Spirit-enabled ability would have been absolutely necessary to carry out such an apostolic commission. Of course, these same abilities, by the will, could also be translated into instruments of chaos. God thereby allowed Himself to be vulnerable to the decisions of Adam.

But, in the choices Adam was allowed to exercise, he was also vulnerable. Ego-driven decisions may have been attractive, but God's community was called to work through the power of loving persuasion. In other words, their means of operation was through medium of invitation. Modern evangelistic efforts may do well to honor this creation principle more than anything designed to manipulate a decision.

Authority without power is meaningless, and vice versa. The power of God's inbreathing is given in order to embrace the ability of signing the Creator's purposes. This gift was given in order that work should become the worship of fashioning the world into images of kingdom life. Those who operate in an evangelical milieu must always remember that we are not saved simply in order to possess eternal life. We are saved in order to live the kingdom life, now and forever.

4. Relationship with God's Image: The Self

Of course, the original and its reflection are not the same thing. Our reflection in a mirror is not the substance of the original. Being made in God's image enables us to understand something of the human struggle. Many psychologists tell us that a fundamental problem within the human struggle is not so much that people love themselves, but that they hate themselves! Root reasons for this may relate to background illusions of self-divinity, but also may find roots in the fact that many people search for meaning in the wrong places. In the agnostic and contemporary view of relationships, unfortunately, they begin in a naturalist sense with the self, and evolve from there onward.

No wonder God simply becomes the product or the enabler of human desires. The idea that the philosophical premise determines the conclusion makes God the product of self-motivated feelings. (In this sense Feuerbach did have a point)!

When Jesus commanded His followers to love themselves (Mark 12:29-31), which was understood by those expert in the law to include loving their neighbors as themselves (Deut. 6:4; Luke 10:27), He was recalling them to a condition that existed in the original schema of creation. The extraordinarily complex and beautiful creature, man, was never designed to know himself apart from knowing others. His predisposition to inner harmony is only explored in the freedom to pursue the otherness of essential relationships. With essential relationships in place, and with God as the primary focus, body, soul, and spirit are in harmony with one another, and not at war within themselves.

Earlier, we considered the fact that God is never diminished in the act of creating. In other words, He isn't fundamentally connected to His creation. In the same way, He is not fundamentally connected to the creatures into which He breathed His life. This is a very clear distinction from the way of natural eastern religions. "The starting point of all their doctrines is that the spirit of man is a part of the eternal, universal, divine spirit, and is, therefore, by nature immortal. There is a 'spark of divinity' in every man . . ."[13]

This would mean that God becomes complete once the spark returns to Him. Or that humanity is complete upon the return to the spirit-real of God. But the reality is that this human creature was never intended to live in a world of spirit; he was intended to live in a physical environment with enormous spiritual potential. His sublime existence is complete in his longing for partnership with God under His sovereignty.

Psalm 42:1 speaks of the human heart longing after God. This psalm proved to be a very moving experience when it was sung at the baptism of Augustine. Years later, in his *Confessions*, Augustine wrote, "Thou hast made us for thyself and our hearts are restless till they rest in thee."[14]

The Adam community is not only responsible to be in partnership with God by maintaining harmony, but in itself, through a sense of otherness. This multi-faceted harmony is an essential sign of how this harmonic equilibrium relates to the world. In our contemporary world, we hear much of the idea that we have to start fixing our internal disorders by beginning with our own perceived needs. We have to spend our lives patting ourselves on the back. That requires a long arm and lots of wind. Television commercials persuade us to buy certain products because "you are worth it." In other words, according to the worldly view, peace within begins by looking within, and is normally accomplished through material consumerism.

This is a false premise. The reason is primarily because the beginning of the quest for serenity is identified in the wrong place. The quest really begins with a relationship with God. This relationship is then expressed in relation to others; it moves outward to the physical environment of which we are stewards. The apostolic, sending God sends His children. Harmony within the self is a byproduct of harmony in relationships, beginning with concord in our relationship with God.

What we observe in the creation story is an inner peace and a gracious harmony within the Adam community. No wonder, when the inner harmony of essential relationships devolves into disharmony within the human condition, all nature suffers the death, sickness, and disease of its leader's disharmony.

Love and the Ability to Choose

Eden, the home of perfect love, finds human expression in its sublime ability to make choices. We could not be really human if we were driven by instinct and not choice. "God said, 'You shall not eat of the fruit of the tree that is in the middle of the garden, nor shall you touch, or you shall die'" (Gen. 3:3). Here is the first indication that life, which was designed for eternal existence, could actually be lost if this gifting was abused. It would not only be lost by making wrong choices, but by *deciding* to make wrong choices. The ability to make choices is a good thing, but perversion of the good is possible. Inwardly motivated choices, made in disobedience to God, have the capacity to alter the harmony of essential relations.

The Adam of Eden employed personal choices in many aspects of his stewardship. Adam even had choices about the things he could do to the garden God had given him. Analogies often break down, but let me risk one for this particular context.

My wife, Verna, and I once lived in a relatively new suburban area of Calgary, Alberta. In our initial scouting for new housing possibilities, we viewed a number of completed show homes. They were lovely, but the principle of the show home was, "What you see is what you get!" We were much more interested in a "spec house." This was a house with all the essentials in place, but the builder had left room for modifications according to the creativity and imagination of the buyer. Nothing of the basic intent of the designer, however, could be changed without some costly consequence.

It turned out that most of the good ideas came from Verna. With my background and her creative input, we shared and agreed on new possibilities for the house. In this situation, we didn't build the house. So in that sense we were not co-creators with the builder. However, we were given the opportunity to be creative with the potential the builder had left open to us.

Similarly, Adam and Eve were not commissioned simply to be caretakers of Eden, but given a charge to be creative stewards upon whom an apostolic community could model their apostolic function. Adam couldn't steward all this by himself; he needed Eve to complete God's purposes. Nor could Eve have fulfilled God's plan by herself.

A Holy Priesthood

The abundance of God's provision must have represented an exotic menu centered in the Tree of Life, because the writer describes every tree as "pleasant to the sight and good for food" (Gen. 2:9). God provided the means for the provisions, but Adam also had to cultivate this sustaining life from the ground. "The Lord God took the man and put him in the garden of Eden to till it and keep it" (Gen. 2:15). But work was no sweat; it was worship. It was unbridled joy.

As we noted, Adam wasn't created in the garden; God placed him there. But everything human beings did in the garden was in cooperation with God, and the whole of their existence was an offering of thanksgiving and praise. No doubt God was never short on offering words of assuring praise to Adam.

The community of Eden was truly a priesthood of creation. "You have made them to be a kingdom and priests serving our God, and they will reign on earth" (Rev. 5:10). Adam's priestly relationship is played out in both communion and cooperation with God.

The apostle Paul speaks of this living sacrifice as "spiritual worship" (Rom. 12:2). The Greek word he chooses, *latreia*, is intended to convey the thought that all life is a sacrificial offering of worship. The apostle Peter describes God's community as "a royal priesthood, a holy nation, God's own people" (1 Pet. 2:10). They are royal because they are children of the King; they are a priesthood because all of their lives are spent in offering creation to God in acts of praise and thanksgiving; they are God's own people because they are His sons and daughters in a relationship of awesome and joyful dependence. They are a holy people (*hagios*, meaning "to set apart for a particular purpose"). They were separate and distinct for God, and for all else in His creation. "For you are a people holy to the Lord your God; the Lord your God has chosen you out of all the peoples on the earth" (Deut. 7:6).

Eden is therefore seen to be the base from which the Adam community looks beyond to the fuller mission of "subduing the earth and filling it." It will remain in the collective memory of the sons of God as the model of God's original purposes. Nothing else ever matched the perfection that Eden modeled. But Eden is the prototypical story that later finds a somewhat incomplete sign in a place called Jerusalem. Later, this city of Zion, for an apostolically chosen people, became the physically identifiable place where God's presence could best be signified. Jerusalem, then, becomes the city from which a connected and commissioned community begins its apostolic mission. It is the temporary Eden existing in signature of God's kingdom, and from which the universal invitation has its focus.

REDEMPTION

CHAPTER 5

How Did Time Become an Enemy?

The Perversion of Good

O ne fundamental principle of creation was that humanity could make free choices. Indeed, how could relationships of love be possible if the principle of free choice was not at work in the center of all relationships? That's the essential nature God implanted in Adam. With some reasonable assurance, we may say that questions concerning the problems of evil are connected with God's decision to create a universe inherently free to be itself.

But can we say that all the subsequent problems are God's fault? Not being subject to time, God most certainly knew all that was to happen. This creation principle of freedom is precisely one with which the powers of evil are happy to engage. Conversely, God "has respected man's free will and has not forced Himself on man. Only thus could He produce beings who are not automata, but are akin to Himself."[1] What we see in this chapter is that, when creation devolved into a series of disharmonious relationships, God already had a plan (1 Pet. 1:20-21), and His timing was perfect.

Satan was surely a creation of God.[2] As a spiritual creature, he existed before (if I can take license with the word) time began. (This will become a very important point when we consider the nature of his ultimate destiny.) The one story does not ever entertain the idea that there could be two gods.[3] "There is no ontological evil."[4] In the book of Job, Satan is described as one of the heavenly beings (Job 1:6). He appears to have some sort of responsibility in connection to the earth and its inhabitants (1:7-8). Apart from decisions emerging from the depths of Adam's nature, Satan was also a source of rebellious temptation.

We realize from the first chapter of Job that Satan was originally a spirit-creature of God's design. What went wrong with him was a self-imposed, egocentric process of self-perversion. In other words, by free choice, Satan became an ego-driven and self-perverted angel of darkness (2 Cor. 11:14). Such a power-centered ego would forever forge a pathway to challenge God's magnificent design. Satan's nature devolved to one of vengeful opposition to God's purposes. (1Pet.5:9) In this continued process, it may well be that success would result in worship being directed toward himself.

The self-perverted Satan flies in the face of God by perverting the good in God's creation. He sets his sights on the worshipful community of Eden. As the priest of creation, Adam is already, quite naturally, capable of offering worship to God. His apostolic purpose is universal. However, the right use of that power is tempered by the inbreathed nature of God in his life. Both the *power* to perform and the very *character* of God are involved in the inbreathing. It was Adam's right use of this nature and power that would ensure an intimate relationship with God and with all that He had made.

In this context, "freedom" denotes a capacity to change or develop what already exists. How else would a God of love operate? If that were not true, then humankind would be just a little pawn in a game that God couldn't possibly lose. We see that the loving God, designing autonomous freedom, allowed Himself to be vulnerable to the implications of creation's decisions.

But this part of the story didn't start with Adam, did it? There is something very intriguing and interesting concerning the nature of evil.

What we will see is not so much the ability of some diabolical creature to produce evil, but of its prideful need to pervert what is already essentially good. In Ephesians 2:2, the power of evil is described as "the ruler of the power of the air," but he may also be described as the prince of perversion.

Many people remain loyal to institutions and nations long after their fundamental values of goodness have eroded. Dietrich Bonheoffer is a good example of a man who withstood the Nazism that had grossly perverted the honorable values of prewar Germany. Many of his fellow clergy, with supposed biblical support, urged their congregations to "accept the authority of every human institution" (1 Pet. 2:13). Like many who speak prophetically, Bonheoffer found himself almost totally isolated. Courageously, in his heart, he also quoted Peter's paradoxical response to the religious establishment of his day: "Whether it is right in God's sight to listen to you rather than to God, you must judge; for we cannot keep from speaking out what we have seen and heard" (Acts 4:20). This statement sounds remarkably like the response of another German, Martin Luther, when making his defense to the Diet of Worms in 1521.

Eventually, on the orders of Hitler, Bonheoffer was executed. They did it during the last few days of the war. Loyalty is easy to pervert, especially in a crowd.

We see another example of perversion in one of the disciples of Jesus. Judas Iscariot had the freedom to choose as his conscience or inclination led him. But in his handing Jesus over to the authorities, we are looking at a man who was possibly filled with honest but *sentimental* intent. It caused him to become angry at Jesus. But why? Being generous, and giving Judas the benefit of the doubt (John 12:26), we may assume that there really was a time when he had a genuine concern to help the poor. He never understood why Mary, with the approval of Jesus, "wasted" costly perfumes to anoint Him (John 12:5). Judas seems to have made other utilitarian decisions. They may have been out of good motivation, but, even after three years of companionship with Jesus, he never saw the bigger picture of Christ's mission. Substance often gives way to sentiment.

A created, spiritual being can become self-perverted through the agency of his own ego. Once able to live in the glory of God's reflected light, Satan became a dark emissary for his own perverted ego. Knowing that the nature of God is one of Light, he set out to counterfeit it. With great cunning, he appears as an agent of Light. "And no wonder! Even Satan disguises himself as an angel of light. So it is not strange if his ministers also disguise themselves as ministers of righteousness" (2 Cor. 11:14-15).

This raises a very important point. Is the Devil responsible for everything that is evil? For example, we know that animals were tearing each other apart long before humans entered the stage of creation history. Robert Capon suggests that it is a serious error "to fob off all the killing and eating to sin—to tie natural badness to moral evil, and to say that, if it hadn't been for sin, all the animals would have been vegetarians . . . We act as if only man were free, only man had knowledge, only man were capable of feeling."[5] There really is a condition we may label as "natural evil." Nevertheless, natural evil does not always equate with an immoral condition, but refers to nature pursuing its own course of self-survival.

Earthquakes must happen, but usually we don't ascribe moral questions to them unless people are killed. When a little child is killed by a drunken driver, it is not God who causes the death, but the act of an intoxicated human who is out of control. Many of the questions we ask concerning evil events are not connected with the nature of God, but the nature of creation that has lost its God-focused bearings (Rom. 1:20).

Egotistical Tactics of Satan

Two trees mentioned in Genesis 2:9 provide an amazing and awesome theological story of the polarization of good and evil. The Tree of Life speaks of the activity and provision of God for the nations. The other tree may well represent human ego and aspiration challenging the normal dependence upon God.

The Tree of Knowledge of Good and Evil is very important. It denotes the dreadful possibility that Adam has all the ability needed to choose its enticing offerings or not. Symbolically, it represents the natural means whereby humanity can evaluate and determine life's primary purpose and values. Obviously, in our contemporary world, there are many enticing individuals and systems that profess how such natural knowledge may be employed. Most are not reticent to tell the church how to change its direction.

The community of God has been baptized into a life employing the supernatural gifting of the Creator, yet, in brazen arrogance, Satan has the audacity to steer the church in the fallen directions of groaning nature (Rom. 8:22-23). However, in looking to God's supernatural revelation, the church cannot be motivated and guided by the fleeting shallowness of contemporary culture. Throughout the story of redemption, one of the obstacles in the marriage dance is that the bride will trip if she doesn't follow the One doing the leading.

A paradox lies within the nature of Adam. He was created good but has equally as much freedom to choose evil. Could it be otherwise if a loving relationship of trust existed between him and God? The ancient writer of Proverbs understood this tension:

> Trust in the Lord with all your heart,
>   and do not rely on your own insight.
> In all your ways acknowledge him,
>   and he will make straight your paths. (Prov. 3:5-6)

Ego-motivated knowledge is power; it promises control. Obviously, these are not values consistent with those of God's kingdom. No wonder Satan wants to steer the sons of God in the direction of natural religions. Those deities can be controlled! Humanity can become divinely powerful!

Adam could have said no to Satan. But the perversion of God's original intent took place. Satan had license to roam the garden. As some have suggested, this may not have been Satan's first attempt at messing up God's creation. C. S. Lewis postulates, "It seems to me, therefore, a reasonable supposition, that some mighty created power had already been at work for ill on the material universe, or solar system, or, at least, the planet earth, before ever man came on the scene."[6] Another commentator, C. Peter Wagner, adds, "Much of the Old Testament is based on the assumption that certain supernatural beings have dominion over geo-political spheres."[7]

But the temptation story did not begin with Adam alone. What I will call the "Eve Syndrome" displays the cunning tactics of Satan.

Satan exploits the gender differences between a man and a woman. (It may be said that, in our contemporary world Satan is exploiting a cultural demand for sameness). Amazingly, Satan is able to draw both the man and the woman into it. It's a way of operating from the sole perspective of the feminine. But as we see, both Adam and Eve are caught up in it. Both are responsible for the desertion of their apostolic calling. The difference in gender is a vital factor for the accomplishment of mission beyond the self.

The taking of the fruit may represent a process of turning inward from a normal God-focus. It's much more than a successful ten-minute snow-job by a smooth-talking, egotistical deceiver.

In Job 1:10, Satan taunts God about Job's false sense of security. Job has a hedge around him. Of course Job exhibits personal righteousness, because there has never been anything in his life to test his ability to make other choices. What's the point of having that ability when there aren't any alternatives?

Here we see the willingness of God to be vulnerable to the very principles of a freedom He purposely designed.

The Eve Syndrome

To a wandering desert people, as Israel became, a serpent is the most feared natural enemy (Num. 21:6-7). It's no wonder that Satan is represented in this way. However, at this point in their story, the Adam and Eve community don't have cause to recognize a natural enemy. Everything can be trusted.

The cunning serpent first approaches Eve, not Adam. However, it is vitally important to point out that, in contemporary life, men also adopt the Eve Syndrome equally. Politically, lauding equality, men often abandon their unique gender characteristics of ensuring communal harmony.

In the garden, the Genesis writer depicts the man as representing the focus of community purpose. Therefore, he is also the focus (not the power-seeking boss) of community life in God. On Adam's part, if he can't trust Eve, whom can he rely on?

In Eastern cultures of that day, as in many of ours, the man and his name provided the recognizable focus of the family as the basic unit of community. Our present struggle is often in determining what theological principles simply evolve from culture, and what revelation God wants to impart through culture—or, even, in spite of it.

The Adam community was much too bright and much too magnificent to be picked off quickly and easily. The fruit of the tree represents a shift from trust in and dependence on God to an ego-perverted reliance on the self. It is a perversion from the outward focus on God to an inward focus on the self. The fruit also represents the lie espoused by Satan that, in being dependent upon God, humanity would be cheated of its natural ability to achieve its divine and eternal destiny. Surely, as Satan reminds them, they have more than enough ability to decide what is good and what is evil; they don't need God to lay it out for them.

To this point, they have clearly demonstrated their enormous abilities. What on earth are they *not* capable of? Aren't they like God Himself? Their ego is being tickled.

It is of enormous interest to note that the writer depicts Satan's primary target to be Eve. Yet Adam, in Genesis 2, is seen to be the focus for the good order of the community. The Eve Syndrome is a tactic not normally based in substance, but couched in sentiment. Sometimes it lies in a self-perceived notion of what is right.

In Adam and Eve's situation, the revelation of the Word of God is relegated to a place lower than the opinion of the individual. The tactic continues to work today when those who live or die on the basis of the Word of God are not challenged on the basis of biblical authority, but self-absorbed sentimentality. There is a ground shift. A subtle change in direction takes place when the dialogue is based in a postmodern view of individual feelings, subjective experience, and personal sentiment over historical revelation.

Eve has a good heart! Quite genuinely, she doesn't want her husband to be deprived of anything that is good. It is on the basis of sentiment that the Deceiver can play his cards. Adam is not likely to distance himself from his wife's actions. He will stand by her because she desires only the very best for him. The subtle trap of sentimentalism is set, and it is through the one person who, with good intent, may more easily fall into it.

In another example, Lot's wife turns back to face Sodom. Probably it is not because her primary motive is arrogant defiance, but a genuine sense of caring for her daughters, who were losing their future husbands (Gen. 19:26). Here, we see that sentiment is not a bad thing, but is not the basis for hard decisions.

In answer to the question of unfettered license without inevitable consequence, we realize that Eve really did turn to God's word! However, as is often the case today, we see how the Word of God takes a secondary place to a personal agenda and self-centered ego.

"God said, 'You shall not eat of the fruit of the tree that is in the middle of the garden, nor shall you touch it, or you shall die.' But the serpent said to the woman, 'You will not die; for God knows that when you eat of it your eyes will be opened, and you will be like God, knowing good and evil'" (Gen.3:4) That is often the tenor of modern discussions on values, particularly when they are dominated by the evolving mores of present culture.

Speaking to the one who gives birth to life, Satan continues His perversions. In effect, he says to Eve, "You, who are the matrix of life, take no account of the word of God; you cannot trust it; you have moved on from there. That was the past. God is the deceiver. Human beings are perfectly capable of finding their own way to natural immortality."

Here is the beginning of the notion that natural immortality is born from the womb of sentimentalism and natural aspiration. How can humanity ever die when it possesses such a natural capacity to produce life? If Adam had not been able to exercise amazing power from God, surely he could not have been tempted to use it wrongly. Could he?

Adam is standing by (Gen. 3:6). His own ego is now being tickled. But the ground has been shifted from the logics of religious philosophy.

Satan has introduced a face to the situation. It is a beloved face. Revelation matters nothing now. Often, values take on a different appearance when a face is introduced into the situation.

Eve is reaching! Adam knows it is just because she wants the very best for him. This is a motivation that is all too easy to pervert. She is a very good and loving wife. He does nothing to stop her.

It is a mutual decision. Adam is equally responsible for the decision. To do nothing is to be implicit in everything.

Satan's deceptive tactic was to convince them that *salvation* (which was a word never before in need of consideration, and is equally abhorrent in the minds of some today) was not a word they would ever need in their vocabulary. They could live out their lives in their own way.

Further, Satan's strategy was to delude Eden's community that, if things got difficult, this God would not seek them out in their troubles. Satan did not know that the great Creator, in His nature, is a seeking God. Indeed, the Genesis writer takes pains to show that, in the nature of God, there is always a passionate desire to seek out those who are estranged from Him.

Nothing Happened!

At least, nothing happened immediately. It *appeared* that nothing had happened. Eve reached out, and there seemed to be no consequences. We may say that the entire temptation process took place over a considerable amount of time. In fact we see, even today, that the tactic of Satan regarding values in the church is to wear it down slowly, but surely. (Dan. 7:25). In the subtlety of this process, it appears that not much has really changed!

The delusion that nothing of consequence has happened impregnated itself upon the human psyche ever since. Satan has successfully erased the collective consciousness and memory of what was once supernaturally possible. Natural effort and natural religion easily move in to take its place.

God had told man that he would die if he made the decision to operate in ways disobedient to His harmonious purposes for creation (Gen. 2:17). Right at that moment of disobedience, however, Eve was still alive, and she continued having a good time enjoying the fruit of the tree. Maybe it had all been a power ploy by God to keep them in a state of dependence. Maybe He had not wanted them to experience their full potential after all. Surely, they could become capable of challenging God Himself.

However, we see very clearly that the choices of the Adam community proved to be expedited by egocentric and self-centered motivation not at all in keeping with the character of Eden. In other words, they had lost the ability to reign in signature of God's kingdom. As they were soon to discover, they were slowly changing.

As seasons went by, Adam and Eve began to note some very strange changes. Eve was developing wrinkles. Adam was getting nearsighted. Neither of them could run around the bed like they used to. Many things that they once considered ordinary were becoming extraordinary. Adam didn't know it, but the commissioned steward of creation's relationships was slowly dying. Maybe something like a DNA of death and decay had insinuated itself into the human condition.

An illusion of long life has become a defensive reaction to the reality of an inevitable death. "I am just eighty-five years young." The desire to possess a meaningful life for an extended time is always admirable. However, in reality, old age is a terrible indignity—a poor impersonation of what once was. In reality, the priest of creation had been rendered impotent. The commission from God was still in His purpose for the Adam community. But the community no longer had the power or the character to perform it effectively.

Instead of bowing the knee in worship, their desire to stand alongside God, eyeball to eyeball, was growing. Maybe God didn't want them to know that they could stand so tall and do it forever! (Gen. 11:4). A perversion was settling in. Nature itself, not its Creator, would become the focus for spiritual life.

The game was up. Consequences of self-centered decisions were about to unfold.

God addressed the serpent with words of judgment. They were words separating him from the divine purposes God had planned for him (Gen. 3:14). Satan remained powerless in the face of the Word of

God. Here, the Lord predicted the warlike nature of future relations with humanity. This passage has resulted in endless debate concerning its prophetic nature.

"I will put enmity between you and the woman, and between your offspring and hers; he will strike your head, and you will strike his heel" (Gen. 3:15). This is mind-boggling language. At that time, no one had ever referred to the offspring of the woman; it was always that of the man. So what did God mean by this strange statement? It reminds us of the passage from Luke concerning the Annunciation (Luke 1:30-37).

Not everyone rushed to the conclusion that the passage prophetically looked toward a messiah from God. Many adopted the idea of a God-Man messiah that unfolded gradually.[8] However, by the time the New Testament was written, there seemed to be little problem with the idea that the birth of Jesus Christ made sense of the statement in question. Being fully God and fully Man, Jesus was a man, born of the will of God and also the seed of a woman: creation's real bride of God.

Of enormous significance is the statement God makes to Adam. "Cursed is the ground because of you" (Gen. 3:17). The cursing of the ground declares the fracturing of one more of creation's essential relationships. The harmonious relationship of humanity with creation would now be a struggle throughout time and is not yet restored. Adam earns his living by the sweat of his brow. Work is more difficult to offer as an act of worship; it is a burdensome act of toil. In that toil, Adam will eventually return to the dust from which he was formed (Gen. 3:19).

Being rendered to dust meant that Adam returned to a state of permanent unconsciousness in connection to all things, including himself. As dust, time would have no more meaning for him. As dust, the necessary constituents of place and space would have no meaning. Time could not exist without place and space. "For the wages of sin is death" (Rom. 6:23).

Plato thought that there was a spark in everyone that could never die because it was connected to the spirit of all oneness. He felt that the *nexus*, a bridge to the divine and highest spirit, became crossable by means of intellectual enlightenment. That's an idea not too far removed from earlier Hinduism, a religion that may have become a profound influence on later Gnosticism.[9]

The late bishop John Robinson said that the Jews tended to think simply of soul and body. Nevertheless, he didn't feel there was an essential difference between the two concepts. Like the ancient Greeks, Robinson became close to the view of natural immortality. He believed in universalism. However, he admitted that natural, pantheistic thought would never be able to achieve personal and individual immortality. Unfortunately, in order to salvage his universalist view of immortality, he had to make some unsubstantiated, or at least questionable, leaps in opting for his philosophy.[10]

We are human beings in all the fullness of what it means to be human. We were never intended to be spiritual beings with no physical connection to matter. As people, not spirits, we are connected beings. We are connected to God, to others, to creation, and to ourselves. It is precisely in this context that we know who we are. Human beings are intended to exist forever in the harmonious relationship of body, soul, and spirit. The apostle Paul expresses this New Testament view: "May the God of peace himself sanctify you entirely; and may your spirit and soul and body be kept sound and blameless" (1 Thess. 5:23).

Predestination, or a Process of Decision

One strike and you're out! Is that the kind of God that Jesus reveals? It seems a little petulant that Adam (and all succeeding humanity) is consigned to such a horrendous fate because of this one covetous and egocentric act. We have made a big issue in highlighting the fact that freedom of choice is fundamental to the principles of creation. Another principle appears in the New Testament that helps to clear things up.

The very nature of humanity has become permanently corrupted. The capacity to make self-centered choices has now become normal. For example, when the apostle Paul speaks of those who will not inherit the kingdom of God, he describes these people as repeatedly acting in the present tense (1 Cor. 6:9-11). In other words, these acts are continually being done, and *by choice.*

In this vein, we see that the Adam community was facing the consequences of the future precisely because of the free choices they had made. It was not because it had been predetermined by God that they do so.

The matter of Original Sin is a very big subject; its influence in western theology has largely been attributed to St. Augustine and reformers like John Calvin, who enlarged much further on the thinking of Augustine.[11] In the extreme, the idea of Original Sin is not only that we are born of a nature predisposed to sin, but, for some thinkers, that we are incapable of making good, moral choices without the prior initiative of God's grace.[12] In some quarters, this is called "Total Depravity." Christian thinkers such as C. S. Lewis, are horrified by the notion of Total Depravity. "The consequence is drawn that, since we are totally depraved, our idea of good is worth simply nothing. He (God) appeals to our existing moral judgement."[13]

Throughout the history of the prophetic ministry in Israel, God's messengers assumed there was some innate goodness in people that was capable of responding to the call for forgiveness and reconciliation (Rom. 2:4). Under the premise of depravity, uneasy responses are made to the suggestion that people such as Gandhi made lots of very good moral decisions, yet were not Christian. Often, the defensive response is that those decisions were made without the conscious understanding of the Holy Spirit being at work.

The idea of Total Depravity, connected to the doctrine of Original Sin, quite naturally led to further assumptions: for example, that creation, apart from the prevailing grace of God, is incapable of presenting any good fruit. Some support for this position may be found in passages like Isaiah 64:6.

> We have all become like one who is unclean,
> and all our righteous deeds are like a filthy cloth.
> We all fade like a leaf, and our iniquities, like the wind,
> take us away.

However, it would be legitimate to view this statement in terms of what God's people had become; truly a far cry from the condition under which they were once included in the shout, "It is very good" (Gen. 1:31).

For the purposes of this book, we temper these theological divisions by going back to first principles. In the garden, the Adam community, not driven by animal instinct, was given a unique human gift of free will. This was a gift that enabled him to *choose* either good or evil. It was a loving gift. That was the whole point of the symbolic Tree of Knowledge of Good and Evil. When we arrive at the New Testament part of the story, we will have to pursue further the meaning of predestination.

The consequences of Adam's decisions have to be met (Gen. 3:14-24). However, not at any time is there an implication that one of the consequences will be the loss of free will. Free will is a creation principle that the God of love will not override. Nevertheless, we must also admit to the reality that there now appears to be a predisposition within the human psyche to turn to the self before it will turn to God. Ask anyone who has raised children!

At some point in Adam's life of decision, God declared the consequences of their actions. It is significant that, at first, they weren't very comfortable in parading their new-won independence from God, so they tried to hide. They were ashamed of their transparency. But no one can escape the ultimate encounter with God. Like the father of the Prodigal Son, God was waiting for His beloved community to return to the intimacy of their primary relationship. The cry of the Father soon became, "Where are you?" (Gen. 3:9)

The Adam community did not simply hide from a searching God, but from the awesome brilliance of glorious Light that illuminated and exposed everything around and in them (1 John 1:7).

It's not that the omniscient God needed to know the answer to His own question; Adam, like us, needed to hear the question! He needed to realize that a perversion and a reversal had embedded itself in his very nature. Indeed, it is not surprising that when the Adam community is out of harmony with the Source, all other essential relations experience discordant relationships.

In the loving nature of God's initiative, the primary direction of humanity's relational encounter is not the human search for God, but

God's search for His people. To spend life in an *inward* search for God inevitably leads to the futility of the aloneness of lost relationships. That's the way to nihilism. It is the fate of natural religion.

Adam and Eve couldn't stay at home anymore. No longer could the Eden community stand as the focus and guardian of all nature's harmonious relationships. Their model home and garden had been sealed off from their use (Gen. 3:24). No longer were they able to enjoy and use it as God had purposed. No longer could they be signatories of Eden's kingdom life.

Eden exists as a distorted memory within the psyche of all humanity. The idea that a life with purpose was intended to last forever still lingers. Many continue to believe in their own immortality. It seems that a process of devolution has set in.

Is it possible that God's magnificent purposes for creation and its priesthood has failed? Is it not possible for moments of light to continue in the ongoing saga of this Adam chronicle? Is it no longer possible for God to find a people, or even an individual, able to be a sign of what once was?

From that very moment His search began, in every nook and cranny of the human story, the longing call of God echoes throughout the cavernous corridors of redemption's story: "Where are you? Where are you?"

There was need for some kind of rescue. There was need for a hope that first-day Light could yet penetrate the darkness of clouded life. The redemption story, envisioned by God before the foundation of the world, was shortly to begin.

CHAPTER 6

First-Day Light on the Mountains of Israel

urely only God Himself could redeem this tragic break in creation's relationships. Only He could restore the calamity of all that was lost. We should not be surprised to find that significant changes took place in the story of Adam and his race. Yet it would be foolish to fob off the need for redemption as a primitive bedtime myth.

Moments of light appear in the redemption story of Israel. The force of these moments is readily apparent in the lives of significant individuals in community. Undoubtedly and often, God reminded His appointed people that He had chosen them. Israel, able to trace its roots through the sons of God, is fundamental in God's redemption covenant for the entire world.

Possibly influenced by a similar Mesopotamian account of a local flood, the story of Noah is one that is loaded with theological implications. "More than 500 deluge legends are known around the world and, in a survey of 86 of these (20 Asiatic, 3 European, 7 African, 46 American and 10 from Australia and the Pacific), the specialist researcher Dr. Richard Andree concluded that 62 were entirely independent of the Mesopotamian and Hebrew accounts."[1]

Ian Wilson adds, "Surely, a real-life Flood must lie behind these stories. The collective memory, scattered over wide geographical distances, is too prevalent, too deep-seated for this not to be the case . . ."[2] Attempting to relate Noah's connection to Abraham and the sons of God, he continues, "The Turkish Ur is only 48 kilometers (30 miles) from Haran, which is the other main family location biblically associated with Abraham (Genesis 11:31)."[3]

Noah appears to have a natural connection with the sons of God (mentioned in Genesis 6). At least, he walks in the relationships intended for them (Gen. 6:8-9). The story speaks of the continuance of human rebellion, of judgment, of God's will to secure a relational remnant, and of a covenant of hope that has its God-made sign of assurance in a normal occurrence of nature. Like the creation story, it is one that emerges from beyond the waters of chaos.

The rainbow, a colorful appearance of fourth-day light, appeared to Noah as a sign that God had not given up on His creation nor His purposes for it. But God had begun again, and at the very basic level of instinct—that of natural faith. Continuing humanity ascribed this universal disaster to the new found power of nature over humankind; an event signifying a reversal of God's initial commission (Gen.1:28) This struggle may well be seen as a basis for natural religion where humanity constantly tries to regain its former control by manipulating the powers of nature. (The story of Elijah on Mount Carmel similarly illustrates the point). Nevertheless, the tiny remnant of Noah was helpless, so God gave a sign of hope in the colors of nature (Gen. 9:11-15).

The story declares to us a principle that runs throughout the entire Bible: On the basis of a faithful remnant, God is willing to maintain His purposes by saving the human race from extinction. But how could God once more sign His purposes through community? This was His kingdom purpose at the beginning, wasn't it?

Predestination: Of Community or Individual?

The Tower of Babel speaks of the disintegration of community and of its essential unity of purpose. It is not coincidental that this story is placed at the very point where the common language, used to proclaim God's purpose to create a universal community, breaks down. The children of God have now lost the way or the desire for such proclamation.

Another lineage is found in this chapter; it is intended to connect the line of the sons of God from Adam to Noah, and then from Noah's son Shem to the Mesopotamian family of Abraham (Gen. 11:10). Abraham seems to be well connected. Ironically, Abraham traced his origins through a race that was on the leading edge of a form of natural religion. It is very popular today. Astrology is a religion that claims human destiny is determined by the movement of lights in the sky—natural lights or, as noted previously, contributors to fourth-day light!

Once again, God chose a people for this special ministry. Clearly, He did not choose on the basis of merit (Deut. 7:7-8). Like the call of the reluctant Jeremiah (Jer. 1:4-5), significant biblical stories often describe, not a call to individual salvation, but God's unique call to leadership within the community.

God's heart, desiring a universal response to the call, is clearly declared in 1Timothy 2:3-4: "This is right and is acceptable in the sight of God our Savior, who desires everyone to be saved and to come to the knowledge of the truth."

It is not coincidental that the call of Abraham appears on the heels of the demise of community, as recorded in the story of Babel (Gen. 11) In His eternal nowness, it was always in the sovereign plan of God for there to be a universal priesthood of creation. Cain had failed to understand why blood was never spilled in Eden. Once beyond the gates of the garden, humanity was in no condition to offer God the fruit of creation, i.e., the fruit of innocence (Gen. 4:4-5). Everything that Adam and Eve had formerly done was an offering of worship. There was no need for blood sacrifices; their entire lives consisted of the priestly offerings of creation through lives of innocence. Therefore, their offerings to God were representative of lives exercised in innocence.

"Only, you shall not eat flesh with its life, that is, its blood" (Gen. 9:4). A very long story emerges after Eden signifying that reconciliation with God was going to be a costly business. Once beyond Eden, a life had to be offered in sacrificial substitution of *atonement*. Much later in the story, we see that God, in loving grace, stepped into the breach to pay such a price.

Abraham, true to the natural religion of his culture, felt that God would be satisfied by the offering of Isaac. After all, this boy was Abraham's only son. But even this costly gift would not bring about satisfaction. A substitute was found in the form of an innocent ram. That concept of substitution was to become an integral part of the Jewish sacrificial system (see Lev. 16:15-19). "The Lord will provide; as it is said, to this day, 'on the mount of the Lord, it shall be provided'"(Gen. 22:14). Abraham's family, in the line of the sons of God, would become the community on earth charged with the apostolic commission of Eden. "I will make you a great nation, and I will bless you, and make your name great, so that you will be a blessing. I will bless those who bless you, and the one who curses you I will curse; and in you all the families of the earth shall be blessed" (Gen. 12:2-3).

The apostle Paul, many years later, offered an understanding of how this blessing of family was extended to all races upon earth, "... for in Christ Jesus you are all children of God through faith . . . There is no longer Jew or Greek, there is no longer slave or free, there is no longer male and female; for all of you are one in Christ Jesus. And if you belong to Christ, then you are Abraham's offspring, heirs according to the promise" (Gal. 3:26-29).

Isaac became the father of Jacob, who produced twelve sons. In the line of the three patriarchs of promise, these twelve sons become heads of an ever-burgeoning family. This family was to become the community of Israel.

What the Bible reveals is that Israel was adopted to be the apostolic community of promise. Truly, by the grace and initiative of God, a community was born to be an instrument of Light to the world. The story of redemption was now placed back into the life of community. "For the creation waits with eager longing for the revealing of the children of God...that the creation itself will be set free from its bondage to decay and will obtain the freedom of the glory of the children of God" (Rom. 8:19,21).

The community of Israel was now on a journey far larger than one in which they were comfortable, and they didn't always remain true to their purpose. Like the journey of their leading patriarch, Abraham, God would not provide them with a blueprint, only a direction (Gen. 12:1).

Faith is the pivotal foundation of this relational covenant (see Heb. 11:1-2, 39; James 2:23). On this very vulnerable principle, God foresaw that His purposes for Israel would succeed. It was their primary and essentially priestly purpose to be apostolic; i.e., to invite the entire world into the community of God's new Eden.

A very important principle of election emerges from the calling of Abraham. Does the call of God equate with a call to enter a community of purpose? Is the question more *what* is the call, rather than to whom it is made? Is the question of predestined purpose more relevant to ask about the community rather than the individual?

"It was not because you were more numerous than any other people that the Lord set his heart on you and chose you [plural], for you were the fewest of all peoples. It was because the Lord loved you and kept the oath that he swore to your ancestors" (Deut. 7:7-8; brackets mine).

The personal call of particular individuals is always associated with a community purpose residing in the heart of God. For example, the reluctant Moses and the equally reluctant Jeremiah were both fearful— not of a call to individual salvation, but of the call to a very difficult ministry within God's community (Ex. 3 and Jer. 1).

From the very beginning, the *community* of Adam had a universal commission. The apathy and disobedience of this community did not negate nor destroy God's sovereign purposes. And so, in God's election, Abraham appears and receives a call. The call and the promises were not solely for Abraham, but for his extended community as it continued in obedience to its destiny (Gen. 12:3). Yet in terms of essential relations of creation, Abraham became a pivotal model for his race. He was called "the friend of God"(James 2:23). Similarly, young Samuel's call was to be a prophet, to remind the community of Israel of its original calling (1 Sam. 3:10-18). The same was true with others, such as Jeremiah. This call was a call to ministry, not individual salvation, and was associated with the earlier apostolic call of the Adam, and later Abraham community (Jer. 1:5, Gen.12"1-3).

All of these individuals could have responded with a resounding no to the call of God. Jeremiah, though he gave reasons to resist his call, replied with a yes, and then moved between bravery and fear throughout much of his ministry. Moses could have been the founding elder of a priestly tribe interceding between God and His people. It was because of his reluctance to say yes to God that the priestly role was passed on to his brother, Aaron (Ex. 4:13-17). Obviously, God remained sovereign in His purposes. He would even use the motivations of gluttonous and power-seeking leaders of other nations to forward His purposes. King Nebuchadnezzar is a good example (Jer. 27:6).

Taking this principle into the New Testament, we see that Judas, whom Jesus knew to be His betrayer (John 13:21-26), most certainly could have resisted the lure of thirty pieces of silver. In the climate of that moment, a Judas could have appeared in any one of a whole range of people. God knew how Judas would respond! In the Book of Ephesians, we see a good example of the call of God being made to a *community* for the effecting of His universal purposes. In Ephesians 1:5, 11, we note that Paul is speaking to a community of saints in Ephesus. He is speaking in the plural.

> He destined us for adoption as his children through Jesus Christ, according to the good pleasure of his will, to the praise of his glorious grace that he freely bestowed on us in the beloved.

> In Christ we have also obtained an inheritance, having been destined according to the purpose of him who accomplishes all things according to his counsel and will.

These two verses enable us to see that the principle of election is not so much about a call to individual salvation, but (as in the beginning) the call to a community to respond to God's original apostolic commission. Indeed, the apostle Paul, in Romans 8:29, uses two words in particular relation to the point we make: *proginosko* (to know beforehand) and *proorizo* (to ordain beforehand). So, by the power of the Holy Spirit, individuals are adopted and conformed into the nature of the real Adam. The sons of God are therefore a community predestined to accomplish God's purposes in signing and proclaiming the kingdom of God. The Lord of all time is sovereign in His purposes.

With Christ as its Head and focus, the community is engaged in the universal task of bringing all creation into the essential relations of creation. Again, in this creation context, predestination relates to the "what" much more than the "who." We speak of Israel as a community called and commissioned by God. The roots of this commission extend through the lineage of the sons of God and all the way back to Adam.

The identity, focus, and purpose of this community later becomes solidified by four supporting pillars. These four pillars can be summarized as law, prophets, priests, and monarchy. Moments of light appeared in all four pillars.

However, before the four pillars could emerge, the people of Israel needed a sign that they could trust Moses in his role of deliverer from Egypt. Here, we see the beginnings of how the light of God's glory shone on all four pillars of Israel. The awesome presence of God would unfold before Israel on two significant mountains of Israel.

Light Upon the Lawgiver

After Israel had resided in Egypt for about 430 years, Moses appeared as a prince, a shepherd, and a deliverer. He is one of the individuals who, more than once, experienced the awesome light of God's glory. It was never natural fire. The fire is that of first-day Light. Such phenomena occurred for Moses on Mount Horeb ("the mountain of God" Ex. 3:1). No wonder he could only walk a little way into its blinding glory. No wonder he had to abandon his shoes in the awe of God's *shekinah* presence. Was it possible to deny God's call to be a deliverer amid such awesome brilliance of Light? The answer is most certainly yes. But God allowed for Moses' feeble excuses not to be a public speaker (Ex. 4:10). The result was that his brother Aaron was given the mantle of Israel's priesthood. God's purposes prevail. "This is why I let you live: to show you my power, and to make my name resound through all the earth" (Ex. 9:16).

They had become a raggedy group. After those 430 years in Egypt, they really didn't have an identity or a purpose; at least, not as a community. The purpose of this tattered community was to cohere into a *sign* that would present to the world a relational life as it once existed in the prototypical community of Eden. Their function was to invite the fragmented world to join the dance! This peculiar group needed deliverance from bondage, a focus in the God they could not name, and values to bind them together into a unique community.

Distinctive signs that God was blessing the leadership of Moses became tangible in the crossing of the Red Sea, in the assurance of God's presence in a cloud by day and fire by night, in God's daily provision of manna and of water, in the giving of the Ten Commandments, and in the central focus of presence in the tabernacle. In these chronological events, the entire community also encountered distinct moments of light (e.g., 1 Cor. 10:1-5). But the giving of the Torah is the preeminent sign often associated with Moses.

"Torah" is a term that has usually been used to describe the Pentateuch as the written literature revealing the Law of God, as given to Moses. The idea that a deity would give a set of laws to enable relationships was something new to this people, or to any people. With God as their focus, they would learn how to live in relationship with Him and with each other.

Not coincidentally, at the very moment the commandments were being inscribed upon tablets of earth, the Israelites at the foot of Mount Sinai were worshipping a pagan god.

It was on Mount Sinai that Moses witnessed the most remarkable demonstrations of the light and fire of God's glory. "Now the appearance of the glory of the Lord was like a devouring fire on the top of the mountain" (Ex. 24:17). Such demonstrations were a powerful assurance of God's continued presence in Moses' call to be leader of a holy nation and a kingdom of priests (Ex. 19:5-6). Moses trusted this promise for the next forty years.

The Torah is a set of laws given by God to enable a loving relationship with Him and, as a result, a similar quality of relationships with others (Deut. 6:4-5; Lev. 19:18; Mk. 12:29-31). But, recalling the idolaters at the foot of Sinai, we must never imagine that natural religion cannot reassert itself in the community again. It does, even today, and it's getting stronger in the mainline churches.

Matthew Fox, a Jesuit priest says this:

> The creation-centered spiritual tradition is truly ecumenical . . . Teilhard de Chardin felt this way when he wrote that 'our consciousness, rising above the growing (but still much too limited) circles of family, country and race, shall finally discover that the only natural and real human unity is the spirit of the earth' . . . In ten years of lecturing and writing on creation spirituality I have seen how excited and amazed listeners get over how deeply this tradition cuts through religious differences and touches spiritual points of convergence.[4]

We are now facing the very same struggles with natural theology that the Israelites experienced of old. The contemporary church surely needs to covet assurance of God's presence in the revelation of both Word and Spirit.

Armed with God's assurances in the law, the priesthood, the tabernacle, and with God's daily provision, Israel should have entered the land that was promised quite quickly from the southern entry point of Kadesh Barnea—probably within eighteen months after crossing the Red Sea (Num. 14:22-23). What else did God need to provide before the people could enter into Canaan? However, because of fear and lack of trust, it took nearly forty years before Joshua, the anointed protégé of Moses, led God's people there via an eastern route over the River Jordan.

They were now in the land where they were called to establish the theocratic reign of Yahweh. Like the Eden of old, Jerusalem was to be a focus, a city from which a universal mission would be launched. From now on the world was supposed to observe the implications of embracing the dance of Eden. It was an astounding opportunity for Israel. How well would this task be accomplished?

In the New Testament, the Jerusalem that had been intended as the focus of God's presence proved to be but a temporal and symbolic sign. It was a sign that would give way to a Jerusalem that is above and is free; a New Jerusalem that comes down from heaven and from above; formed by God, as was Eden. (Gal. 4:26; Rev. 21:1-2)

Light upon the Priesthood

The seemingly strange story of Cain and Abel is for Christians both remarkably prophetic and also figurative. In Genesis 4, we read that Cain killed his younger brother Abel simply because Abel's offering was acceptable to God. The offering of Cain was not.

Each brother offered a sacrifice arising out of his own effort in living. Abel offered a blood sacrifice while Cain offered produce from the ground. What was wrong with the offering of Cain?

Cain was offering to God the fruit that his parents had offered at the time of their innocence. In Eden, there was no need for a temple, no need for blood sacrifice. But the offerings of innocence were no longer possible. No longer were they in the garden of Innocence where such fruits could be presented to God.

A substitute offering of life was now needed—something outside of Eden. Cain's offering was a perverse parody of what once had been. That's why only Abel's offering was acceptable to God. From then on, no one would be able to offer to God the fruits of innocence.

Or would they? Would it ever be possible? If so, and until then, substitutionary sacrifices would be necessary.

Prefaced in the sacrifice of Abel, God would initiate such blood sacrifices of reconciliation for His chosen people. Aaron, the brother of Moses, appears as the first priest of this community. He was called from the Levitical family among Jacob's sons. His priesthood is centered on a system of blood sacrifice (Gen. 9:4-5).The continuing priesthood of Aaron had a primary purpose of reconciliation and atonement. Even in nations devoted to natural religion, some system of priesthood was devised as a means of mediation between the deity and his people. The Levitical priests of Yahweh uniquely offered sacrifices for the sin that caused estrangement from God and others.

The idea of estrangement from personal relationship with a deity is an original concept unheard of in natural religion. This system is questioned in the New Testament, where we note the fulfillment of blood sacrifice is in Jesus, and a better covenant of creation's innocence is employed. However, the roots of this system are apparent in Old Testament thinking.

At the time of Abraham, Scripture introduces Melchizedek, a mystical figure who continues to represent a priesthood of the innocence of creation. Melchizedek is both priest and king of Salem. "Salem" was probably Jerusalem (Gen. 14:18). It was an early Bronze Age city. Shalem was the name of an ancient deity, but later the name became associated with the Hebrew word *shalom*, meaning peace.

Were "priest" and "king" not the dual roles of Adam in Eden? We are immediately drawn to the idea that Mount Zion could become the center for the ideal ministry of a priest and king of peace. Giving a blessing to Abraham, this priestly king offers him bread and wine, not a blood sacrifice: an offering of the fruits of creation that may represent the fruits of innocence in Eden.

Melchizedek is prototypically a continuation of the royal priesthood of creation, to the Most High God. Blood sacrifice is not in the venue of his ministry. "Abraham, the 'friend of God' (Isa. 41:8), accepts the blessings of this Canaanite priest and recognizes the priest's God as his own. Yahweh, God of revelation, the God of Abraham, is also to be recognized as God Most High (Hebrew: El Elyon), God of the universe, the God of Melchizedek."[5] Melchizedek, as a king and priest of the Most High God, merits Abraham's tithe of the spoils of war. Nowhere else in the Old Testament, do we see the hint of the elevation of creation's offerings of innocence over the blood sacrifice of substitution.

The stage had been set for the hope that one day a priest-king of creation would once more offer the fruits of innocence that could not be offered by Cain. Under the headship of Aaron, this priestly tribe exercised a variety of rites and roles on behalf of the people (Num.

3:5-10). The sacrificial system, necessitating the offering of blood, was of primary importance. "For the life of the flesh is in the blood; and I have given it for you upon the altar to make atonement for your souls; for it is the blood that makes atonement, by reason of the life" (Lev. 17:11). The very costly spilling of blood was a requisite, and a means of securing the reconciliation of relationships.

It was also the priest's function to perform the male initiation rite of circumcision. "This is my covenant, which you shall keep, between me and you and your offspring after you: Every male among you shall be circumcised . . . when he is eight days old . . . So shall my covenant be in your flesh an everlasting covenant" (Gen. 17:9-13). Even Jesus was brought to the temple to enter the rite of covenant (Luke 2:21). Mary and Joseph may not have known that the spilling of *this* blood was but an initial sign of a new covenant that Jesus would offer in the innocent sacrifice of His own blood.

Did God shed His glorious Light on this priestly pillar of Israel? Would God's brilliance of glory ever show up on Mount Zion? We recall two examples. The first was at the dedication of the original temple. When Solomon's temple was completed on Mount Zion (about 950 BC), we note: "When Solomon had ended his prayer, fire came down from heaven and consumed the burnt offerings and the sacrifices; and the glory of the Lord filled the temple. The priests could not enter the house of the Lord, because the glory of the Lord filled the Lord's house" (2 Chron. 7:1-2).

Many years later, around 740 BC, Isaiah had a vision of the temple which forever changed his life direction. "In the year that King Uzziah died, I saw the Lord sitting on a throne, high and lofty; and the hem of his robe filled the temple" (Isa. 6:1).

We see then, that the priesthood, focused in the high priesthood of Aaron and his Levitical descendant Zadok, had a dual purpose: not only to minister as mediators through whom sacrifices were offered, but also to be guarantors (signs) that God was faithful to His covenant promises with Israel. Not surprisingly, therefore, Israel's priesthood is at the very heart of the nation's major feasts: Passover, Weeks, Tabernacles, Hanukkah, and Purim.

Light upon the Monarchy

David stands out as the iconic monarch par excellence. He brought the ark of the covenant from Hebron to Jerusalem. Jerusalem becomes the place from which the ideal king will reign as once he did in Eden. That's the same picture presented in Revelation, the last book of the Bible (Rev. 21:1-6).

Michal, David's wife, never understood the ecstatic joy of David as he led the procession up the hill of Zion (2 Sam. 6:20-22). Dancing (apparently) naked before the Lord's presence, for one brief moment, David, as king, was embracing the dance of Eden. Nakedly unashamed and transparent, he was innocently absorbed into the arms of God's glorious presence. It was a sign of what God knew to be the norm of a dancing community in new creation.

Samuel had been very uncertain concerning the desire of the people to have their own king. They wanted to be like the nations around them. But, as citizens of the kingdom, they were called to live under theocratic rule. How else could they dance the dance? To Samuel, God was their king.

Having settled in Canaan, they appeared to be a people developing a memory of who they were called to be. But memory seemed to last for one generation alone. "Another generation grew up after them, who did not know the Lord or the work that he had done for Israel" (Judges 2:10).

At least twice in the Book of Judges, we see words such as, "In those days there was no king in Israel, all the people did what was right in their own eyes" (Judg. 17:6; 21:25). For about two hundred years (some believe it to be about four hundred years; see 1 Kings 6:1), God raised up judges among them instead of kings. Of particular note are Gideon and Deborah.

The grumblers of Israel looked over the fence, and they wanted what all other nations possessed. They grumbled to Samuel, who reluctantly heard from God that the people were not rejecting him as a judge, but rejecting God as their king (1 Sam. 8:7).

Of the tribe of Benjamin, Saul was the first king. But, because of disobedience and because he resorted to the occult for advice (a return to natural religion), the anointing for kingship was taken from Saul (1 Sam. 16:13-14).

Quite remarkably, and in fulfillment of prophecy, David, from the tribe of Judah, succeeded Saul. Predictive prophecy was on the side of the young man from Judah. "Judah, your brothers shall praise you; your hand shall be on the neck of your enemies; your father's sons shall bow down before you . . . The scepter shall not depart from Judah, nor the ruler's staff from between his feet, until tribute comes to him; and obedience of the peoples is his" (Gen. 49:8, 10).

David was not to build the temple (1 Chron. 28:3), but he supplied much of the foundational material for his son, Solomon. At the dedication of the temple, the fire from heaven had a dual purpose. First, it was the awesome Light and presence of God to assure His people of a blessing on the monarchy. Second, it was an assurance that God's presence could be found equally upon Mount Zion as it was on Mount Sinai.

However, as is often the case, the promises of God were conditional upon the responses of His people. The astounding and eternal promise, given to Solomon was such a conditional promise. "I will establish his kingdom forever if he continues resolute in keeping my commandments and ordinances, as he is today" (1 Chron. 28:7; see also 1 Kings 9:4-7).

In 1 Kings 11, many reasons are given why this eternal promise was torn away from Solomon. Interestingly, Solomon, the builder of the great temple, isn't mentioned among the Old Testament saints in Hebrews 11. Like Adam, he seems to be omitted. But God's purposes were not defeated. How could the Light of God shine, once more, upon a ruler from Judah? It took a long time, but it did.

Light upon the Prophets

The purpose of a prophet was to *forth-tell*, or proclaim, the Word of the Lord. However, it was also to *foretell* what was in the knowledge of God for His people. After all, the God who knows the beginning from the end, in His eternal present, is able to reveal the future to His prophets (Isa. 9:6-7; Amos 3:7). Of course, there were times when the ancient prophets didn't live long enough to see their own prophecies come true (Jer. 31:31-34; Isa. 7:7-9, 14).

In the life of this struggling, theocratic nation, there is a tension between the prophet and the king. It is intended to be a healthy tension in order to ensure the purposes of God for His community. A significant principle of the foretelling ministry is that the Word, which is given in a particular context for a particular time, sometimes has far more significance for the future. God's people have to trust in order to know.

For the genuine prophet, God is the source of visions. Prophets such as Isaiah and Ezekiel saw visions, and those visions were part of the one story held in God's eternal nowness. Some examples are Isaiah's vision of the peace and harmony of a restored creation (chapter 11) and Ezekiel's vision of the river flowing from the temple at Jerusalem as it feeds the nations of the world (chapter 47). Remarkably, instead of the river (which has its sole source in the area of the temple) becoming more shallow as it moves further from the source, the water becomes deeper. Does that remind us of the streams flowing from Eden to feed the whole earth? And does it remind us of the river flowing from the New Jerusalem of Zechariah 14:8, Revelation 22:1, and John 7:38-39?

Broadly speaking, the prophetic ministry of God's community had a fourfold character. First, prophets exercised an apostolic call. This involved inviting the entire world into a universal community of God (Gen. 1:28; 12:3; Isa. 26:18). This primary apostolic call became a major problem in the life of Israel.

Second, this invitation involved a specific call to Israel to live a prophetic life that necessitated an attitude of *repentance*. But what did that mean? Repentance was always in connection with the covenant they had received from God. In syncretistic fashion, Israel was always snuggling up to other cultures for their approval. (Today, have things really changed?) Therefore, the prophets called upon the Israelites to return to their peculiar roots in God.

Third, the prophets called Israel to *demonstrate* for the world the character of God's kingdom, once lived in Eden. In other words, Israel was to be a light and sign to the nations. It was a universal commission, so that the world might respond to God's invitation to live in the harmonious and essential relationships of Eden.

Fourth, the prophets continually reassured Israel that God, in sovereign power, continued to involve Himself in their history. The prophets' message was not simply a reminder of what God *had* done; it was an assurance of what He would do in the future (Isa. 48:3; Ezek. 25; Jer. 32:37-41).

Clearly, therefore, the major role of Israel's prophets was to reveal the will and Word of God to His chosen community. Nevertheless, there were times when the Word was addressed specifically to an individual, especially to a monarch. One example was the encounter the prophet Nathan had with King David regarding an adulterous relationship. The relationship resulted in murder and the death of an innocent child (2 Sam. 11:14-15). When directly confronted by God's prophet, David repented (Psa. 51).

The standing of the prophets in the community was always of a charismatic nature. Genuine prophets of God could or should not be institutionalized. If they acted as institutional chaplains, they would not avoid stooping to the level of a popular seer (2 Chron. 18:7).

Among a people who supposedly came under theocratic rule, the history of the kings of Israel in the north and Judah in the south proved to be a litany of good news-bad news events. The good kings were those who listened to the prophets and who worked to eradicate the enticing natural religions of their neighbors.

God's intent was to raise up a community, not only to speak invitingly and prophetically to the world, but also to live a prophetic life in demonstration of kingdom essentials. Canaan was intended to be a land that would reflect, if imperfectly, the character of life in Eden. One prophet stood out as being representative of the entire prophetic ministry.

Elijah may not have been as busy as his successor, Elisha, nor may he have performed as many signs and wonders as did his protégé, but one occasion in his ministry stands out like a beacon in the natural versus revelation dynamic. The place was in the northwestern part of Israel; it was called Mount Carmel. After a three-year drought, Elijah, bravely and mockingly, challenged the natural prophets of Baal. The challenge was a duel of sorts: whose God or gods could save the people of the land?

Baal's prophets prepared a sacrifice and called on their gods to send fire. Nothing happened.

Elijah prepared a sacrifice and poured water on it. Then he called on God. The fire of the Lord consumed the offering and everything around it (1 Kings 18:38). Soon, the rains appeared. The natural prophets of Baal were routed and put to shame.

The event proved climactic in the struggle between those who followed natural religion (led by King Ahab) and those who turned to the God of Self-revelation. It was a magnificent moment of light. From that time on, Elijah became synonymous with the prophetic ministry of Israel. At the time of Jesus, many were still looking for Elijah's prophetic ministry to return (Mal. 4:5; Matt. 16:13-14).

The period between the return of the exiles (ca. 538 BC) and the heraldic mission of John the Baptist (ca. AD 30) cannot be described as a complete restoration of the four pillars of Israel. Despite a growing hope, never again would the Jews have their *king* from the line of Judah; at least, not in the normal way they had anticipated. "The anticipation of a return of Davidic rule and national independence, held by a few people in the time of Haggai and Zechariah, had proved unfounded. The faith of the community survived, but it had all but lost hope for any significant future."[6] Apart from the possibility of some parts of the Book of Daniel, the voice of prophecy became relatively silent in the inter-testament period. However, the law was honored, and a priesthood returned to its ministry in the temple.

A little later, after the destruction of the temple in AD 70, the exiles of the Diaspora, who were more likely to take their primary apostolic mission seriously, were literally forced into a ground-shaking ecclesial reform. There were no more kings and priests in their system. But through the genius of the recently emerged Pharisees, their emphasis on law, prophets, and prayer made Judaism possible for Jewish people throughout their Diaspora, far from the assurances offered in Jerusalem. From that time on people of Israel, wherever they were, could find God in Word and Prayer, in a synagogue!

Promised Light for a Future Remnant

Despite years of conflict, exile, assimilation, and loss of freedom, Israel's hope remained that God would be a light shining upon their future. "Arise, shine, for your light has come, and the glory of the Lord has risen upon you . . . nations shall come to your light, and kings to the brightness of your dawn" (Isa. 60:1,3).

Isaiah also looked to the day when the nation would know peace. First-day Light was their hope. "Violence shall no more be heard in your land, devastation or destruction within your borders . . . The sun shall no longer be your light by day, nor for brightness shall the moon give light to you by night; but the Lord will be your everlasting light, and your God will be your glory" (Isa. 60:18-19).

One day, on the eighth day of his life, a baby boy received the Jewish rite of circumcision. Standing nearby, Zechariah, the father of John the Baptist, "was filled with the Holy Spirit and uttered this prophecy" (Luke 1:67-79). In that prophecy he said that God's Messiah would be called "the prophet of the Most High." His purpose would be to "prepare the way of the Lord," and that God would "give light to those who sit in darkness and in the shadow of death."

Similarly, and shortly after, there was a man in Jerusalem who constantly looked for deliverance for God's people; he prayed at the temple for the Lord's Messiah to appear. It happened right before his eyes. Mary and Joseph brought the baby Jesus to the temple to be circumcised. When Simeon saw the Lord Jesus, his eyes lit up; he held the baby in his eager arms and prophetically breathed over the child. This child, he said, would be "a light for revelation to the Gentiles and for glory to your people Israel" (Luke 2:32).

Thirty years later, John the Baptist pointed to his cousin Jesus, and declared, "Here is the Lamb of God who takes away the sin of the world" (John 1:29). John also said, "I baptize you with water for repentance, but one who is more powerful than I is coming after me; I am not worthy to carry his sandals. He will baptize you with the Holy Spirit and fire" (Matt. 3:11). And, "He must increase, but I must decrease" (John 3:30).

Jesus appeared, and soon after, John the Baptist exited from the stage of Israel's history.

"But you, O Bethlehem of Ephrathah, who are one of the little clans of Judah, from you shall come forth for me one who is to rule in Israel, whose origin is from of old, from ancient days" (Micah 5:2).

Doesn't this text remind us a little of the nature of Melchizedek? It appears he also was something very special, in terms of his nature (Heb. 7:1-3). The apostolic hope for a universal community was alive in the remnant person of Jesus Christ. For the writer of Matthew's gospel, Jesus was not only the suffering servant of Isaiah, but the anointed Messiah of Israel's future hope.

In this brief summary of activity in Old Testament times, we see that knowledge of God is clearly not acquired by means of philosophical conjecture. Rather, such knowledge is experienced in stories of how God reveals Himself in and through the lives of real persons of historical authenticity. There are many stories impregnated upon the consciousness of this community, which have profoundly affected that consciousness of being unique in identity and purpose.

Certainly, even when there are clearly different traditions involved, we can appreciate through these stories what God wants us to know of Himself. Going forward, we will be almost completely absorbed by one Person; the Lord Jesus Christ. What connections are made between Jesus and the failures of Adam? In what way may we see Him in His divinity? Has God revealed Himself to us in a real Person? If so, then what is our response?

CHAPTER 7

Who Is This Jesus?

The Stage Was Set

*J*esus *is* the Story! In proclamation, in signs and wonders, in death and resurrection, He is the summary of all that is meant in the story of creation, redemption, and restoration.

In the apostolic charge to Adam, and later in the call of Abraham, we see clearly that the nation of Israel really was intended to pioneer the creation of a redeemed and universal community. Biblically, we also observe that this nation remained in a prominent place of honor to the very end.

However, God's ultimate rescue of His purposes is focused in a one-Person remnant. Jesus sacrificially spent His entire life, ministry, and death embracing and signifying the dance of Eden's innocence. As we have seen in the story of Eden, the dance included a charge to draw together a universal community under the lordship of Eden's rightful king. The time was drawing near for His appearance.

Five occurrences in chronological time had made the world a less provincial-minded place. First of all, many of the Jews who had been taken into exile were free to either remain in their new lands or return to their homes in Judah. Maybe, for some of this remnant community, there was a glimmering sense that God's first-day Light could yet shine throughout the entire world.

Second, through the imperial ambitions of Alexander the Great, the common language and culture of Greece was becoming the norm throughout the West, the Mediterranean, and the Near Eastern regions of the world.

Third, the Romans, who adopted much of Greek culture, established easy trade routes throughout all the regions they had conquered. Because there was now a common language, international trade could be accomplished.

Fourth, there was an expectancy growing in Israel that God was going to send them a deliverer. They believed a messiah may soon arrive. In the Diaspora, there was a common language, and on almost every street corner there was an opportunity for philosophical debate.

Fifth, the Pharisaic sect of Judaism had established itself during the previous two hundred years. Largely through them, synagogues had been established in most Roman areas of commerce. Synagogues proved to be a significant starting point for many apostolic penetrations in the universal spreading of the gospel.

The known world was becoming accessible. Never before in the history of civilization, and particularly in the life of Israel, had a universal and apostolic mission been more possible. How about that for *kairos* timing? "When the fullness of time had come, God sent his Son, born of a woman, born under the law, in order to redeem those who were under the law, so that we might receive adoption as children" (Gal. 4:4-5).

All creation once more would see the most extraordinary and powerful light reflected upon its face (John 1:4). This would be a moment of light that would shed its light on the mountains of both redemption and restoration. In fact, the entire ministry of Jesus would be a moment of light. Jesus, the inbreathed and real Adam, had entered the stage of history. First-day Light was shining in the darkness once more (John 1:15).

But a Virgin Birth?

God, of a certainty, chose the most common and unremarkable way to introduce Himself. But this was what He had planned even before time began. In the very moment God decided to create the universe, in order to fulfill Old Testament revelation, He also decided to pay an enormous price for universal redemption. Knowing the future, He knew that He would clothe Himself with the same physical nature He had designed for Adam (Phil. 2:6-7). But His entry into the world would be through the cursed birth pangs of a woman (Gen. 3:16). This would be the way He would sign His kingdom character upon creation. *Suffering* was the pathway God chose to vindicate His sovereign purposes.

The virgin birth is clearly recorded in Matthew and Luke, but not as the pivotal event in Christ's appearing. If people didn't believe in the fact of the resurrection, then the virgin birth would be very low in their priorities. Nevertheless, most of the Christian world celebrates the virgin birth of Jesus, the Light of the world, and at a time of the year when much of the world's population (i.e., the northern hemisphere) is at its darkest point.

Without dwelling heavily on the birth narratives in Matthew and Luke, we must highlight the importance of the star—the natural light that shone over Bethlehem. In the account recorded in Matthew's gospel, the writer was most certainly not honoring the ancient art of astrology. He was using the story to underline the fact that the magi, once having seen the "light for revelation to the Gentiles" (Luke 2:32), had to bow prostrate before the glory revealed in the baby Jesus. It was Jesus who was the real star of Bethlehem.

But, in the prologue of John's gospel, it is John's language that demands attention. He makes it very clear that the eternal identity and the earthly work of the One who is the Light must not be confused with the one who heralds it, namely John the Baptist (John 1:8). In fact, this verse shows clearly that no one else could ever shine as the Light of the world. Guided by natural light of the fourth day, the wise men bowed before the glorious Light of the first day. They could never go back the same way again (Matt. 2:12).

But was this really a virgin birth, and was it necessary? To many, it sounds preposterous. Why did He come to us this way?

It's all connected with the creation story. From that horrific moment when Adam began to devolve from his original nature and from his kingdom possibilities, God posed the question, "Where are you?" In an awesome moment of light, God's incarnation in Christ answered the anguished cry of all humanity: "Here I am!" The true Light was not ashamed of innocent transparency. Indeed, the entire story of God's incarnation is the story of Jesus' glorious dance of innocence.

Nowhere in the history of religious thought do we observe anything that parallels the awesome incarnation of God in Jesus (Isa. 7:14). "The Jews were not given to the heroism and virginal birth stories of the superstars of Greek mythology. Mythical story, of this sort, is better found amongst the Indians of New Mexico; the ancients of China; and the Hellenistic legends of Greek heroes like Hercules, Perseus and Bellerophon."[1] A godlike hero, displaying the courage and vices associated with heroism, was not in the mind of Israel's prophets. Jesus was no hero. He was the suffering servant (Isa. 53), and the anointed Savior (Isa. 42:1-4). Matthew 12 reaffirms this in verses 17-21. That's why Jesus can never, ever be considered a superstar.

We must consider the efficacy of the virgin birth a little more. After all, two synoptic writers found it important. It wasn't outlandish for them to accept that the God who created the universe by the breath of His Word could make possible a virgin birth. It is difficult to see how the God of redemption could have achieved this miraculous work without considerable cost to Himself.

A little girl once ran into the house on a cold and wintry day. She was crying. Her mom, a little disturbed by this, asked her what the problem was.

"I try very hard to feed the hungry sparrows, but every time I throw the bread crumbs, the sparrows fly away. I love them, Mommy. What can I do to show it?"

Her mom replied, "Maybe, in order to feed the sparrows, you have to become a sparrow."

In other words, in order for God to become fully involved with the human story, He had to *become* the human story! And that's what God's moment of incarnation is all about.

No one knew the truth of Christ's birth more than Mary and Joseph. But it took the miraculous apparition of an angel to Joseph in a dream before Joseph was convinced. He proved to be a wonderful father, exactly the father figure needed for the formation of Jesus' humanity. Mary, chosen by God from among all the women of the world, proved to be the perfect mother figure. She was overwhelmed because, amid the excited gossip about an imminent messiah, she couldn't believe that she had been chosen, and especially without the aid of a man.

The Hebrew word *almah* and the Greek word *parthena* meant "virgin" to Mary. "How can this be since I am a virgin?" (Luke 1:34). A literal rendering of *epei andra ou' ginosko*, with its prefacing question, would be, "How can this be since I do not know an adult male?" (In Hebrew thought, the verb for "to know" also refers to physical intimacy; see Genesis 4:1.) Even more astoundingly, she was to bear God Himself (*theotikos*). Luke traces the lineage of Jesus all the way back to "Adam, son of God." No wonder we are drawn to understand *why* Mary quietly "pondered these things in her heart" (Luke 2:19).

Who had ever spoken of the seed of a woman? Wasn't the seed of the man all that was required to make a baby? Of course, modern science has changed all that thinking. But the writer of Genesis 3:15 records that God said to Satan that the seed (or the offspring) of a woman would bruise his head. After the baptism of Jesus, Luke continues with Christ's genealogy, showing that Mary's offspring would be the one to cause the bruising of Satan. He would be the Son of the Most High, the Son of God. In terms of priesthood, similar metaphorical language is used to describe Melchizidek—see Hebrews 7:3. Jesus was the Son who would reign on the throne of David in an everlasting kingdom. What an astounding lineage Luke records! (Luke 3:23-37).

The entire, single story of the Bible, as predicted by the prophets, is now entirely focused in one Person: Jesus Christ.

Luke's record of the angelic annunciation reveals that the one who was to be born would be both fully human and fully God. He would be the Son of the Most High. As such, He would be given the earthly throne of David forever! (Luke 1:32-33). God would be in Christ, reconciling the world to Himself (2 Cor. 5:19).

This notion of miracle may not sound quite so outlandish to a *modern* scientist, but we must stress the theological point that God has voluntarily entered into our dimension of life because we were no longer capable of reaching up to His. Such an act from above requires a miracle.

Through the use of the term *theosis*, Eastern churches tried to explain deification, or union with God.[2] Irenaeus and Athanasius put it this way: "God became man in order that man might become god."[3] Westerners sometimes are a little disturbed by this language. However, the small 'g' is used of the deity in this context because Eastern theologians are very eager to stress that God is ultimately unknowable.[4] We can never enter into complete union with God because we will always be created beings who thirst everlastingly for the joy of knowing the original and eternal Creator. There will always be a distance between the Creator and the created.

Deification, therefore, is all about being rescued in order to become what we once were: inbreathed and living in the reflection of God's light and glory. It's all about the fact that Christ has come to us in order to lead us back to God; to make captivity captive (Eph. 4:8).

Rescue *necessitates* a divinely appointed miracle. "Christianity claims that in the extraordinary conception of Jesus we see the truth of which all those pagan stories are parodies. Of course this is shocking. Of course it is an affront to other worldviews. It only makes sense within the Judeo-Christian worldview, specifically within the worldview that is opened up by the resurrection of Jesus."[5]

The entire incarnation of God in Christ was truly a moment of light.

"And the Word became flesh and lived among us, and we have seen his glory" (John 1:14).

Jesus in the Wilderness

Adam lost his inbreathed power. But Jesus emerges from the waters of baptism, and humanity in its fullness is empowered once more (Luke 4:1).

Before Christ's ministry even begins, Satan attempts to attack Jesus in the wilderness in a similar manner Satan used with Adam in the garden of Eden. From the luscious paradise of a garden to the very austere wilderness of stress, wilderness was the major arena in which temptation really could take place. (Early Eastern fathers felt that it was important to face the demons within by meeting them on their own ground—in the wilderness and desert regions.)

Of course, Jesus immediately recognized who Satan was; not because, deceivingly, Satan appeared as an angel of light, but because all of Satan's words were contrary and offensive to the principles of God's kingdom. Adam was taken in by deceit and the perversion of his own ego. But, by observing Satan's encounter with Jesus, all humanity is given the opportunity to recognize Satan for the cunning liar that he is. This is primarily because Satan's words do not conform to the revealed Word of God (Luke 4:5), and neither do they conform to the revealed nature of God's kingdom (Gen. 3:4-5).

Satan's attempt to work on the ego of Jesus fell far short. Jesus was very secure in His identity. He had nothing to prove to a religious or philosophical establishment (Luke 23:9). But our primary interest in this crafty and arrogant encounter is in seeing how the entire story of redemption was under attack. Jesus, the Son of God, undergoes harassment in His humanity and in His divinity.

Recall that Luke traces the genealogy of Jesus beginning with Joseph, through David, and back to God. Matthew proceeds backward to Abraham. However, both authors agree on Christ's human and divine natures. Also, both agree that, unlike the old Adam, the real Adam did not succumb to Satan's wiles (Heb. 5:15).

The first temptation was stated this way: "If you are the Son of God, command this stone to become a loaf of bread" (Luke 4:3). "If you are the Son of God" is significant in that the definite article "the" is used. This word choice is the assurance that His eternal divinity and His humanity are under attack. Had Jesus given in to the Devil's taunt, then He would have signaled the end of God's plan of redemption. Jesus' mind was on eternal things of the kingdom, and not on short-term solutions.

The Devil offered Jesus a simple way to solve the problem of world hunger. It is a problem of which Satan is diabolically the chief agent. How could a compassionate person resist such an offer? The compassionate Jesus is not a sentimentalist. He never denies that Satan has the power to give what he offers.

Had Jesus given in to this easy solution, what would it have meant for God's plan of salvation? Did Satan really believe he had the power to change or take hold of the ultimate nature of God's kingdom on earth? The kingdom principle in Eden was that God provided, but His children would cultivate fruit in a life of worship. Satan wants nothing less than worship. The second temptation bears out the point of Christ's dual nature. The Devil offers Jesus the kingdoms of the world (vv. 5-7). In an ancient garden, did not God previously offer Adam stewardship of this massive enterprise? (Gen. 1:28). But stewardship is not enough for Satan. What an arrogant usurper! Who had allowed Satan to roam the earth in the first place? (Job. 1:7). And then, who was it who was called to win back the kingdom with the price of His own blood? Again, a successful attack on Christ's mission would have meant that Jesus had sold out God's redemptive purposes (Phil. 2:5-10). The short-term goal would certainly have relieved Jesus of the cost of dying for the sake of humanity's redemption.

In the third temptation, it appears that Jesus could have been enticed. After all, He still possessed what Adam had lost. Had Jesus acquiesced, it would have meant that humanity could have secured for itself the control or the restoration of all time. Humanity could *naturally* live forever, after all. The consequences of detracting the worship focus from God's kingdom authority would have been disastrous. No longer would faith in God be needed. "Do not put the Lord your God to the test" (Luke 4:12).

Putting the wilderness temptations in their kingdom perspectives, we realize that it is Jesus, both man and God, who says no to Satan. Like us, He has the perfect freedom to say yes to the Devil, but He doesn't. He makes decisions from bigger perspectives than those of His own ego. He makes His decisions according to His obedience to every word proceeding from the mouth of God. In contrast, Adam made his decisions according to the lying promises of Satan.

Jesus, as a man, really did calm the storm; He really did walk on the water. But He did so as the real Adam. The one story requires that sort of identification of God with humanity through God's inbreathing. This is the reality that was reflected upon the world. Pondering Peter's brief, pre-

Pentecost encounter with Christ, when He walked on the water, makes us wonder how much of Adam's original ability still resided in Enoch. How much have we marveled at such glimpses or signs in Elijah and others to this very day? "Do not put the Lord your God to the test."

Who Do They Think He Is?

It's not surprising that the people of Israel didn't accept the dual nature of Christ very easily. The religious establishment rejected it without much thought. Christ was rejected thoroughly by His own people (John 1:11). They could deal with ideas of God speaking through creation, through history, and through the prophets (Heb. 1:1), but they found it very difficult to embrace the thought that God had become human. Emmanuel: God Himself is with us? (Isa. 7:14).

Not surprisingly, the apostle Paul found it necessary to give an explanation of the need for divine rescue when he wrote to his Greek-thinking converts at Philippi. He said, "Who, though he was in the form of God, did not regard equality with God as something to be exploited, but emptied himself, taking the form of a slave, being born in human likeness" (Phil. 2:6-7).

It's not that the gospel of Jesus Christ was more sophisticated than humanity had ever known, but that the Trinitarian God of Jesus was much more complex than rational thinking could ever comprehend.

The god of Babel will always be too small. Truly, the nature of the Trinitarian God defies adequate description. It won't be explained fully by the story of a community on a journey, or by the theoretical logistics of a faith borne in rationalism.

Examples of two different persons presenting two different Christs are found in the persons of Albert Schweitzer and Rudolph Bultman. Are these two persons at the root of the strange, modern expression, "the Christ in you"? It's as if Christ were a different person in everyone.

The truth is the reverse: We are all different persons in Christ (Gal. 4:19).

In the early part of the twentieth century, Albert Schweitzer made a genuine attempt to find the Christ of faith in the historical events of His life, particularly as the events related to His Jewish context. Schweitzer was on a quest for the historical Jesus. It was in this context as a Jewish man that "the self-consciousness of Jesus underwent a development during the course of his public ministry."[6] In his quest to uncover the historical context in which Jesus ministered, and of the perceptions His followers had of Him, Schweitzer determined, "Our conclusions can only be considered valid so long as they are not found incompatible with the recorded facts as a whole."[7] It sounds fine, but will the facts do all the talking? Are they enough?

Quite differently, Rudolph Bultman felt that there was another way to uncover the Christ for all people. His approach to the Christ of faith was quite simple. Reinterpret the so-called miracles of Jesus, and you finish up with someone you can believe in. Miracles are not needed to give credence to Christian belief.

Bultman was far less interested in facts. He believed his purpose could be achieved by demythologizing Christ's so-called miracles. For him, the miraculous intervention of God was an anachronistic notion. As such, in the embers of modernist thought, miracle was no longer needed in a more sophisticated understanding of the Christian story. The resurrection of Jesus is sometimes thought of this way.

Bultman believed that miracles equated with simplistic mythologies inherent in primitive religion. Christians could abandon them in favor of the system he called "de-mythology." The intent of his schema was to recover deeper meanings behind mythological concepts. "De-mythologizing makes clear the true meaning of God's mystery."[8] But will faith without the facts of history be enough?

The reality is this: the Christ of faith can only be discovered through fact and faith—that is, if we want authentic Christian experience. When we tread the way of revelation, we walk the pathway of faith paved with the well-worn stones of history.

The intentions of both Schweitzer and Bultman were admirable. However, in some sense, both attempted to transfix the image of Christ into a papier-mâché of their own making.

They were not alone in forging paths in such directions. Indeed, the nineteen-sixties and seventies saw a huge surge in existential thinking. However, we cannot point back to pioneering atheists such as Jean Paul

Sartre as the sole voices exalting individual experience. Can it be said that individual experience may be regarded as the arbiter of truth? Some Christian thinkers believed in the idea that "my present reality is the way that determines the process of truth." Indeed, the very idea that subjective, individual human experience becomes the focus of truth's integrity has been relished by postmodern minds. This notion may have scientific roots in Heisenberg's uncertainty principle." In common thought, it translates to mean, "Reality is the way I observe it to be." For example, this interpretation is inferred in a recent movie entitled, The Life of Pi. At the end of the movie an ambiguous choice is given to adopt a different ending, if that is what suits the observer best. But the real history and truth of the story is important. At one time Jesus posed a question with historical reality in mind.

Late in His ministry, Jesus asked His own disciples the ultimate question: "But who do you say that I am?" (Matt. 16:15). He would not have asked them that question earlier. He was more likely, in those early days, to say, "Go, and tell no one" (Matt. 8:4). Jesus wanted the effects of His kingdom life and His demonstration of kingdom signs to do all the talking (John 14:11). His dual nature had to emerge before them. Had Christ's claims to ontological divinity been broadcast, His signatory ministry would never have got off the ground.

But now the twelve were faced with the most awesome question requiring a decision. Peter (besides Jesus, my favorite biblical character) wasn't very shy! He was never bashful about speaking on behalf of the other eleven. Peter said, "You are the Messiah, the Son of the living God" (Matt. 16:17).

In the Matthew account, Jesus appears to offer a much longer reply than we see recorded in the same accounts in Mark and Luke. For over 1,700 years, this difference has been a major point in deciding the supremacy of Peter in the universal Christian community. However, never did Jesus appear to exalt one person to a place of headship in His community. (It should be recognized that Jesus may well have acknowledged Peter as the spokesman for the Twelve). James and John discovered that a place of supremacy was not consistent with the nature of the kingdom or of the Trinity (Mark 10:43). Indeed, the late Raymond

Brown, a Roman Catholic theologian, speaking of Peter, makes this historical comment:

> Certainly he was not the original missionary who brought Christianity to Rome (and therefore not the founder of the church of Rome in that sense). There is no serious proof that he was the bishop (or local ecclesiastical officer) of the Roman Church-a claim not made till the third century. Most likely he did not spend any major time at Rome before 58 when Paul wrote to the Romans, and so it may have been only in the 60s and relatively shortly before his martyrdom that Peter came to the capital.[9]

The closest we come to a hint of special recognition within the community of the Twelve concerns three of the apostles. Peter, James, and John appear as special witnesses to three important events in the ministry of Jesus. These events are the raising of Jairus's daughter (Luke 8:51), the agony of Christ in Gethsemane (Mark 14:33), and the transfiguration (Luke 9:28). Peter does not stand out on these occasions. (See 2 Peter 1:16-18, and note that Peter speaks in the plural regarding being a witness.) In none of these situations is there a hint that Peter was given a position of supremacy.

Let the scholars continue this debate concerning a possible misinterpretation, or an acontextual view, or even an interpolation of Matthew 16:18. The real problem is that Christ's disciples had not yet begun to understand the nature of His kingdom. Subsequently, shortly before His betrayal, when Jesus washed the feet of His disciples, the event blew their minds. The kingdom is all about serving one another!

Who Does He Think He Is?

The apostle Paul addresses the question of Christ's uniqueness in the following way: "For in him all the fullness of God was pleased to dwell" (Col. 1:19). And again, "For in him the whole fullness of deity dwells bodily" (Col. 2:9). His use of the Greek phrase *pan to plaeroma* means that absolutely nothing of the fullness of God's deity was left behind.

Until the latter part of His ministry, Jesus downplayed His divinity by preferring to *let it appear*. In describing Himself, He used the term "Son of Man" with some frequency. In choosing this approach, He was showing that He was truly the real son of God; that is, in terms of the relationship associated with God and the family of Adam—Jesus' humanity (Gen. 6:2; Luke 3:23, 38). It was also the terminology often used by the prophet Ezekiel when speaking of the ideal prophet and watchman of Israel. Later, Jesus began to assert the nature of His divinity.[10]

For two thousand years, the church has fully acknowledged the dual nature of Christ. But many of the theological problems we encounter in the contemporary mainline church are associated with a poor appreciation or experience of the Trinity. Biblical writers were wise to avoid long theological explanations of this incomprehensible mystery. However, they did not back away from the reality that once Christ had appeared on the stage of history, a new apologetic for the nature of God had to be acknowledged.

In the baptism of Jesus, we see both the fullness of God and the perfection of humanity. God was well pleased. "The Holy Spirit descended upon him in bodily form like a dove. And a voice came from heaven, 'You are my Son, the Beloved; with you I am well pleased'" (Luke 3:22).

Doesn't that sound like God's "It was very good" after Adam appeared on the scene? Indeed, this particular occasion leans toward acknowledging the humanity of Jesus. Would Jesus, in His divinity, have any need of baptism? Would God speak of God by saying how pleased He was concerning God? The life offered by Jesus (John 10:10) is a reversal of the consequences inherited from the Adam of Eden. It is precisely what God intended for His creation. Secure in His identity, Jesus could say, "And this is eternal life, that they may know you, the only true God, and Jesus Christ whom you have sent . . . So now, Father, glorify me in your own presence with the glory I had in your presence before the world existed" (John 17:3, 5).

We remember that the reason Jesus died was precisely because He claimed to be the Son of God; i.e., in His divinity. And, to the leaders of the religious establishment, He declared it (Mark 14:61-63; John 19:7). The high priest was angry, and Jesus died for asserting such "blasphemy." To the representative of the world's secular power, Jesus answered affirmatively that he was the king of the Jews (Matt.27:22-24). Pilate, afraid of his standing before Caesar, caved in to the crowd.

What had Jesus said and done in order to elicit a reply to that astounding and ultimate question? Jesus maintained the Spirit-filled ability to do what Adam once did, but lost. Jesus was truly the charismatic Christ. Secure in His humanity and divinity, He could face further taunts of Satan as the man of Eden and the eternal Son.

Would it not be valid to ask that, if Jesus was more than a prophet or a guru, He would surely have to *show* He was capable of doing the things that Adam subsequently failed to do? We are here thinking about the power of Jesus as a human being. Signs and wonders of the Spirit had been evident in many of Israel's individuals. Moses, Elijah, and Elisha are good examples. But could there be a remnant Person who would actually be the model for an entire reborn community?

Language is important. Instead of making use of the more spectacular word "miracle," both John and Luke prefer to use the word "sign" (*saemeon*). The call to kingdom life is a call to live in signature of the power and obedience of the real Adam.

Bringing Creation Under Control

Throughout His ministry, Jesus never did say that His kingdom was complete by virtue of His arrival. Hence His teaching on the Lord's Prayer (perhaps more aptly named the "Kingdom Prayer"—see Luke 11:3-4). As God had given Adam the task of working on nature, so Jesus and His community would *demonstrate* what God had intended at the beginning. It was from the House of Israel, the new community of Eden focused in Jerusalem, that Jesus would create an apostolic community for His universal mission.

Jesus was not given a new mandate from God. Indeed, after His baptismal inbreathing, Jesus returned to His home in Nazareth. In the synagogue, He astonished His familiar neighbors with the words of Isaiah: "'The Spirit of the Lord is upon me, because he has anointed me to bring good news to the poor. He has sent me to proclaim release to the captives and recovery of sight to the blind, to let the oppressed go free, to proclaim the year of the Lord's favor.'" (Luke 4:18-19) "Then he began to say to them, 'Today this scripture has been fulfilled in your hearing.'" (Luke 4:21)

We note from this mandate that Jesus' mission was summed up in the words "proclamation" and "service." Service to others included the justice mission of a hoped-for Jubilee.

Jesus subsequently signaled the apostolic character of His mission when speaking to the diminutive Zacchaeus: "I came to seek and to save the lost" (Luke 19:10).

D. M. Baillie commented on the words of Claude Montefiore. Montefiore was an Anglican bishop who grew up in the Jewish faith. With such a tradition, he saw a striking difference between the Old and New Testaments. For him, Jesus presented the God who was a seeker who would actually go into the wilderness in search of His children. Commenting on this observation, Baillie added, "Now that does not consent well with a theology which speaks only of the human quest of the Divine, and which will say no more even about the climax of the quest than that it is the supreme discovery by the supreme pathfinder."[11] Baillie's observation seems to strengthen the case that the progressive nature of the Bible affirms the proposition that there is but one story with its focus on Jesus.

Soon after the baptism of Jesus, John the Baptist found himself in prison. Not surprisingly, he was now questioning if he had been right in taking the role of Jesus' forerunner. No wonder he sent his disciples to Jesus for an assuring clarification. In reply, Jesus quoted a familiar messianic Scripture: "The blind receive their sight, the lame walk, the lepers are cleansed, the deaf hear, the dead are raised, the poor have good news brought to them" (Luke 7:22-23).

Wasn't this precisely the ministry that Isaiah had foretold of the anointed Messiah? (Isa. 61:1-2). Were not these acts signs of the kingdom? Let the facts speak for themselves.

Jesus is the healer of nature gone wrong. Mark begins his gospel with breathtaking alacrity. In a matter of three chapters Jesus had exorcised unclean spirits; healed Peter's mother-in-law of a fever; cured several other people; cast out more demons; healed a leper and a paralyzed cripple; and healed a man with a withered hand. Much of this He did to show people of the religious establishment "that you may know that the Son of Man has authority on earth to forgive sins" (Mark 2:10). His authority did not reside in the religious structures. However, the powers of darkness most certainly feared it. This was clearly an authority of a charismatic nature.

Chapter four of Mark is very significant. In this chapter, Jesus demonstrates His authority over nature itself. Miracles are a significant and essential part of that story. The miracles of Jesus demonstrate the wholeness that God would have continued to exercise through the inbreathed Adam. Jesus, the real Adam, declares this in bringing together the meaning of "authority" (*exousia*, Matt. 28:19) with "power" (*dunamis*, Acts1:8). All authority in heaven and in earth was given to Him, as was the power to perform it (Matt. 28:18; Luke 3:22). Was not this the same authority and power that was given to Adam?

Are People Able to Walk on Water?

Mark introduces us to a remarkable event. Jesus is with His disciples in a boat under dangerous conditions. The boisterous winds are battering their vessel with merciless violence. Jesus rebukes the winds and waves by the power of His Word: "Peace! Be still!" Then the wind ceased and there was a dead calm" (Mark 4:39). Does not this remind us of the apparently disordered beginnings in the creation process? Then, the Spirit brought order and meaning into the situation.

Similarly, on another occasion, Jesus shows His mastery of chaos and of the barriers to God's purposes. He walked on the unruly sea.

I have a profound admiration for Dr. Hugh Ross and his scientific contribution to contemporary Christian thinking. However, I do not always share his biblical interpretations. In chapter ten of his book on the cosmos, Dr. Ross explains how Jesus, in His divinity, is able to transcend the limitations of a four-dimensional universe.[12] As a physicist, when he explains this to a layperson such as myself, he makes a wonderful case. Ross explains how it is possible, when He is not confined to four-dimensional limitations, for Jesus to walk on water.

Having shown in mathematical terms how this is possible, Ross then makes an enormous theological leap. He attributes the miracle to the unfettered divinity of Christ.

My major problem with this leap of interpretation is that the incarnational identification of God with humanity becomes weaker. In Ross's view, Jesus may simply don His divinity hat when encountering natural difficulties. As human beings, we are all faced with situations of chaos and disorder. There is hardly any consolation for us when, in similar situations, we see that Jesus overcame difficulties by donning His divinity. Wasn't He tempted in all points as we are? (Heb. 4:15).

The first Adam did possess the ability to overcome such difficulties, but as a human being (Gen. 1:28). We recall that, in this particular incident, Jesus also invited Peter to walk on the water. What a cruel invitation that would have been if the challenge were not possible. Surely, the invitation was given to Peter precisely because the problem could be overcome in his humanity. (I refuse to spiritualize this event when, as an historical event, it is of such significantly theological importance.)

For one brief moment of light in the human experience, Peter really did walk in creation authority. Well, he did so until he took his focus off Jesus, and then he surrendered to the limitations of his fallen nature (Matt. 14:22-33). But for one glorious moment, like Jesus, Peter was a breathtaking sign of what was possible through the Spirit.

That situation is very similar to the situation of the believing church of today—at least, when it moves in Spirit power. Such signs can happen now, but not in a measure signifying that the kingdom has arrived in its fullness. We need to take heart that God can surprise us with such signs.

By taking a large swath to show Christ as the Word of creation and as the real Adam of perfection, John writes his gospel around seven major signs. Chapters 2-11 are wonderful examples of how this theological schema is presented. These chapters present Jesus in relation to the seven signs of the kingdom and seven days of creation, including the Sabbath.

For John, the finished work of Jesus culminates in the resurrection of first-day Light. In John's mention of seven signs, we see that Jesus stands as the true, cosmic Christ. He straddles the apex of all time as the heart and focus of new creation (Eph. 1:10; Col. 1:17).

1. *Chapter 2:1-11.* Changing water to wine: Jesus had come to recreate new wine (the vibrancy of new creation) from the feebleness and spent ability of the old order.

2. *Chapter 4:46-54.* Healing of the nobleman's son: Jesus is the source of healing and of Eden's restoration. How did He perform this miracle when He wasn't even there? Is this a hint of multidimensionality in Adam, or does it distinctly demonstrate the unlimited power of the Word in time and space? As did the divine Son in creation, Jesus, in His humanity, had the authority to see the miracle before He gave the command.

3. *Chapter 5.* Healing of the crippled man on the Sabbath: Jesus is Lord of the Sabbath; He is the pioneer of restoration's advent. First-day Light was made for humanity, not the other way around.

4. *Chapter 6:1-59.* Feeding of the five thousand: Jesus is the Living Bread, the Word of Life for God's people and for all time. That includes the ancient wilderness people (vv. 58-59). The twelve baskets remaining supplied Life for the entire apostolic witness to the world.

5. *Chapter 6:16-21.* Jesus walks on the water: Not bound by the waters of chaos, the real Adam has complete authority over all creation, as He does in the new creation.

6. *Chapter 9.* Jesus heals the blind man: As in the beginning, He is the Light of the world, illuminating the world's darkness and gloom by the power of the Word. "I am the light of the world" (John 9:5). In other words, Jesus *is* creation's true Light.

7. *Chapter 11:1-44.* Jesus raises Lazarus from death: He is the essential sign of resurrection to new life, the Alpha and Omega of creation and its restoration. And, unlike Lazarus, who experienced a *resuscitation* of the old life, Jesus was the "first fruits

from the dead" (1 Cor. 15:20). After doing apostolic ministry in Cyprus, Lazarus was eventually buried at the Church of St. Lazarus, Lanarka. But Jesus rose with a *restored* body (i.e., the one essential sign of the body fitted for the new creation).

In Jesus, God has given us a glimpse of what creation was intended to be, and what it will be at the restoration. In a much better way, through Jesus, humanity reigns in a new creation. Jesus is the head of this restored community. But it is one fashioned from and through the old community of Abraham (Gal. 3:29). It will be through this apostolic priesthood that a Spirit-enabled community will continue to sign kingdom life until the day of the Lord is fulfilled.

Interoperaed in the signs of who Jesus is, John connects *word* and *action* when recording the astounding claims Jesus makes of Himself. Clearly, for John, verbal claims meant very little unless they were validated by signs of authentic kingdom life.

> I am the way, and the truth, and the life. No one comes to the Father except through me. (John 14:6; see also Matt. 11:27)

> I am the bread of life. (John 6:46)

> I am the light of the world. (John 8:12)

> Before Abraham was, I am. (John 8:58)

> I am the good shepherd. (John 10:14)

> I am the gate. (John 10:9)

> I am the resurrection and the life. (John 11:25)

Not surprisingly for some, the notion that John did not write this gospel is very attractive. The above statements are so awesomely profound that they leave little room for the kind of inclusivity such people desire. The case for authorship commonly ranges between the single writing of John (the brother of James) to a dual authorship. Raymond. E. Brown notes that there was also a theory that there may have been six authors of John's gospel.[13]

For many of a more liberal persuasion, John's gospel represents the reflections of a mid-second century community in Ephesus. The entire Gospel of John is contingent upon its astounding prologue (1:1-14). It is written with the consistency of a Jew writing to Jews.

The gospel summarizes, for this second-century community, what they feel Jesus has become to them. Is this not a truly existential basis for biblical theology? What does it say about the historical integrity of the book, or the honesty of first-person language?

Scholars such as Robert M. Grant are convinced that John's gospel was written around the time of Rome's invasion of Jerusalem (AD 70).[14] D. Moody Smith notes the distinctive nature of John's gospel and relates one theory of its origins. "Nevertheless there has been a wide consensus on such things as the likelihood that the Gospel of John represents a distinct form of early Christianity arising out of a Johannine circle or community and that this community possessed traditions about Jesus independent of, if not related to, the synoptic."[15]

John Robinson may have pressed his case too far. However, in his view, the teaching of Jesus clearly points to Himself as the new Temple of Israel. Robinson cannot see how the fact of the temple's desecration would not have been noted in a later-dated Gospel of John. He therefore concludes that John's gospel was written prior to AD 70, and at a time when the claims of the fledgling community could be challenged![16]

Churches of Eastern orthodoxy are convinced in their assertion that John brought Mary, the mother of Jesus, to her new home in Ephesus. From the time of the ascension to the period of the temple's destruction, at least thirty-five years elapsed. Clearly, the young John had a considerable amount of time to reflect on the life and ministry of Jesus. He didn't need another fifty years!

Regardless of an early or late first-century dating, the final content of John's gospel relays a further tradition. Historically, it supports and broadens the gospel focused in the historical Jesus. Important historical facts of Jesus' life are there, and especially as concerns the resurrection.

If the first New Testament writings were penned somewhere between AD 55-60, then the apostolic teaching and experience were commonly understood at least twenty-five years before the first writings were penned or circulated.[17] The vast majority of so-called "Christian-related" Gnostic writings, which later challenged the church, did not begin to be written until after the second century was under way. Whatever challenges they may or may not hold up to the church, the Gnostic gospels cannot be considered as possessing *any* apostolic or historical authority.

The powerful statements of John shock people today equally as much as they did in the time of Jesus. What is often described as a gospel summary, John 3:16, is also a summary of the dignity of free choice offered in God's creation. John's gospel is both inclusive and exclusive. Eternal life is for the *whosoever* that believes. But the corollary to this statement is also true; eternal life is *not* for those who disbelieve.

What may be said about Jesus' connection to the four pillars of Israel? Surely, if Jesus is the fulfillment of Israel's history, then He must be significantly connected to its four pillars. The entire Bible, as one story, becomes pointedly one story in the person of Jesus Christ. But we will not begin with Christ's relation to David, the great king. We will begin with the king in Eden.

CHAPTER 8

Is He the Real Adam of God?

The Real Adam, King of Israel

*I*n His humanity, Jesus saw himself as king, but what sort of king? First of all, He was the real Adam, the king of creation. Mark sees Jesus as the Adam who was not subject to anything in nature at all. Adam had been given authority over all creation; in disobedience he failed, but the real Adam didn't. No wonder Christ's disciples were in awe, "Who then is this, that even the wind and sea obey him?" (Mark 4:41). "In the Old Testament the sea is hostile to God, and God's victory over the primordial ocean is celebrated in song. So too in the New Testament, Christ's kingship is seen in his calming of the sea . . ."[1]

In Matthew's gospel, Jesus claimed His authority to be from above, not from His followers. "All authority in heaven and on earth has been given to me" (Matt. 28:18).

When Christ comes again, He is to return as the real Adam and as King and Master of God's new creation (Mark 13:24-26; Rev. 11:15). However, Jesus does have a connection with David, the great king of Israel. In Luke's genealogy, Jesus' lineage goes all the way back to Adam, son of God. Matthew, who is writing specifically to Jews, dates the lineage back to Abraham. But both make the connection to David.

There is no doubt that Jesus saw Himself as the Lord of King David. Therefore, His ministry showed Him to be the promised ruler of a new Israel: "David himself, by the Holy Spirit, declared, 'The Lord said to my Lord, Sit at my right hand, until I put your enemies under your feet.' David calls him Lord; so how can he be his son?" (Mark 12:36).

Jesus perceived His position to be greater than that of King David. In Jewish eyes, David was the ideal king; nevertheless, David was subject to Jesus (Mark 12:35-37). Speaking of a future, eternal reign, He taught about His own place in this restored community of God (Matt. 13:41; 16:28; Luke 22:30). On other occasions, He also spoke of Himself as judge and ruler in God's kingdom (Matt. 25:31-35). Secure in the authority given to Him, He consistently challenged others to grow in the essential characteristics of God's kingdom (Matt. 6:33).

From Old Testament perspectives, Jesus saw Himself to be the center of a predicted messianic reign in the new creation (Zechariah 9:9). On the occasion when he rode on a donkey into Jerusalem He did nothing to dispel the jubilation of the crowd: "Hosanna! Blessed is the one who comes in the name of the Lord! Blessed is the coming kingdom of our ancestor David. Hosanna in the highest heaven" (Mark 11:9-10).

The entry into Jerusalem (the new focus and sign of Eden) was an eschatological sign of the coming kingdom. If this meaning is not understood, then the occasion stands as a pathetic parody of a pretended authority. The Holy City of Jesus was to be a New Jerusalem, a Jerusalem above, a Jerusalem that is free! (Gal. 4:26).

Prophets much later than David saw the picture:

> My servant David shall be king over them: and they shall have one shepherd . . . and my servant David shall be their prince forever. I will make a covenant of peace with them; it shall be an everlasting covenant with them; and I will bless them and multiply them, and will set my sanctuary among them for evermore. (Ezek. 37:24-26)

> For here we have no lasting city, but we are looking for the city that is to come. (Heb. 13:14)

And therefore Jesus saw His universal commission to His disciples to begin from Israel's old city and the symbolic replica of Eden. "All authority in heaven and earth has been given to me. Go therefore and make disciples of all nations" This quotation from Matthew 28:18-19 has similar illusions in other biblical passages. (Gen. 1:28; Matt. 28:18-19; Luke 24:49; Acts 1:4, 8).

Without a shadow of doubt, the apostles of Jesus began to see a little more clearly that He was to be the king of a new creation. Although this kingdom would appear in a moment of restoration, it is very real. In some way, it is connected to this present world. It is, in fact, the kingdom that God has prepared from the foundation of the world. Jesus is to occupy center stage in it. He was fully aware of the fact. Unabashedly, He asserted that He had the authority to judge and rule in this kingdom that He Himself will bring to consummation (Matt. 7:21-23; 25:31-46; 28:17-20; Luke 21:27; 22:28-30; 23:42-43; Rev. 5:9-10). But how does Jesus fulfill the meaning of Israel's four foundational pillars?

The Real Adam Is Our High Priest

In all major versions of the Greek New Testament, the word for priest, *hieros*, is used in just three ways. Never in the New Testament is the word associated with a specific order of Christian ministry. However, the New Testament mentions the word in relation to three concepts: (1) the priesthood of the Temple; (2) the finished high priesthood of Jesus (Heb. 5-7); and (3) the priesthood of all believers (1 Pet. 2:9).

In this sense, as it was in the beginning, priest followed the original pattern of Adam and Eve. The entire Body of Christ is the appointed priesthood of creation. In Christ's connection with the priesthood of Melchizedek, the entire priesthood of believers is also the priesthood of creation, but not of blood sacrifice. The connection of priesthood with Jesus is, to the writer of Hebrews, now that Jesus has completed the Aaronic blood sacrifice, associated with Melchizedek and no longer with the blood sacrifice of Aaron (Heb. 7:11,15-17). If this were not true, then the finished work of Jesus would not be finished at all. It *is* finished, and is always efficacious as an offering of creation's innocence, which only Jesus, not Cain, could offer.

Peter and Paul agree that the primary function of the present New Testament priesthood is kerygmatic; it is one of universal *proclamation* of the gospel of reconciliation (2 Cor. 5:19-20; Rom. 15:16; Acts 2:38-40; Acts 4:18-20, 1Pet.2:9). Wasn't this also true of Adam's commission?

In the Book of Revelation, the writer looks to a picture of *consummation* with a kingdom of priests reigning on earth and in priestly service to God (Rev. 5:10). Isn't that the way it was in the beginning?

However, in the completed work of Christ, it is Jesus as High Priest and Victim who offers the grace of God to a needy and penitent world. He is the Abraham (priest) and Isaac (victim) that never really happened.

Moses believed the whole nation of Israel was called into a priesthood (Ex. 19:6). But, in the ministry of Jesus, we see Him as the great High Priest of a nation of priests, existing on behalf of all nations (Matt. 28:19-20). It is only in seeing Jesus as the High Priest (in the *finished* offering of Himself, Lev. 7:6) and the perfect Victim (Who was slain, Lev. 1:3) that we understand His new covenant work as High Priest.

We see Him also to be the focus and head of a new and universal priesthood. It is a restored priesthood of creation. As in the beginning, it is a priesthood consisting of both male and female; it is a priesthood with a mission. It is called to be a priesthood in order to "proclaim the mighty acts of him who called you out of darkness into his marvelous light" (1 Pet. 2:9). This is the apostolic mission to which Abraham had previously been called (Gen. 12:3). The priest holding greatest significance for Abraham was Melchizedek. In Jesus, we see God's priesthood of love reaching to all the nations of the earth.

The New Testament plainly points to the sacrificial priesthood of Jesus as the one mediator who is connected to the blood sacrifice of the Aaronic priesthood. But the Old Testament, recognizing the genealogical mystery surrounding Melchizedek, does not appear to connect the sacrificial priesthood of the future Aaron with the eternal priesthood of Melchizedek. This is made abundantly clear in Hebrews 7:6. However, the writer to the Hebrews does speak of the completion of this Aaronic priesthood in terms of the finished work of Christ (Heb. 7:11-24, 9:12, 24).

The original priesthood of the Adam community is figured again in connection with the eternal priesthood of Melchizidek. It is the rightful New Covenant priesthood of Jesus. The new covenant is celebrated in the mystery offering of the fruit of new creation's innocence in bread and wine.

Of course, once beyond the gates of Eden, Cain couldn't do it. And, ultimately, neither could Abel (Heb. 12:24). Surely, Abraham, the father of Israel, prefigured this by offering a tenth to Melchizedek and by receiving the fruit of creation from his hand—namely, bread and wine.

In His own body and blood, Jesus offered the innocent sacrifice of creation. Jesus was the innocent and perfect Paschal Lamb. In other words, it was not simply and exclusively a priest, on behalf of the people, who was offering the sacrifice of substitution. It was Jesus, the High Priest, in the anticipation of having offered His body and blood in completion of the Aaronic sacrifice, and who, like Melchizedek, gracefully offered to the priesthood of all Israel the restored offerings of Eden's innocence. Christ's priestly offering of Himself is the innocent offering of bread and wine.

It is now, in Christ, that His entire priestly community is graced to enter into the celebration of the fruits of His innocence. It is a mystery of new covenant that connects and completes the Aaronic work of redemption in Christ's own body and blood (Heb. 5:5:6). It is the celebration of a priesthood no longer limited to gender, but consisting of the entire redeemed priesthood of a new Eden.

Therefore, at every service of Holy Communion, the duly appointed celebrant, on behalf of the entire priestly community, in thanksgiving for Christ's finished work of redemption (John 19:30, Heb.7:22-25, 9:25-26), is graced to present to the people the remembrance of Christ's sacrificial act of atonement in restored, worshipful fruits of innocence. Christ has graced them with the innocence of His own life.

Like King David, should not the celebrants literally dance from the altar in joyful transparency? Surely, King David represents an outstanding sign of an Old Testament character. This is the Adam person who was privileged to sign the very first dance of Eden. In transparent innocence, David was not ashamed. But this terminology, in penitence, is now seen as an act of innocent worship. It is celebrated by the penitents at every service of Holy Communion in an awesome ministry of redemption and restoration.

Praise and thanksgiving can now, through the reconciling work of Jesus, be offered in a state of redeemed innocence (Heb. 13:15-16). It is then best understood in the light of Romans 12:1-2. Jesus alone is our Mediator, standing between God and His people. He does so for all time by offering to God's people the fruits of Eden's innocence. What a dance! The Lord's presence is profoundly and mystically with those who do.

> For this reason he is the mediator of a new covenant, so that those who are called may receive the promised eternal inheritance, because a death has occurred that redeems them from the transgressions under the first covenant. (Heb. 9:15)

> You are a priest forever according to the order of Melchizedek . . . Accordingly Jesus has also become the guarantee of a better covenant. (Heb. 7:17,22)

The eternal banquet of a new covenant, alluded to by Jeremiah, is now focused upon an intimate and eternal relationship with God through Jesus Christ (Jer. 31:31-34; Heb. 8:8-13). Further, it is brought, as Jesus implies, to fullness of meaning in the priestly sacrifice of His own body and blood.

And so, on Calvary's cross, Jesus incorporated the now-completed (and ended) ministry of the Aaronic priesthood with the eternal and everlasting priesthood of Melchizedek. Therefore, at every communion service, the entire priestly community is accounted as the innocents of Eden when they, in penitence and worship, are graced to enjoy the benefits of Christ's finished work of redemption and creation's fruit of innocence.

Jesus Offers a Mystery

As the High Priest of new creation, there was an awesome sense of mystery when Jesus touched the ordinary stuff of the earth. At the

Last Supper, He astounded His disciples when He offered them the daily, common elements of bread and wine. Wasn't this just like the offering of Melchizedek to Abraham and the new covenant promised by Jeremiah? The "new covenant" words of Jesus had not been heard since the time of Jeremiah! However, when the Passover meal had reached the point of drinking from the bitterness of the cup representing the cost of redemption, Jesus refused it and passed it back to His disciples) "for I tell you that from now on I will not drink of the fruit of the vine until the kingdom of God comes." (Luke 22:14-18, Exod.12:13) Indeed, this was the cup that Jesus was reluctant to take in His Gethsemane struggle. (Luke 22:42) The completion of this sacrificial act would permanently connect the Aaronic Passover of the blood, a passing over of God's judgment with that of the Melchizedek's offerings of innocence. It was a connecting of fallen creation with its restoration in Christ's blood. Indeed, the command of Jesus to do this in remembrance of me, was truly an anamnaesis (a memory, a recalling of Christ's finished work of redemption). In the finished work of Christ, (i.e., His death in the offering of His body and blood) the blood sacrifices of Aaron are now permanently ended. (Heb.7:15-17, 2224-25) But is this celebration simply a memorial?

The Holy Communion was a celebration of the full gospel story, not simply the part which emphasizes the story of redemption. And so, the offerings of Jesus are also the creation offerings of innocence in bread and wine. (Creation and restoration). Like David, the priesthood of believers in celebration embraces the dance of Eden's innocence. And the very Word that spoke creation into being, also said, "This is [*touto esti*] my body which is given for you" (Luke 22:19; brackets mine). *Touto esti* (in the present tense) bears the same force as the words God spoke to Moses at the burning bush, "I am who I am" (Ex. 3:14).

Great reformers have tried to explain, or explain away, the real presence of Jesus. But as all things were made through Him, He said, "Let there be light," and there was light. At this transforming celebration, the Word also said, "It is," and so it is! The saving manna of Moses was also the life-giving body of Christ (Ex. 16:4; John 6:30-35). It is so because the Word said so! Why argue what Jesus has declared to be, or even try to explain what will always be an incomprehensible mystery?

It is a mystery connecting, in the body of Jesus, the spiritual offering of the fruit of innocence. In saying "This is," Jesus is not speaking of emblems or of a daily meal, but of spiritual realities connecting the Jewish paschal offering with the spiritual food of restoration's innocence. The writer to the Hebrews sees the Aaronic priesthood to be one, now completed in the light of Melchizedek's eternal priesthood of innocence. It is eternally ministered in Jesus (Heb. 7:17, 23-27). Therefore, partaking in this bread and wine, we are graced to be identified with Christ's fruit of innocence.

Celebrants of the Holy Communion walk to the Lord's Table in thankful remembrance of Christ's finished work of salvation. They walk away in the sublime joy of being fed with the eternal and real fruits of Christ's innocence. A priesthood representing sacrifice is no longer necessary. A priesthood standing between God and His people is no longer necessary. "It is finished." (Heb.7:25, 7:27, Jn.19:30)

Apart from the high priesthood of Jesus, and the priesthood of all believers, surely it is not accidental that the New Testament *never* refers to a priestly order of ministry in the new covenant community. One of the church structures we encounter in the New Testament is noted in the Pauline church of Corinth. Here, elders (*presbuteroi*) are instructed to conduct worship decently and in order (1 Cor. 14:10). Although structures varied in Jerusalem, Corinth, Antioch, and possibly other places, an eldership is common to all New Testament forms. Following the synagogue model, elders had appeared in a wide range of ecclesiastical structures before Paul began his missionary journeys (Acts 11:29-30).

Surely, the Catholic-Protestant tensions concerning eucharistic theology must both be challenged with the question, "How did the ministry of elders (*presbuteroi*), not priests (*hiereoi*), evolve to an order of priesthood in the late second century?" The notion of there being an order of priesthood is not observable in any of the diverse church forms during the apostolic age. Some, condescendingly, describe this era as belonging to the primitive church. What was primitive about its remarkably diverse structures? They were close, and accountable enough for the church in Antioch to make an appeal for apostolic clarification to the church in Jerusalem (Acts 15:1-2).

We must also note that there is no etymological connection between *hieros* and *presbuteros*, except by the later and continuous usage of incorrect association. By the mid-second century, there was a powerful institutional move to separate professional ministry from amateur; who are sometimes called "laypeople." *This is a term never found in the New Testament.* Although the wider church was somewhat diverse in its structures, the one order which was common to all was that of eldership—the *presbuteroi* (plural).

Quite possibly the purposeful but gradual separation of professional from lay ministry inspired a restoration of a professional, Levitical priestly class. We remember that this tribe of priests was indeed the religious class of Israel; it stood between God and His people.

Whatever the tradition or form, the astounding *mystery* of the Eucharist must be maintained. Magic can be explained, but never mystery. "This is" becomes a spiritual mystery; it always will be, and is, therefore, above all simplistic or sophisticated explanation. The community of Christ therefore regularly celebrates this mystery of sacrifice and restoration (Acts 2:42).

We can't explain the mystery of Christ's presence any more than we can explain its so-called absence. If a chemist tested the bread and wine after it has been consecrated, he or she would conclude that it was constituted of all the elements of common bread and wine. But those elements now possess a changed spiritual reality! From Thomas Aquinas to Ulrich Zwingli, in different ways, apologists did attempt to explain the real presence or the real absence. Spiritual realities cannot be analyzed by any natural form or by any natural language. When we "do this," why do the natural elements become the spiritual reality of Christ's body and blood? Because the Word said so!

Whatever disagreements exist in denominational thinking, we should at least agree that the connection of the Last Supper with the promised new covenant of Jeremiah is all about the recovery of the eternal and essential relationships of Eden's innocence. These spiritual realities are the fruit of the innocent condition that Christ has won for us. These new covenantal signatures, offered at considerable cost to God, are the lively assurances that the penitential recipients are now accounted as innocents of the new Eden. It's all about presence! Except for an invitation to penitential confession, "Where are you?" is a question never asked at this celebration.

Much of the theological disagreement concerning the Eucharist that has occurred since the sixteenth century may have been avoided had there been an equal consideration of a Melchizedek-creation theology, centered on Eden's restored fruit of innocence.

At the Last Supper, Jesus made possible precisely what Jeremiah had predicted. He offered to His disciples the fruits of His own innocence. "This cup . . . is the new covenant in my blood" (Luke 22:20). The new covenant anticipated by Jeremiah took flesh in that astounding moment of light. Jesus, the Bread of Life, said so (John 6:35). The final steps on the path of redemption began from a banqueting table.

From the moment of Christ's resurrection and ascension, a restored priesthood of creation would continue to invite the world to a lavish celebration that would last forever. The Last Supper was an anticipatory moment celebrated at a table of everlasting abundance. Those who participate in this banquet feed eternally without the sweat of their own labor or the signature of their own effort.

Jesus, as Priest and Victim, has offered the sacrifice of Himself, once and for all. Through this offering, Jesus draws into Himself a universal priesthood, a priesthood of proclamation. "Be a minister of Christ Jesus to the Gentiles in the priestly service of God, so that the offering of the Gentiles may be acceptable" (Rom. 15:16). This eternally graced priesthood, as in Eden, is now declared to be "a royal priesthood . . . God's own people, in order that you may *proclaim* the mighty acts of him who called you out of darkness into his marvelous light" (1 Peter 2:9; italics mine).

The Real Adam Is Both Prophet and Lawgiver

In His dissertation, sometimes called the Sermon on the Mount, Jesus said that He had not come to abolish the law, but to fulfill it (Matt. 5:17). What did He mean by that?

Surely He could not have meant that He would demand strict obedience to the old covenant. Surely He wasn't asking His followers to obey every Levitical law and the myriad of tedious laws that were added on by the Pharisees. Of course not! In His wonderfully perceptive way of explaining God's principles for creation, Jesus reinterpreted how the essence and purpose of law was simply to enable God's people to live in the personal embracing of the relationships attributed to Eden's dance. Jesus' view of kingdom character goes all the way back to a harmonious Eden. Jesus, in obedience to the Father, was able to fulfill those impossibly high standards of kingdom life in which Adam had failed (Heb. 4:15).

Jesus' view of law was a matter of heart relationships. "I will put my law within them, and I will write it on their hearts; and I will be their God, and they will be my people" (Jer. 31:33). A good example of how Jesus got to the heart of relationships is gleaned when we make a quick comparison of the character difference between the Decalogue (Ex. 20:1-17) and the Beatitudes (Matt. 5:1-12).

Nearly every one of the Ten Commandments is prefaced with a negative tone of admonition. These commandments, as a call for changed behavior, are prefaced by the words, "You shall not."

No doubt Jesus preached the principles of the Beatitudes many times and in a variety of places. Clearly, He felt no need for restraint in times when He was challenged on matters of law. "You have heard that it was said . . . But I say to you . . ." (Matt. 5:27). It was Jesus who could delve into the very heart of the Law and even clarify it. We observe in Jesus an approach emanating from a heart condition. It is His pattern of life. Behavior would proceed from the basis of heart relationships, just as it once did in Eden. "Blessed are those . . ." In Him there is a call to certain types of behavior representing a quality of joyful relationships. Jesus taught His listeners that their primary focus was to live out the principles of the kingdom of God. "But strive first for the kingdom of God *and his righteousness* . . ." (Matt. 6:33; italics mine).

Jesus used this famous Sermon on the Mount to encourage His listeners to live by such motivation and standards. Much of the Sermon on the Mount appears to be addressed to His disciples, not the crowd. He was not casting pearls before swine. The call of Jesus was to total commitment to life in the kingdom of God (see Matt. 5:1-2; Luke 6:20). Sometimes in the same context, as Jesus intimated, we may cast pearls where they are not appreciated (Matt. 7:6). In other words, the character of a life with Jesus at the center is a kingdom-focused life. Jesus positively attributes happiness (*makarios*, also translated as "blessed") to those who *are* living with a covenant focus and a kingdom motivation.

It is incomprehensible to imagine how anyone can live up to the teachings of the Sermon on the Mount. But these standards, which are impossible to attain to perfection, point to the fact that, in order to live the kingdom life, God's community has to rely on His life-changing grace alone.

After the seemingly impossible standards He had set, the exasperating admonition to be perfect, as is our heavenly Father (Matt. 5:48; 2 Cor. 13:9), is a call to a quality of discipleship that reaches kingdom standards of relationships. The standards are not lowered to levels of sentimental individualism or to the petulance of a fickle culture. Nor are they lowered to the easily attainable level of a Barabbas crowd.

Unfortunately, in the much perverted concept of inclusiveness, there are many in the church today who would gladly lower the standards of this kingdom teaching to a level that costs little in terms of holiness, effort, or sacrifice. It's all about grace!

Clearly, all of humanity stands in need of God's grace. The one Person who may offer it, is the One who attained its impossible kingdom standards.

The apostle Paul didn't invent the idea of justification by faith (Rom. 1:17, 5:1). Nor did he initiate the idea of living joyfully in the grace of God (Eph. 2:8). Habakkuk had already caught a glimpse of this (Hab. 2:4). Jesus intimates it in everything He says and does.

God, by grace, accounts us worthy to receive the full status of adopted children—that is, sons of God—even though our individual efforts will never, in this old order, match His standards of "essential relationships."

What about the power of personal decision that was given in Eden? In our fallen nature, we realize that, by itself, personal decision does not have the ability to secure an eternal relationship with our holy God.

However, on behalf of all humanity, Jesus met the impossible standards of the Sermon on the Mount. He is truly the *real* Adam. The God-given ability to decide can never secure our salvation, but the complete work of Jesus is an invitation to enter into His decision for us. And His desire is for everyone to be saved, even though many, by decision, will not accept Christ's offer (1 Tim. 2:3-4). Salvation is all of grace (Eph. 2:8-9).

In terms of history, we see that Abraham proved to be the patriarch of promise. In his journey, which was in God's agenda, Abraham pioneered both elements of faith and reason. Jesus completed this journey of promise. "And if you belong to Christ, then you are Abraham's offspring, heirs according to the promise" (Gal. 3:29).

The prophetic tone of hope may be observed in many places throughout the New Testament. In 2 Peter 1:19, the message is also likened to a lamp shining in a dark place. The Word is truly a lamp to our feet and a light to our path (Ps. 139:105).

All the synoptic writers show Peter, James, and John witnessing the transfiguration of Jesus (e.g., Mark 9:2-8). Before their very eyes, Jesus is bathed in glistening light. The event was a signature prelude to the victory of the resurrection and ascension.

Reflecting on this astounding moment of light, Peter, like John, sees an inextricable connection between Light and Word (2 Pet. 1:16-19; John 1:5). The three apostles are privileged to gaze upon the same glory that shone upon the first day of creation, and also on the prototypical mountains of Israel.

Standing with Jesus were Moses and Elijah. They represent the only two foundational pillars that were to remain in the future life of Israel: the law and the prophets. After the sacking of Jerusalem in AD 70, there was no longer a priesthood or a monarchy.

The entire event is prophetic. It is symbolic of a Judaism that is to continue without a mountain embracing a city and a temple. At least, not as they had known it. That principle exists to this very day, apart from the belief of some orthodox Jews and others who continue to hope for a king and priest in Zion. Judaism reveals itself in the light of law and prophets. The Pharisaic vision of a Judaism existing through synagogue worship had succeeded. But, on this mountain of transfiguration, the brilliance of dazzling light was given to Jesus, not Moses or Elijah. Jesus is the very *shekinah* Glory that illuminates the two mountains of those pivotal figures (i.e., Sinai and Zion).

Clearly, the mountain of transfiguration appears to signify a dazzling pinnacle of revelation declaring completion. This teleological event completely focuses the story of Israel in the light of Christ. Not coincidentally, the account ends with the following words. As the images of Moses and Elijah fade away, the three followers of Jesus hear a voice from above saying, "'This is my Son, the Beloved; listen to him!' Suddenly when they looked around, they saw no one with them any more, but only Jesus" (Mark 9:7-8).

Greek texts clearly denote the use of the passive voice when referring to Christ's change of appearance. It was made possible by an act from above. Christ is acted upon by the Father. And God's desire, through the Spirit, is to reveal the Son, the Light of the world (John 16:13-14). It is therefore no accident of the pen that Moses and Elijah are then seen to fade right out of the scene.

The entire story of Israel is now summed up in the One who is its Adam and Eve, its Light, its Word, and its Glory. And, as Jesus said, the law of Israel is also now summed up in the words, "You shall love the Lord your God with all your heart, and with all your soul, and with all your mind . . . And a second is like it: You shall love your neighbor as yourself. On these two commandments hang all the law and the prophets" (Matt. 22:39-40)

"I give you a new commandment, that you love one another. Just as I have loved you, you also should love one another" (John 13:34).

Does this mean that the story of redemption is now over? Surely such consummation could not possibly occur until Jesus assumed the full role of the obedient servant of Isaiah (e.g., Isa. 53). Wasn't Jesus born in order to die?

The sacrifice of Christ could not be simply a sentimental myth or a beautiful theological story. It had to be an indisputable fact of history.

CHAPTER 9

When Is Redemption's Story Complete?

*J*esus was the perfect icon of kingdom life. Yet although He fed the multitudes, He went to bed each night surrounded by throngs of starving people. Although He healed the sick, He went to bed each night surrounded by all manner of disease and disorder. Although He raised several people from the dead, He went to bed each night as thousands faced a dark night of fearsome death. Although He preached about new birth, He went to bed each night with millions living in ignorance and darkness. Although He taught and lived the meaning of peace and justice, He slept in a world gripped in the vise of horrendous conflict and injustice.

His entire ministry had been one of kingdom signature. His works proved to be signs of the kingdom yet to be fulfilled in His completed work.

In Jesus, God gave us a glimpse of what creation was intended to be, and what it will be at the restoration. But now, the time had come for an earth-shaking sacrifice; it would be one that would change the course of reconciliation history forever. And where would this sacrifice take place? On Mount Zion, of course! It was the very place (once called, Moriah) where Abraham could not offer his only son in sacrifice.

As we follow the Easter events from Friday to Sunday, we are privy to momentous moments of light summarizing the entire meaning of creation, redemption, and restoration.

Calvary Was a Decision

When we call Calvary a decision, the question is, "Whose decision?" Jesus didn't have to go to Jerusalem; at least, not unless the will of the Father was of the first order in His life (John 8:28-29). As a matter of fact, Jesus had already told His disciples that it was necessary for Him to die in order to rise again (Matt. 16:21-23). At that time, they didn't have a clue what He was talking about. As usual, it was Peter who spoke up in a naive, though well-meaning, attempt to protect Jesus.

In Luke's gospel, Jesus, knowing what was before Him, deliberately trod the path to the Holy City because "it is impossible for a prophet to be killed outside of Jerusalem" (Luke 13:33). But Jesus didn't see Himself as a heroic martyr. He knew He was to be the Savior and the suffering Servant for the world. Having said this, Jesus must have known the theological tension that would arise by His acceptance of this role.

If Christians may assume to say so, Jewish scholars have always been perfectly correct in identifying the suffering servant as the community of Israel. Even Jesus declared to the Samaritan woman, "Salvation is from the Jews" (John 4:22). However, we must also acknowledge that, up to the time of Jesus, the suffering of the Jewish nation had come largely through their *disobedience* to God. "And many nations . . . will say one to another, 'Why has the Lord dealt in this way with that great city?' And they will answer, 'Because they abandoned the covenant of the Lord their God, and worshiped other gods and served them'" (Jer. 22:8-9).

On the other hand, we see the opposite occurring in the life of Jesus. It really was upon a single Person that suffering was inflicted; and through the fruits of *obedience*. "We do see Jesus . . . now crowned with glory and honor because of the suffering of death, so that by the grace of God he might taste death for everyone" (Heb. 2:9).

Subsequently, the new community of Israel, the offspring of Abraham through faith in Christ, was, in the same way, called to tread the path of suffering in obedience to God. Paradoxically, in the heart and mind of

God, signs and wonders of the kingdom would be best worked out on the pathway of a cross. "If we have died with him, we will also live with him; if we endure, we will also reign with him" (2 Tim. 2:11-12).

This biblical narrative is really one continuing story.

It was only after Calvary, and in subsequent glimpses of the Easter moment, that Peter began to see this one story clearly. "He was destined before the foundation of the world, but was revealed at the end of the ages for your sake. Through him you have come to trust in God, who raised him from the dead and gave him glory" (1 Pet. 1:20-21).

For some, the fickle crowd acclaiming Christ's entry into Jerusalem parodied the reality of Jesus' sense of mission. The theologian Edward Shillibeeckx believes that Jesus saw—in His limited success in Galilee, His betrayal, His rejection, and the whimsical nature of the crowd—the ultimate failure of His past ministry.[1] Shillibeeckx goes on to describe the second phase as no less of a failure. The ministry in Jerusalem is "an attempt to salvage the 'fiasco' in Galilee."[2] Quite regardless of Shillibeeckx's opinion, the fact is, Jesus believed He had done everything that the Father had told Him to do. (John 5:19, 17:4) Deliberately walking into a deathly trap (Luke 22:42) was hardly the action of a predicted saviour living with the guilt of failure. It is important for us to stress that, if we don't believe Jesus saw Calvary to be the necessary climax of His redemptive ministry then, what occurred in Jerusalem may well be the continuation of a so-called fiasco.

The crucifixion, in the mind of Jesus, was to be the highlight and the climactic moment of light in the entire story of redemption.

The idea that suffering would figure prominently at the heart of faith goes against the grain of our stoic, me-centered, wanton, and feely culture. Suffering, not triumphalism, is the norm of the Christian journey (Rom. 8:18; 2 Cor. 1:7-8). We see the identification of God with humanity more profoundly in the suffering of Jesus than in any other part of the human experience. The cross was the will of the Father (Matt. 16:21). Jesus knew this before He entered Jerusalem. Fully cognizant of the role prophetically laid before Him, Jesus walked the way of Zion in active obedience to the Father's will, and also in the knowledge that He was to be "delivered up, according to the definite plan and foreknowledge of God" (Acts 2:23).

Even though the Father didn't offer it, Jesus may have easily justified to Himself another course of action. In another garden, called Gethsemane, Jesus refused the desirable fruit of self-centered survival. Satan was in *this* garden too. Silently, without argument, Jesus accepted God's cup of redemptive sacrifice.

"I always do what is pleasing to Him" (John 8:29).

The Barabbas Syndrome

Why did Jesus choose the cross? It was because God had already determined that it was necessary. Some may desire to blame the Jewish establishment, or Pontius Pilate, or Judas Iscariot. Or they may want to blame the crowd for its fickleness in choosing Barabbas. All of these factors are contributory to the death of Jesus. Here, we see what we may call the Barabbas syndrome appearing in stark and ugly form.

What does "the Barabbas syndrome" mean? The crowd will always choose a Barabbas over Jesus.

The crowd is much more easily manipulated than are thoughtful and prayerfully minded individuals (1 Pet. 3:15). It's interesting that, when it suited their own agenda, the religious establishment incited the crowd on the basis of an appeal to its lowest instincts. Isn't this still happening in Protestant liberalism? According to Matthew, the members of the religious establishment enticed the crowd to respond to Pilate at the level of *eros*. Eros, a Greek word denoting sensual love, speaks a lot of making choices at the level of the emotions or of self-centered sentiment. It is never used in the New Testament to describe the way of discipleship.

Jesus, in the post-resurrection appearance to Peter, challenged his disciple at the level of *agape,* which is total and uncompromising commitment (John 21:15; also used in John 3:16). Agape denotes the way of the cross. Peter wanted to settle for *philia*-a middle-of-the-road word denoting friendship or being a good pal (John 21:15-17).

Taking the Sermon of the Mount as another example, we see that Jesus calls for the very highest in humankind in order to live a kingdom life. It can be lived out by God's grace and forgiveness alone.

For some, there remains a question concerning who was the founder of Christianity—Jesus or Paul? The assumption is that Paul could be the one. But, on the basis of "justification by faith" (Rom. 5:1; Eph. 2:8-9), a concept sometimes attributed to Paul, we note that Jesus was at this point long before Paul. For example, Jesus was fully aware that Habakkuk had predicted this concept (Hab. 2:4). And, in His Sermon on the Mount, Jesus calls His followers to an impossible condition. "Be perfect, therefore, as your heavenly Father is perfect" (Matt. 5:48). In other words, the followers of Jesus cannot ever claim this perfection, but may be accounted, by grace alone, as standing in full acceptance under the overshadowing mantle of Christ's perfection.

What we see in the Barabbas incident is that members of the religious establishment compromised the tone of social acceptance. They were forerunners of a church leadership that has come to set the tone for the church becoming more willing to be chaplains to the culture rather than prophets within it.

In the contemporary Western world, the media has become the most powerful tool to entice the crowds with the agendas of a new social establishment. The Barabbas syndrome really works for the media. And, in equally subtle ways, the syndrome also continues in most mainline churches of today. The crowd, allowing scriptural ignorance and their own sentiments to reside at the very easy level of a Barabbas, appears to be very tolerant in the discussion of higher standards. In contrast, people who love enough to call for the highest in us, who challenge us in empathetic love, may appear to the crowd as being very intolerant.

Jesus stood before the curious crowd, the religious establishment, and also the Roman authority. He was prepared to go the way of the cross. As God's ultimate icon, He appeals to our highest impulses.

We sentimentalize a Barabbas while we fashion Jesus into a plastic image of our own making. For a crowd, sentiment easily triumphs over truth and righteousness. For this crowd, Barabbas never poses a challenge to their chosen lifestyles. He appeals to the lowest in all of us.

It appears that this Barabbas theology is prevailing in many Western churches today. If only the best of Roman justice and ideals had prevailed on that day, Barabbas would have taken the place of Jesus. The name of Barabbas means "son of father." But what father?

The Passive Christ

"The story of the death of Jesus and of what led up to it and flowed from it, which occupies such disproportionate space in the Gospel (a third of Mark and nearly half of John), reflects the decisive importance for the early Christian preaching of the death and resurrection of Christ."[3] This period proved to be the most significant turning point in the earthly ministry of Jesus. It is the period in which He allowed the powers of destruction to go unimpeded in their ravenous desire to consume Him (1 Pet. 5:8).

To the point of His betrayal, Jesus had been actively in control of His life and ministry. Verbs associated with Jesus are usually in the active mood. He initiates the course of events. He is at the center of activity; when He is around, something is always happening. He is fully in charge of the outcome of each event. "It is the activity of Jesus which maintains the momentum. He is constantly moving from place to place, from situation to situation; and always it is His intervention in word or deed which changes the situation."[4]

Once Jesus is handed over in the garden of Gethsemane, a change in grammatical mood, particularly in Mark, is evident.

> The change of manner consists in this, that from this point to the moment of Jesus' death on the Cross, a period which occupies, in Souter's text, one hundred lines of narrative, Jesus is the grammatical subject of just nine verbs. And the reason for the change is not, of course, that Mark has now gone on to a different story and that Jesus is no longer there. Jesus is there all the time, at the very center of the story. But now, He is no longer there as the active and initiating subject of what is done. He is there as the recipient, the object of what is done.[5]

The Suffering Servant of Isaiah 53 was "oppressed and he was afflicted, yet he did not open his mouth; like a lamb that is led to the slaughter, and like a sheep that before its shearers is silent, so he did not open his mouth" (Isa. 53:7).

In spite of opposition in Jerusalem, and particularly from the time of His cleansing of the temple, Jesus had not shied away from public ministry. But the nature of the Paschal Lamb had to become apparent to worldly powers before it was offered in sacrifice. He was to be led like a lamb in a passive manner.

Some commentators don't want to be too hard on Judas Iscariot. They have a point. John Vanstone makes some interesting observations about the language used to describe Christ's betrayal.

In the gospels, the verb "to betray", *prodidomi*, is used only once, while the verb "to hand over," *paradidomi*, is used on thirty-one occasions. *Paradidomi* is a relatively harmless word, and it is this word that is used to describe the act of Judas. "The word is by no means the kind of derogatory or offensive word which we should expect from writers who thought so very ill of Judas . . . Whatever the reason for the familiar mistranslation of *paradidomi*, as 'betray,' it remains a mistranslation. The verb is ambivalent, neutral, colourless; and we shall continue to translate it as, 'to hand over.'"[6] Quite possibly, Vanstone is reminding us that, in the selection of this particular word, we all understand what it means to hand over Jesus. Peter did.

Upon His arrest and confrontation with Pontius Pilate, Jesus was faced with the question of whether or not He was the king of the Jews. The Romans had been forced to put down a few guerrilla skirmishes in the recent past. Pilate needed an answer.

In one of the few words Jesus spoke during this time, He replied, "My kingdom is not from this world. If my kingdom were from this world, my followers would be fighting to keep me from being handed over to the Jews" (John 18:36).

Pilate didn't have a clue what Jesus was talking about. What is a spiritual kingdom in a polytheistic world?

There's every possibility that Jesus could have avoided being crucified. The Jews had a fair number of sects among them; one more wouldn't have been a problem. However, Jesus seemed to be saying something more than any sectarian leader. At His trial, the high priest asked Him, "'Are you the Messiah, the Son of the Blessed One?'" Jesus said, 'I am; and you will see the Son of Man seated at the right hand of the Power, and coming with clouds of heaven'" (Mark 14:61-62)

Now, that really did seal His fate. Surely this response, and the angry tirade it elicited from the high priest, can only be understood if Jesus' messianic claim is also a claim to His Deity. In Christ, God became vulnerable. God was silent.

Why Should God Pay a Cost on Calvary?

The thought of God paying a cost for our redemption has often been downplayed. Not all people intentionally try to diminish the finished work of Christ, but Peter Abélard (1079-1142 AD) maybe, unwittingly, fell into this trap. Consequently, his *opinion* on the meaning of the cross is proving to be an easy way out for many present-day revisionists.

The idea of exemplarism has become popular. Abélard leaned "toward an exemplarist theory of the Atonement according to which the suffering of Christ was our supreme example, though little more."[7] It is not at all uncommon or surprising to hear eloquent and passionate cries to follow the supreme example of Jesus.

But if this sacrifice were merely to be of the caliber of selfless sacrifice, doesn't Gandhi fit in there too? Yet even Gandhi, when confronted with his assassin, desperately shouted, "No!"

In comparison, Jesus becomes the Christian example of sacrifice in the purpose of God. Maybe we don't hear from those revisionist pulpits that the subsequent Council of Soissons rejected Abélard's opinion (AD 1121). (The Oxford Dictionary of the Christian Church, p.3) When notions of exemplarism are held up, we shouldn't be surprised that the connection is missed between the empty cross and the finished work of redemption. To make such a correlation would be to admit that all persons need to be rescued from a situation they cannot resolve on their own.

Archbishop William Temple pondered the meaning of the "nice man" of his generation. "Why anyone should have troubled to crucify the Christ of Liberal Protestantism has always been a mystery."[8]

In preferring to think that, basically, everyone is good, we miss the point. God, in His holiness, could no longer bear our company. And yet, in Jesus, He paid the utmost price in order to secure it.

In consequence of our estrangement, we can hardly bear our own company. At its best, the church will never minimize the substantial cost paid by God for our redemption. But what does all this talk about cost really mean?

Does God Owe Evil a Debt?

It all sounds very legalistic and technical, doesn't it? At least, it sounds a bit like a kidnapper demanding a huge ransom so that a rich man may get his kid back. Is it really possible that God owes something, or that He has to pay a price to the powers of evil? Well, that's precisely the language of people like Irenaeus. That notion has remained in the minds of many to this day.

Actually, the idea of ransom does have a place in New Testament thinking (Matt. 20:28; 1 Tim. 2:6). However, it's over elaborated when interpreted by theologians such as Irenaeus, Origen, and Gregory the Great. They use the word in the context of the slavery of their own day. Their use of the word gives the impression that God, somehow, got the better of a deal between Him and Satan. And, in spite of that fact, Satan secured some satisfaction.

But here we must stress that the primary point of "ransom" is that God paid a price for our redemption. Ransom, according to Michael Green, "is our rescue from a perilous predicament through the very costly self-giving of Jesus. Rescue and costliness are the point."[9] According to Baillie, "It is something infinitely costly, a giving up by God of His only Son in the process of dealing with our sins."[10] The "rescue" is deliverance from the penalty of fracturing our relationship with our holy God and His creation. We must not elevate the technical approach over the relational recovery. A legal standing with God (such as a baptismal certificate) does not give greater credibility if it does not result in the restoration of a personal relationship with God.

Earlier, we thought of the impossibility of aspiring to the standards that God has set. A sentimentalist view of the problem might go something like this: God is all loving. His love for us is unconditional. Therefore, a loving Father would simply look at His errant child and say, "It's all right. Don't worry about it. It really doesn't matter."

A simple example is the story Jesus told of the Prodigal Son. This story is analogous to the history of Israel as a nation (Luke 15:11-31). The loving father, waiting for the return of his errant son, didn't need to hear the penitent words of this son, but the son needed to say them.

What does all this say about God's standards for relationships? On the other side of the question, what does it say concerning the awesome holiness of God being insulted by a casual or deliberate view of sin? What does it say about Him leaving us to suffer the consequences of our own choices?

It says that His requirements for living the essential relationships of creation are not worth the paper (or the tablets) they are written on. They don't have any worth at all. It says there are really no standards or requirements for us to meet in engaging with the awesome and holy God. It says that, ultimately, God's standards don't require a cost to meet them. There is no point in redemption.[11] We really don't have to accept personal responsibility, because a loving Father would simply say that everything will be okay anyway.

The fact is that God's laws do matter. Everything is not okay. We really do matter to Him. The standards of the kingdom do not lower because we cannot or will not measure up to them.

Jesus demonstrated this with His Sermon of the Mount. Then He blasted all our sense of self-righteousness with, "Be perfect, therefore, as you heavenly father is perfect" (Matt. 5:48).

God, in Christ, pays the impossible price for us because we are of ultimate worth to Him. But to whom is the price paid? God owes Satan absolutely nothing. Satan doesn't have any bargaining power when God enters the arena of satisfaction. God pays the price to Himself in order to satisfy His own standards of relationships.

"Satisfaction is an appropriate word, providing that we realize that it is he himself in his inner being who needs to be satisfied, and not something external to himself. Talk of law, honor, justice and the moral order is true only in so far as these are seen as expressions of God's own character. Atonement is a necessity because it 'arises from within God himself.'"[12] God is satisfied that the price was commensurate with the standards He set. Humanly speaking, the price is impossibly high because the standards of relationships are of immeasurable worth. And the price was fully met in and through His beloved Son.

We see that the Paschal Lamb, offered at every Passover feast, had to be perfect, without all blemish. This is a lot more than a technical or legal transaction; it is a costly restoration of relationships made possible by God alone. That's what justification by faith is all about (Rom. 5:1). God really was in Christ reconciling the world to Himself (2 Cor. 5:19).

The Cross and Culture

A well-known mega church in the United States recently admitted that they have produced many thousands of converts, but have now realized they have made very few disciples. What has this got to do with the cross of Calvary?

There is a stoic denial of suffering that pervades our culture in the West. Such an idea runs counter to the demands of walking the way of the cross. Will the church of latter days have the stomach for the suffering and pain that has already started in the East? Will it petulantly deny that suffering is of the very essence of the gospel, or will it produce another, much more palatable gospel? (Gal. 1:7). Will the institution of the church be seen more and more as a willing chaplain to the wants of a fickle culture?

Truly, ours is a culture that seeks spirituality over truth. Maybe, if we briefly identify some of the dominant marks of our postmodern culture, we may be shocked to find just how much of it has already invaded the present life of the church.

What does it mean when Jesus tells us to take up our cross today? "You will be hated by all because of my name . . . and whoever does not take up the cross and follow me is not worthy of me" (Matt. 10:22, 38). The NIV translation refers to taking up "his cross." No one else can take up the cross of Jesus.

Many Christians of the third world and the southern part of the globe may more easily answer questions concerning the relation of the cross and suffering. The apostle Paul tells us that we are children of God and joint heirs with Christ, "if, in fact, we suffer with him so that we may also be glorified with him" (Rom. 8:17).

We do observe in a fringe of the population a willingness to embrace both morality and absolutes arising from their growing sense of mystery. For example, in a generation born to the Baby Boomers, we may observe a passion and commitment that has spear-headed a major revolution in the Middle East. Nevertheless, this brief look at the meaning of the cross will challenge us to demonstrate to our entire culture why the meaning of Christ's death is a necessary ingredient in the church's witness. This message is at the very centre of relationships restored.

Consumerism

God loves the world; He doesn't hate it. We aren't Docetists who think physical things are evil. God really did make a material world, and He put us in it. The prophetic role of the church is not adequately exercised in a church that studiously avoids the reality of the material.

Biblical prophets never displayed a Gnostic revulsion to material things. However, they did remind the community of God how to be responsible stewards of the things He had given. Maybe, in today's world, we realize that we are not called to be environmentalists, but stewards of God's creation. This concept is far more demanding, and calls for a syntheses of all essential relationships!

When Christians devote equal time and effort to acquisitiveness as do others, what message does it give to the world?

Christians often fall prey to media images that blur the distinction between need and greed. How then, are we seen to be different from the world? Are we really so different when we place higher value on those who are best able to consume? (James 2:1-4). Does the church rise above the superficiality of consumer values by investing its own life in sharing with the needy and those suffering injustice? Can the church minister this way with no thought for gain? Some Western aid results in further wealth for the givers; interest rates on loans are one example. When we read of the post-Pentecost community sharing in order to meet the needs of others, we are not reading a manifesto for communism. What we read is that there is a cost in loving one another.

What sign do we present to the world when we will not sacrifice the gluttonous lifestyle so common to our goals in life? There is a price to be paid for change. Our ethical priorities seem out of place, and our leaning to what is largely an Old Testament prosperity gospel sounds positively obscene. Can you imagine the enormous difference that would be made if churches of the West made the problems of poverty and homelessness the *priorities* of stewardship? When new carpets and better sound systems are sacrificed for such priorities, what message does that give to the world? Given the choice, do we plant churches where people can afford them, or where people *cannot* afford them?

The values of the world tell us that our sense of worth is related to our ability to consume. We acquire the advertised product "because we are worth it."

The cross speaks of our infinite worth in the sight of God. God, who knows the very number of the hairs on our heads, considers each individual life to be deserving of His sacrificial love.

There is a verse in Romans that could strike terror into our hearts, if not properly understood. "So then, each of us will be accountable to God" (Rom. 14:12).

Some years ago in Snow Lake, a little mining town in northern Manitoba, I was conducting a teenage Bible study in our home. It was an eight foot wide trailer. We got to one of their favorite topics: "Obey your parents in the Lord" (Eph. 6:1). I let them rattle on about their "rotten parents" who made them come home early, who made them do chores, who made them study, who made them . . . ! To most of the teenagers in the town, one fifteen-year-old girl was a hero. She could do anything she wanted. She could come home when she wanted; she could drink booze and play around with young men. She was there and said nothing.

After about half an hour, she threw up her hands and screamed, "You guys are so lucky!"

Silence descended with a thunderous crash. "Why do you say that?" I asked.

With tears in her eyes, she replied, "If once, just once, my mother or father, told me to get home by eleven, then I would know that they love me."

About fifteen years later, I happened to see her again, holding the hand of a little girl. She looked beautiful. "Are you married?" I asked her.

Quickly, she retorted, "No! Who would have me?" Time didn't prove to be a healer for her. After all those years, she had not acquired a confidence in her own self-worth. As years progressed, she simply became more and more crippled. And it all started when her very busy parents had not loved her enough to call her to account.

Accountability means worth.

For those in Christ, accountability to God will not be an occasion for cringing before an angry judge, but an honest facing of how they have used or misused the gifts that the Father has given them (Matt. 25:19). If God calls for an account of one's life, then He cares about it, and it holds enormous worth to Him.

The cross speaks of a love that credits our life with value. It credits the world with value. God loves us so much that He came down to us when we could no longer reach up to Him. Christ bridged the gap when we were incapable of crossing sin's barrier. He saved us when we had failed to save ourselves. He redeemed us when we had lost the power of purchase. He accepted us when we could no longer accept ourselves.

Individualism

Ever since the garden of Eden, the wants of "me" have become more important than the needs of the community. The Trinitarian God created community from the pattern of His own relational nature. In the primal sense of community, we cannot conceive of identity in terms of individuality. We are created with a sense of dependence upon God and others. God's very nature is one of otherness.

In this fashion, the church exists primarily for the benefit of others. But the prevailing attitude of society is one of me-ism. What is good for me? In our postmodern era, we are hardly dominated by the motivation of putting the needs of others first! In congregations where most of the time, energy, money, and other resources are spent on their own needs, how is the Christian community seen to be different?

Individualistic arrogance prevails everywhere, including the church, and it is the primary reason for the breakdown of community. Some congregations are told to live like "King's kids." Children of the King deserve the very best. Miracles come on demand, provided you have enough faith. And if you can't name it and claim it, then it's a problem of *your* faith. This prosperity gospel looks obscene when we think of committed Christians in developing nations whose basic struggle is one of *survival.* Is their faith inferior to that of us gluttonous and waist-bulging Christians of the West? Nowadays, the sense of the universe with *me* at the center sometimes begins from very early days.

Some years ago, a bright and caring friend suggested that we are now living in a child-centered world. My questions were, "How are we helping our children face the realities of this cruel world? When they grow up, how will they cope with the truth that they are *not* the center of the universe? Are we helping them when they feel they have a right to whatever they want? Are they not destined for a grinding and hurtful time ahead? Will they become a petulant and demanding generation of adolescent adults, resentful of annoying inconveniences of life?"

I think we wonder if many of the children of today have learned what it means to live a life of sacrifice for others. It's a refreshing change when we see these young people expending themselves in sacrificial love for others. Is it any wonder that, in order to attract this generation into the life of the church, we fall for the ploy of enticing them with a gospel of comfort? The reverse may be more of a truism. A great many people of this generation need and desire a challenge.

The cost of discipleship seems to be remarkably elusive in a me-centered and feely church. No wonder efforts in evangelism may be couched in accepting a syrupy Jesus, or in being enticed to attend a comfortable church, or in joining a particular community because "we can help solve your problems." We must wonder how this Jesus can ever be resisted. How often do we hear that suffering with Christ always precedes reigning with Him? (2 Tim. 2:12).

In recognizing their own very serious problems, Christians of underdeveloped nations have much to teach us regarding their suffering for the gospel of Jesus. They also have much to teach us about joy.

How much is the church of the West seen to be in the forefront of ministering in the gap between rich and poor? How much are its leaders actually seen to be sacrificial in their lifestyles in order for most church resources to be directed outwardly? This challenge is particularly pertinent to certain styles of television evangelism. Where is there a genuine apostolic focus? How do the words of Jesus strike us when we pride ourselves on our born-again experience but sacrifice little or nothing for the poor, the lonely, and the sick? "Truly I tell you, just as you did not do it to one of the least of these, you did not do it to me" (Matt. 25:45).

We have seen clearly that biblical creation theology lauds community, not individualism, as a reflection of the very nature of God. However, our present culture has learned only too well the lyrics of the song, "I did it my way." Our arrogance and prideful individualism are offensive to a holy and righteous God.

A perversion has occurred when the wants of the individual become more important than the needs of the community.

When individualism runs rampant, what we observe in all societies is a loss of identity, contempt for values from a higher source, sexual inequality, racial discrimination, the despair of loneliness, a lessening of commitment to relationships, and the frenetic seeking of status measured in material wealth. We hear it from Christian pulpits too.

Both the Old and New Testaments speak of values, promises, and challenges that are primarily addressed to the community of God. The Old Testament is replete with conditional promises by God to a community called to observe His criteria for signing a life of justice, righteousness, and peace.

However, time and time again, preachers speak on these Scriptures as if the words are addressed to individuals alone. When preaching becomes absorbed by the goal to be relevant to people's perceived needs, such preaching contributes to a very individualized spirituality. Often, it is a spirituality lacking in a social context.

No wonder biblical revisionists, even when their Christology is weak, have been given enormous energy in demonstrating compassion and justice. It's the only gospel they have left. "The vocation of Christians is to be builders of communities that join with them what is highest in themselves within another and within the whole human race. The most basic thing that Jesus does when he liberates us is to make us caring people who then have the commission to build communities in the place where we live and play and work."[13]

Quite apart from its evangelistic potential, it is for reasons such as these that the church needs to rediscover the immense value of structures that are primarily based around the small home group. The basics of Christian community are learned and practiced in these foundational organisms. When organized properly, the agenda of the congregation emerges from the groups rather than hierarchical leaders.

We are not here speaking of churches that simply run home groups, but churches whose very structures emanate from the relational insights and ministry concerns discovered in these smaller communities.[14]

Apathy

In many ways we have become a passive and impatient society. We want things done for us, and we want them now. The idea of *commitment* is not always easy to see. Yet the very life of the gospel demands it (Matt. 10:38-39).

Commitment in the human psyche hasn't completely gone out of the window. Some years ago we were impressed by Chinese students who gave up their lives in Tiananmen Square for the cause of freedom and democracy. When perseverance and commitment such as theirs is not apparent, often apathy, disillusionment, and despair set in to the psyche of the culture. This despairing syndrome may resolve itself in self-destruction. It is presently happening among young native people of Canada and the despairing revolutionaries of Syria. One newspaper journalist describes the native population of Canada as "Canada's Tibet."[15]

A personal example of this despairing and suicidal attitude came to me one day. A mother of a seventeen-year-old asked me to see her boy.

"He has no interest in anything; he just plays video games and sulks a lot."

I arranged to see him, and he was obviously not even remotely interested in talking with this old goat. I coaxed him very slowly with questions for about half an hour. Reluctantly he engaged with short, obviously bored replies.

Suddenly, in a most unprofessional demonstration of counseling, I blurted out, "I think I know why you are bored."

One eye opened. "Why?" he drawled.

"Because you are boring! I wouldn't have you as a friend; you would be a real drag!"

My strange retort opened up a wealth of feelings and anger. It helped me to get on to the meaning of life with purpose. The result was that this bored young man gave his life to Jesus and became a lively and helpful member of our youth community.

The late David Watson wrote, "A Communist once threw out this challenge to a Christian: The gospel is a much more powerful weapon for the renewal of society than is our Marxist philosophy . . . How can anyone believe in the supreme value of this gospel if you do not practice it, if you do not spread it and if you sacrifice neither time nor money for it . . . ? We believe in our Communist message and we are ready to sacrifice everything, even our life . . . But you people are afraid to soil your hands."[16]

In many of our Western churches, we have a serious problem with the developing of basic discipleship. In point of fact, all too many churches have very little idea of how to make disciples, even from among their present membership (Matt. 28:19-20). The making of disciples is a process requiring classroom theory and practical marketplace application. An ongoing process such as this is all too uncommon in churches, where institutional success is measured by revenue, attendance, programs and decisions for Christ.

Relativism

In a globalized economy, absolute values are thrown out, but the perverse freedom of politically correct religion is loudly heralded.

While lauding individual values, society has been encouraged to become intolerant toward any suggestion of absolutes. Truth is therefore relative to each individual and culture. There are no absolutes except those being lauded in a globalized world that is consumed by values serving a universal economy. When the church displays insecurity before such intolerance, it also begins to espouse the same attitudes; it begins to lose its distinctive and prophetic identity.

The individual Christian exists, not to join the correct political party, but to be sacrificial according to the teaching of Jesus. The church exists *prophetically* to inform the world, and to *demonstrate* that all meaning consists in Jesus Christ. Jesus is not *a* truth; Jesus is *the* Truth (John 14:6).

The greatest man in the history of the world died for making that statement! The Christian faith rises and falls on this fact. There really are Christian statements of an absolute nature, although not as many as some people think. Nevertheless, these statements are absolutes because they don't exist relative to anything else.

The church has never been called to act as a chaplain to the world; it is called to speak prophetically and to live prophetically before the world. We are called to show the world that a sign of Eden still exists.

The world has every right to reject what it sees and hears. But it has to see and hear first. In ensuring precisely that, the church itself has to be prepared for crucifixion. It has to be prepared for rejection and death. *It is not in the business of survival.* It adopts the mind-set of crucifixion because it believes in the power of Christ's resurrection.

A subtle form of relativism today is in the area of spirituality itself. We are pressured on all sides by non-biblical spirituality. The media, educational system, social institutions, business demands, all call us to hold spirituality as an individualistic and private enterprise. This is one example of how well-meaning institutions, including the church, may become perverted and act as cultural chaplains.

The postmodern era has produced a vast number of people who are spiritually hungry. Yet cultural spirituality not only denies claims to absolute truth, it also forbids the appearance of such values before the public and in the social arena. The above influences and institutions will tell us what is politically correct—for now, at least.

In a culture that changes about every twenty years, we can't be dogmatic about our present belief—if we follow the lead of the culture. Relativism has its basis in the popular pluralism that dominates Western thinking. The manipulators of a globalized economy foster these attitudes. Possibly too much blame is pointed in that direction, but it is abundantly clear that the major values of a world economy and those of Christ are at odds.

The analogy that arises from this vacuum of absolutes is that of a God (in whatever form) who waits at the peak of a mountain to welcome all who come to the top. It really doesn't matter which pathway is taken.

For the thinking Christian, this approach is not only intellectually insulting but insultingly sloppy. Which God will be there? There will be unbelievable contradictions.

The fact is that God has chosen the pathway. It's a reversal of this pathetic analogy. God has already decided to meet us. But where?

At the bottom! It's at the bottom of the mountain where we meet with the saving God (2 Cor. 5:19). It is Jesus who leads us to the top, to the One and only God whom He has revealed to all humanity.

Entering the waters of baptism, Jesus signified a death to self. In His death on the cross, all the idols of culture come under severe scrutiny, and that's because the cross not only has the power to expose, but also to redeem them. The message of the cross challenges people of all cultures, and it challenges the entire lifestyle of the church.

The church may or may not be successful in demonstrating to the world the way of the cross. However, in throwing out the challenge of the Way in relation to culture, I must add that there are many wonderful signs emerging in the West.

For example a form of neo-evangelicalism is emerging and forging superb inroads into social areas of depravity and injustice. This movement combines the personal spiritual gospel with that of the real-felt needs of society (James 2:17; 1 John 3:16-18). As with the example of Jesus, success or failure, is not its motivation. Kingdom imperatives require faithfulness in living out the implications of this Jesus gospel. A radical renewal of the meaning of the cross and of its required lifestyle is therefore paramount—that is, if our primary desire is to be an anointed and authentic sign of the kingdom. This most certainly means that the church will often operate in countercultural directions.

Feelings

If it feels good, do it! This is a really big one for today. It's all about Eros. Not only has a feely-based culture created an extraordinary me-centered therapeutic industry, but it has also bolstered an unflagging consumerism. This equates the power of purchase with the perceptions of self-worth. Rightness is all too often determined by the criterion, "How do you feel?"

From a counseling perspective, that is usually a good question, and it often leads to positive and healing responses. However, in our culture, the question is often posed in order to eliminate personal feelings of guilt or responsibility. Consequently, people are not led to grow and learn through their difficulties or sin, but are affirmed in those sins.

It doesn't take an Einstein to realize that, when values are based on individual feelings, the contradictions that ensue in a community will most certainly devolve in socially disastrous directions.

Modern church synods have often been profoundly influenced in debate, not on the basis of substance, but on the basis of individual feelings such as, "I am deeply hurt by your position." Often, such a statement is designed to cripple real dialogue.

Having had the privilege of speaking in many churches, I find that pastors often share a common complaint. After all their sermons, they find it more difficult than ever to get people *committed* to areas of ministry. For a small percentage of Christians, there really are legitimate reasons for noninvolvement. However, more often than not, reasons such as these are given: "I can't commit myself for more than a short time," or "I didn't feel like coming last week."

Feelings and weak will are accepted as a basis for doing or not doing ministries. Of course, on that basis, there is no reliability or accountability. Nor is there a determination to struggle through training processes and through success or failure, all of which make ministries more effective.

One of the greatest tragedies of putting feelings before commitment is that of marriage. The breakdown of the basic unit of society is raising enormous problems. Remarkably, the statistics are the same in both believing and non-believing communities. Children often grow up with insecurities because feelings dominate the lives of their parents. Social problems occur with much more frequency among the children of parents who have put feelings before commitment.

Of course, this is not to say that there are not disastrous marriages; sometimes, emotional health and physical abuse cannot be dealt with so long as the couple stays together.

From a biblical perspective, the pathway of growth in mature, Christian discipleship is never equated with feelings, but with the power of decision in walking the way of the cross.

Commitment and Culture

The word "commitment" is becoming less fashionable these days. A culture may live with diversity, but not with contradiction. The result will be cultural suicide.

The same is true for the contemporary church. We see this dilemma in the revisionists of our day. As prophets to the world, their voices have been rendered silent. The main reason is because their voices are no longer needed. Their voices sound the same as those of the world.

While we have suggested that, from a theological point of view, most revisionists are aligned with old-fashioned modernism, from a sociological point of view, they are clearly postmodern in their attitudes. It is a perfect combination for the rise of a brand-new form of religion. The religion is inevitably one of chaplaincy to the culture, at least for a while.

A glaring question needs to be asked: how do we live in the world but not of it?

Surely, we are not to abandon the culture in which we live. How can we engage in dialogue if we are apart? Commenting on the issue "of, but not in," Don Posterski notes, "Many contemporary Christians have abdicated from the world. Often out of good intentions to be 'godly,' we have confused the biblical injunction to 'be separate' with social segregation . . . Clarity comes when 'not of the world' while being 'in the world' is understood to mean 'different from the world.'"[17]

George Hunsberger offers a way to witness by going into and through the culture's pluralistic assumptions. He believes it to be a more effective stance than one formed out of resistance and opposition to those dynamics. He encourages a style that moves alongside "the principles that govern a pluralistic society: acceptance of diversity . . . appreciation of options . . . and interaction with alternatives." He goes on to say, "the tolerance factor in pluralism is an open opportunity for evangelism, not a barrier that stymies it."[18]

We have strongly suggested that Jesus really did sign the meaning of all four pillars of Israel. In Christ, we see that there cannot be a biblical distinction between two stories, called "covenants." In Christ, there is but one story. Also from God's perspective, i.e., of viewing the entire story in God's eternal present, there can only be one story. Having considered something of the procession of this story, laden in facts of history, it cannot reveal its meaning unless it is highlighted in the way of the cross.

> He was destined before the foundation of the world,
> but was revealed at the end of the ages for your sake. (1
> Pet. 1:20)

> This man, handed over to you according to the definite
> plan and foreknowledge of God, you crucified and killed
> by the hands of those outside the law. (Acts 2:23)

The question is, does the church continue to take part in the crucifixion of Jesus?

CHAPTER 10

The Time Road from Calvary to Hell

O n a dark plain, under the shadow of a rocky cliff called Golgotha, the inevitable clash between the kingdoms of the world and the kingdom of God was mercilessly played out. The cross of Jesus Christ shows up the counter-nature of our contemporary culture. When Pilate raised the question of truth to Jesus, he couldn't see the Truth before his own eyes. The Truth lay in a Person, not in philosophical ideas (John 14:6; Heb. 13:8).

But in order to consider the bedazzling questions that are needed in this chapter, we will have to reflect on some of the words Jesus spoke from the cross.

Why Have You Forsaken Me?

The scene at Calvary does not appear to be one of triumph. In spite of His powerful and compassionate healings, His teachings, and His miracles, there was hardly anyone to say good-bye. A few women remained; for a while, at least, all but one of His twelve apostles had lost their nerve. Where were those whom He had healed and delivered? The loneliness of a hell had begun.

Humanly speaking, the scene was one of abject failure. Jesus, now dying, was surrounded by indifferent executors of state law and by a religious establishment rubbing its hands in awkward self-justification. Here was an establishment convinced it had stamped out the challenge to its own view of truth. But also we see the detached and dispassionate establishment of Roman secularism. For them, compassion or vindictiveness had actually given way to an easy political solution. It's not surprising that Good Friday is sometimes viewed among the religious as simply an historical sign of exemplary sacrifice.

Jesus knew that the path of Calvary was clearly and indisputably *the sign* of abject failure. The cross of Jesus stood starkly in signature of the wretched failure of all humanity. Jesus was intended to walk the path of human failure and to face its miserable consequence. How may the shallow theories of exemplarism possibly account for Jesus' kenotic and desperate cry of loneliness?

In a moment of despairing abandonment, He cried out a well-known passage from the Psalms: "My God, my God, why have you forsaken me?" (Ps. 22:1; Matt. 27:46).

What an astounding reversal! Throughout the redemption story, across all time from that awful day in Eden, the longing voice of God has cried, "Where are you?" And now, in this awesome moment of pain and of Eden's reversal, the real Adam cries, "Where are *you?*"

The sinless and innocent Christ, on behalf of despairing humanity, began to experience the hell of separation from God. For the first time in Christ's experience, darkness blanketed the light of God's glory.

Angry and despairing humanity, not knowing the meaning of this reversal, often reiterates the question. However, it is often not shouted amid the pain of separation, but in frustration and anger at a God not being there when required. But a genuine sympathy does exist for those in pain and anger. We remember that six million Jews suffered horrendous injustice and death in the Holocaust. Many of their surviving relatives, in frustration and pain, became atheists. How could God desert them in such an hour?

But God did understand. In Christ, God also suffered separation from the beloved crown of His creation. The One who took the entire sin of the world upon Himself was suddenly separated from the awesome presence of the holy God. God, in His eternal nowness, already knew the pain. He knew it from the beginning of time.

However, in His humanity, Jesus experienced what was the inevitable consequence of humanity's condition. It was a moment of unordered darkness. And that meant, for all humanity, hope, or even meaning, could exist no longer.

The disciples had witnessed the cruelty of crucifixion before, but when they witnessed from afar the death of Jesus, "it was also their own death because Life had been taken away from them; they could no longer live but merely exist."[1] Further, "If it were possible for Christ, with all that he represented, to die upon the Cross, this meant that human hatred was stronger than Divine Love; human hatred had managed to repulse Divine Love, to banish him from the habitations of man, had rejected and killed him at Calvary."[2]

Forgive Them

"Father, forgive them; for they do not know what they are doing" (Luke 23:34). Deserted by many who loved Him, the closing thoughts of Jesus were for the redemption of all who were lost. How many people who were there even heard those astounding words of reconciliation? How many even cared? For most people, this was just an ordinary day. Probably, they passed by with scarcely a glance. The soldiers were professionals. The one difference between this day and all others was that the Jewish establishment wanted the execution over before four o'clock.

The remaining disciple and the women in waiting could have hardly heard what He said. However, they knew that these words were also for them. It would take a little time for them to realize that those words were for the whole world.

Normally, the entire scene would be considered to be a recipe for disaster. The blame game of Eden was bound to emerge among them. Quite possibly, in attitudes of self-justification, everyone would have gone his own way, would have gone back to the way he had been before he met Jesus. The purpose of the Twelve, as the foundations of a new Israel, may well have evaporated forever.

But He forgave them! In forgiveness, all was not lost. Jesus showed us that forgiveness is the way of reconciliation.

With those words, Jesus made possible a new humanity that, as the real Adam, He could present to the Father in a priesthood of offering and victimization.

> From one ancestor he made all nations to inhabit the whole earth. (Acts 17:26)

> He has abolished the law with its commandments and ordinances, that he might create in himself one new humanity in place of the two, thus making peace, and might reconcile both groups to God in one body through the cross, thus putting to death that hostility through it. (Eph. 2:15-16)

With these words of reconciliation, Jesus went to the cross, thereby ending the institutional meanderings of the religious pathway. In Christ, our real Adam, we have the Leader, the Jewish leader, of a universal procession marching together from Calvary to the heavenly Zion (Isa. 35:8-10; Eph. 4:8).

With Me in Paradise

There are some very important clues at Calvary regarding our condition after death. The two thieves who died beside Jesus represent the condition of all humanity in relation to Christ's work of atonement. Both of them died on crosses, and both agreed they got what they deserved. One died by himself and sealed his eternal fate. The other died with Jesus and with a hope for God's kingdom inheritance. Jesus promised him a place in paradise. It was a *place* where life could be lived forever. Jesus responded, "Truly I tell you, today you will be with me in Paradise" (Luke 23:43).

Here, we must remind ourselves of our former literary view of creation terminology. In this context, "today" and "moment" are synonymous terms.

Before we consider Jesus' astounding statement, we must make note of three things.

First, the promise was not extended to the other thief. Of course, we are not allowed to make judgments about the eternal destiny of anyone (Matt. 7:1-2), but this passage provides little or no support for those who say that entry into heaven is simply a matter of time. Some believe that even if it takes a million years, everyone will get there. Universalism (the idea that everyone will eventually get to heaven-because, ultimately, God's love is irresistible) finds no support here. As we are to see more clearly, *time* has ended during the dying ember of unconsciousness, or self-awareness. Therefore, without some miracle of restoration, time's dimensional constituents of *place and space* are clearly absent. In the absence of these elements, all that might remain would be a purely spiritual existence. Although Gnostics believed in such an existence, Jesus did not. The very nature of His post-resurrection appearances proves the point. The other thief, by virtue of his own response to Jesus, was not promised the gift of paradise.

Second, the passage lends support to the principle that, for the most part, and within the context of closing time, we cannot know who has decided for a relationship with God in Christ. The dying thoughts of the thief conversing with Jesus were directed toward the lordship of Christ and His kingdom. This man perfectly epitomizes a teaching that Jesus had formerly given. It was about the master who hired laborers to work for a daily wage. In the final hour of the day, he hired people who received the same reward as those hired earlier (Matt. 20:1-16). God's fairness is His business.

It is all about a God who will never resist anyone desiring a genuine relationship with Him. That principle applies no matter how late in the "day" the response to God's invitation is received. Salvation has absolutely nothing to do with deserving; it has everything to do with the grace of God.

Clearly, it's beyond our knowledge to know how Christ may or may not encounter persons in the closing moments of their earthly existence. It may well be that such an encounter with Jesus will occur in a moment of judgment at the same cross of reconciliation. Our moment of judgment, as did creation, will occur in that "day" and in the context of time.

Third, "today" is the Lord's way of saying that the salvation of time had been restored to the penitent thief. He had already called out for the eternal gift. The day of re-creation had begun (1 John 5:12; John 11:25-26). That thief had already entered into the day, or the moment, of Calvary's finished work.

We would lose the meaning of this Easter moment if we insisted that "today" should be defined within a particular chronological parameter. Today is part of the entire meaning of Easter recreation, and of this astounding moment of first-day Light. For that particular thief, it would be a moment with Jesus that would last forever.

"It Is Finished"

It was at Calvary that Christ's final shout may have sounded to some as a whimper of defeat: "It is finished" (John 19:30). The history of the church has proven otherwise. This was truly a shout of victory. With these three words, the real Adam, our great High Priest, King, Prophet, and Lawgiver declared the completion of the redemption story (Mat. 3:15). But at that particular moment, no one really understood the triumph of the cross. And wherever the cross is memorialized in sentimentalist terms, the same holds true today. Why would Jesus utter this agonizing cry of finality in the closing moments of His ministry?

In spite of Jesus' living in signature of kingdom life, the problems surrounding the cross were massive. There was overwhelming evidence all around Him that the problems of essential relationships were not lessening.

In our present and wonderful age of instant communication, thoughtful and compassionate people understand that they, with increasing frustration and despair, exist at despairing levels of fractured relationships. Jesus had not consigned the poor to a hopeless future of poverty (Mark 14:7). He simply spoke realistically of the nature and destiny of a self-centered humanity living in spiritual poverty. In fact, social conditions were destined to get worse.

I want to venture three reasons why this cry of Jesus was absolutely correct in its biblical context, and for all other moments of time.

Finished: Its Relation to Law

It must be done to fulfill all righteousness (Matt. 3:15). Those were the sentiments Jesus relayed to the reluctant baptizer. John the Baptist knew that the One standing before him was to take away the sins of the world (John 1:29). Jesus was fully aware of His own relation to the legal requirements of the law. In fact, near the beginning of His ministry, He told His eager listeners that nothing would depart from the law until all things were fulfilled.

This was the moment All of the law was summarized in Jesus. It is quite possible that the specific law of which He spoke was the Decalogue. Ever since that moment, neither Jews nor Christians have felt that the Ten Commandments have become obsolete.

The Decalogue and the Sermon on the Mount still serve, in very practical ways, to show the ethical behavior required to remain in relationship with God and with others. Anything less is abhorrent to the nature of the holy God.

What we particularly observe in the very few laws of Jesus is the motivation to enable the keeping of the law. It is the compelling force of love. It often eludes all of us. And that is because we allow feelings, not will, to dominate our motivation.

What Jesus was speaking of is the *consequence* of not meeting the requirements of the law. Although, for some, Paul's letter to the Romans may have seemed a little pedantic and forensic, he was taking a very careful approach to emphasize a major gospel principle: whereas sin and law highlight the breakdown of creation's essential relationships, grace makes possible the restoration of those relationships.

Paul sums it up this way: "There is therefore now no condemnation to those who are in Christ Jesus. For the law of the Spirit of life in Christ Jesus has set you free from the law of sin and death. For God has done what the law, weakened by the flesh, could not do: by sending his own Son in the likeness of sinful flesh, and to deal with sin, he condemned sin in the flesh" (Rom. 8:1-3).

The work of Jesus could not possibly be finished had He not come alongside the human situation in these ways: first, by identifying with the condition of sin that was deeply embedded in all human nature; and second, by identifying with the consequences of choice arising from that condition.

The failure of humanity to rise above both of those situations necessitated, not only rescue from its perilous condition, but grace to move on without the crippling curse of condemnation.

In relation to the former covenant, the cross is God's perfect icon of reconciliation for all time. To cite one example, there is no longer any need for a peculiar order of priesthood within the community of God. Jesus alone continues as the Mediator of God to humanity and humanity to God (Heb. 7:25-27). Jesus is the High Priest of a royal priesthood. Having offered the sacrifice for all time, He continually mediates the intercession of His priesthood back to God.

Finished: Its Relation to Sign

The cross is the perfect icon and tangible means whereby *reconciliation is assured.*

Although Paul had a good understanding of the world's pluralistic thinking (we didn't invent it in our century), he realized that its natural philosophy and the redeeming message of the cross were not compatible (1 Cor. 1:18). Not surprisingly, this was to be the determining factor that represented the hallmark and sign of his entire ministry. "For I decided to know nothing among you except Jesus Christ and him crucified" (1 Cor. 2:2).

The cross was the perfect icon of Christ's kenosis—that is, the total outpouring of Himself for the sake of others. Clearly for Paul, Jesus understood that His baptism could not lead anywhere except to death (Rom. 6:3-4). But as the cross was the redemptive signature from death, it also signaled the gateway to resurrection life.

Two beams, one perpendicular and one horizontal, represent the perfect icon of reconciliation. One beam stretched perpendicularly, an end rooted firmly in the earth and the other end stretching fully toward the heavens. Possibly scores of criminals had been pinned to that very beam. This beam meant nothing to the dispassionate Romans and spectators.

The body of Jesus hung upon the well-used wood, and in one awesome moment of light, His body connected earth to heaven and heaven to earth. In that moment, oblivious to the indifferent soldiers and gaping bystanders, the hope for salvation from the human predicament was emblazoned upon all of the pages of human history. The healing blood of Jesus seeped into the soil of a groaning creation and, through His outstretched body, the awesome chasm between God and His creation was closed.

The other beam stretched horizontally across the perpendicular. Thinking of the essential nature of humanity, we see that humans are directly related to God and also to the earth. The iconic representatives of all humanity, Jew and Gentile, stood on either side of the cross. The Greeks, representing the rational, natural, and intellectually narcissistic philosophy of the world, were on one side, and the Jews, representing a faith played out in the medium of story and law, were on the other side. In terms of human hope, neither system had achieved universal reconciliation of essential relationships. The entire human condition was impotent in securing the fellowship of relationship's restoration.

The four pillars of Israel represented a hope of what was to come. In themselves, they had not guaranteed the promises of God to an unfaithful and apathetic people. All the promises were wonderful, but the responses were not. On the other side, all the wisdom of an Aristotelian world had not unlocked the mysteries that were intended to bring the informed into union with the holy and righteous God.

The arrogant results and the failure emanating from the Enlightenment period force us to realize that the wisdom of all ages has miserably aborted human hope. Neither element of hostility, Jew or Gentile, could touch each other. Humanity was lonely!

With arms outstretched, Jesus embraced in His own body both Jew and Greek. In this final ministry of *theosis*, the great High Priest raised both Jew and Gentile into the arms of a waiting Father. The cross is truly our shame, but it is also God's glory.

We are not stretching the words of the writer to the Ephesians. Here, he really is saying *that all nations are invited* to become one race through the redeeming blood of Jesus Christ: "For he is our peace; in his flesh he has made both groups into one and has broken down the dividing wall, that is, the hostility between us" (Eph. 2:14-16).

In Christ, our real Adam, we have the Leader of the human procession that marches together to Zion (Isa. 35:8-10; Eph. 4:8).

Earlier in this book, we asked questions about the origin and nature of evil. We concluded that a loving God, in making a world free to be itself, had lovingly allowed for the possibility of evil to be present in His creation. Indeed, perfect love could not exist without the exercise of free choice. Omniscient God, in His eternal nowness, surely knew of the horrendous suffering that was to follow. We also concluded that a loving God also had to allow for the possibility of evil; the very nature of love demands it. God has faced up to His responsibilities for that decision.

But is it enough that Jesus was dispatched to a relatively quick death? When reading the daily newspaper, we don't take long to realize that hell's fury is not yet spent. Violence and hatred persist.

Jesus absorbed the cost of evil's furious rage completely and for all time on the cross.

At Calvary, the Savior of the world suffered the fierce lashings of hatred, fear, lies, rejection, bigotry and suffering of all time. There is no period in all chronological counting that was not covered by the sacrifice of Jesus on Calvary.

Finally, as is the destiny of the entire human condition, the Life of the world suffered the awful insult of death. The holy and awesome God could not bear to look upon the face of His own Son. The despairing cry of Jesus, "My God, my God, why have you forsaken me?" was a piercing wail of abandonment. It was truly the cry of all humanity as it cried after God, "Where are *you?*" Hell persisted for Jesus in that moment of desolation; it continued until the moment He was raised to lead captivity captive (Eph. 4:8).

Humanity was in hellish loneliness. But when was that? The man, Christ Jesus, suffered excruciating separation from the lifelong and intimate relationship He had with the Father. All those who share an eternal separation from God know something of that suffering. He uttered those words on our behalf.

Paradoxically, His understanding of the cry, "Where are you?" must have grown immensely in that dreadful moment of time. He had never experienced anything like this in His entire life. This was truly to be indicative of the tormenting pain to be experienced by all who reject God's free and loving offer of reconciliation. On the cross, the real Adam traversed the time-long procession of all those who, dejectedly, looked back to the gates of Eden, and now closed to them forever.

The Cross: Its Relation to Time

The cross speaks of the efficacious suffering of God for all time.

In our introductory discussion on the nature of time, we concluded that all of it exists in God. He sees and experiences all of it in the eternal now. What this means in redemptive terms is that, in one moment of light, Jesus drew into Himself the pain and the sin of all ages. All time, past, present, and future, met in that one moment in God. To see this in any other way would mean that God, even after heaven and earth had passed away, would still be dealing with the consequences of humanity's sinful nature. It would mean that God continues to suffer, and, for God and man, the *consequences* of Christ's sacrifice on the cross have not been fully met.

Clearly, in that moment of which we speak, God also experienced all the fullness, and all the effects of creation's brokenness. It's astonishing! How could the writer of the book of Revelation, with his limited knowledge of time, speak of Christ suffering from the foundation of the world? (Rev. 13:8). Theology makes powerful sense when God reveals it to us. The cross of Jesus Christ proves to be the astounding moment when all time is redeemed.

Maybe the reality of this revelation can be illustrated in the following way. In that moment and on that historic cross, God, in Christ, suffered the agony of humanity's departure from Eden. He suffered the anguish of His despairing children in exile. He suffered the agony of His Son's abandonment at Calvary. He suffered the death of all those martyred for the sake of His gospel. He suffered the pain of His dying people at

Auschwitz. He suffered the cries of starving children in barren Ethiopia. He heard the anguished cry of mothers brutalized by sadistic rapists. He heard the despairing cry of the vagrant in the city. He suffered the murderous vengeance of Rwandan Christians in conflict with each other. He felt for the Ugandan babies dying of AIDS. He suffered with the poor as food was destroyed for a future profit. He felt the despair of a gasping creation choking in the pollution of death. He was pained to see it repeated again, and again, and again.

Amazingly, in that apparent moment of defeat, and for all time, the entire redemption story was gloriously won in a magnificent moment of light.

Paradoxically, at the very end of the sixth day, that one hour of darkness is, for all time, the ultimate sign that the Light in humanity had been fully extinguished. If the Light and Life of the world had died in the real Christ, then all hope had died in all humanity.

On the sixth day, God completed His work of creation and rested on the Sabbath. The ugly yet paradoxical sign of the real Adam's obedience was that Jesus finished His work of redemption on Friday. In time for the Sabbath, His body was laid to rest in a dark tomb of life's hopelessness. If this was the destiny of the real Adam, then how could life ever hold meaning for anyone else?

A defunct meaning of time now loomed its largest; its very vagueness of meaning would signal enmity to all humanity.

Yet, in that incredulous and paradoxical *moment* of apparent defeat, the obedient Christ, in triumphant cry, shouted, "It is finished." In hope, and faith, He saw Himself leading a procession of the redeemed as they sang their way to Zion's reopened gates. Jesus believed it, but He had to die in order to know it. In that moment of atonement, Christ's redemption crossed the awesome barriers of time in rescue of the saints of old, the present, the future, and all, at the very point of their extinction.

Is it just fanciful philosophical thinking, devoid of any solid bases, to think that the pain of all time could be encapsulated by Jesus in that awesome moment? The astounding accomplishment of Christ's victory is that, in one moment of light, Jesus took upon Himself the pain and insult of all time.

From a mathematical perspective, Hugh Ross postulates how God, who exists in multidimensional ways, can do this.

> A significant part of what transpired in Christ's payment of all that our death warrants took place in God's extra-dimensional realm . . . With a second time dimension, God could move along, that is, experience, these twenty billion lines. He would possess a plane of time that could encompass all of them. Thus, while Jesus suffered on the cross for six hours on our time line, He could have experienced the suffering of twenty billion infinite timelines in two other dimensions of time.[3]

God has no further need to experience the pain of past, present, and future. It is all done. "It is finished!" He doesn't grow with future experiences; He has experienced them in all their fullness and for all time. He doesn't continue to be the suffering God.

We understand how God, in Christ, completed His work once and for all. We realize that all the fullness of time itself was redeemed in that awesome moment of abandonment.

When Jesus died, He was surrounded by a world bearing the cruel marks of despair, oppression, and injustice. But in a moment of time, the victory was won. It was finally signed on a hill called Calvary. The ravages of chronological time would yet play themselves out in their gluttonous demands on the world, but it is now a world possessing an ever-enduring icon of hope. Humanly impotent, and upon two wooden staves, Jesus won the victory for all time, and for all that is incorporated in its redemption.

With total abandonment and confidence in God, Jesus, the Priest and Victim, shouted, "It is finished." And, in that awesome moment, the veil of the temple was torn in two (Matt. 27:51).

The Great High Priest had laid Himself ready for God to restore an entire priesthood of believers to first-day Light of new beginnings. Christ's work in the redemption story was now complete.

"Father, into your hands I commend my spirit" (Luke 23:46). It was another glorious moment of light. Christ, the Light of the world, had begun His descent into the nihilistic darkness of hell while His mortal body was still bound to the cross.

We should never minimize the astounding force of Christ's final statement. He had voluntarily turned His face toward Jerusalem. He did so in total and absolute confidence in the Father's plan for creation, redemption, and restoration. Making way for His own death required an enormous capacity for trust and faith in the sovereignty of God's plan.

Jesus believed in the resurrection, but He had to die in order to experience it. He had to trust in order to know it.

How Did Jesus Descend into Hell?

It was Saturday, God's Sabbath rest from the work of creation. The body of Jesus had been laid in a hollow and stone-cold tomb; it was sealed in the nihilistic darkness of nothingness. Ironically, this cruel condition was guarded by the forces of the religious establishment (Matt. 27:62-66). The *rest* of Sabbath was now a metaphor for the death of the human condition; the very crown of God's completed creation was lifeless.

The tomb of Jesus was a hollow sign that all natural hope of meaning in immortality was firmly and absolutely dead. The real Adam was dead! The tomb's covering stone, sealed shut, was an immoveable sign that nothing less than a miracle from above could change that reality.

Doesn't it stretch the credulity of believers to ask them to believe that Jesus actually descended into hell? What can this possibly mean?

The meaning of the cross is that, at the very moment of Christ's finished work, all time has been redeemed. The hopeless condition of humanity, for all time, has been claimed back. And its benefits are promised to all those who respond to Christ's invitation.

Well, that sounds good for us, but what about all those people who died before the time of Jesus?

The apostle Peter seems to ponder the same question when he asserts, "For this is the reason the gospel was proclaimed even to the dead, so that, though they had been judged in the flesh as everyone is judged, they might live in the spirit as God does" (1 Pet. 4:6).

Recognizing the importance of time, we note here that that the gospel was proclaimed to the dead. In other words, these people, at some point in their dying, earthly existence, still had a consciousness of life, and therefore of time. So was it possible for God to snatch them back from the fire? (Jude 23).

After Jesus died on the cross, a stone-cold body was laid in a borrowed tomb. Does this mean that the eternal second Person of the Trinity was dead? Of course not! The dead body of the man, Jesus Christ, lay lifeless in the tomb of helplessness. Everything that was *human* was dead. In Gnostic, not Christian fashion, a soul had not escaped in order to whisk its way to heaven.

However, while the dead body of Jesus lay in the tomb, Christ in His divine and eternal present encountered people of all times, past, present, and future, and at the very point at which, for each individual, death was to claim its natural course to nothingness. Christ, in His divinity, is always the Lord of time. Therefore, His descent into Hell speaks of the divine Christ's point of meeting with all those who face everlasting extinction at the very moment of separation from mortal consciousness. This is their moment' of judgment.

In the finished work of Christ, redemption is intended to be possible for all. It is for this reason we are to view Saturday not only in chronological terms, but as the necessary connection in the entire story of the Easter moment. After all, in the playing out of this entire moment, the dawn of first-day beginnings was to emerge. Connected with Christ's resurrection, many saints of old became incorporated into the God-graced fellowship of restoration.

We read in Hebrews 11 how the writer speaks of the great saints of old who walked the path of faith. There are many others, of course. If they could not be invited apart from the finished work of Jesus, then how could they be invited at all? Jesus, in His eternal present, met each person at the point of that person's extinction, the very point at which hell exacts its fullest toll.

If all time exists in God, then it is no great feat for God to meet anyone at any point in human, conscious awareness of present time, What this means for the individual is that, at the moment of extinction, they also meet God in judgment and final invitation. The activity of God.

The activity of God is not confined to chronological time as we see it. At some point in this Easter moment, Jesus Christ met Abraham, Sarah, Moses, Rahab, David, and all the rest. In His eternal moment, separated in chronological time, Christ, the first fruits from the dead, gives people, of all time, the opportunity for repentance and reconciliation. They also had to be invited in this...no resurrection at all. They also had to be invited in this way because Jesus, by His grace, is not only the Inviter to salvation, but the Pioneer and Perfecter of faith (Heb. 11:40;12:2). Apart from Him, there is no restoration at all.

But what about the little Hindu lady from rural India who died last night? Will the saints of Hebrews 11 share an eternal home with people whose god is not the God of Jesus? After all, this little old lady had never even heard of Jesus. If Jesus really is the way, truth, and life, and for all people, how may this lady see or hear Christ's invitation?

Clearly, without resorting to sentimentality, the same principles are in place here. God, as the sovereign Lord of all time, does make an opportunity for all people, at the point when time still resides in their consciousness, to receive the invitation to share restoration life with Jesus. Jesus really is the Alpha and Omega of life.

And so, to the very last moment, our loving God presents Himself and reaches out to all who seek and desire Him. Indeed, many in such a position may gladly embrace life in God's kingdom.

"I love those who love me, and those who seek me diligently find me" (Prov. 8:17).

Jesus, in His divinity and as Lord of all time, meets all people in their ebb of receding consciousness. Then, what is it that this 21st century lady and the Old Testament saints have in common?

In that moment of receding consciousness, they are all caught up into God's eternal nowness. In that moment, for everyone, they meet the *resurrected Christ* in this, their moment of revelation and accountability. (Heb. 11:39-40)

A chronology of thousands of years on both sides of the cross is embraced in that one moment. No one from any age will be able to accuse God of not presenting an opportunity to meet the inviting Christ; that is, the One who is the Light of the world. That is why the thief on the cross, and those working for but one hour, and those who are on the ebb of life, and those who have died previously, and all those yet to be born, are all embraced by God in that one moment of hope and *final* decision.

In other words, as we have previously intimated, In the mystery of time's restoration, people like King Saul and Jezebel as well as King David, Rahab, Mary, Martin Luther, Mother Teresa and Joe the planet traveler meet the inviting Jesus at the moment of death's eternal unconsciousness. It really is the final moment of decision in response to Christ's invitation.

As we see in the parable of the rich man and Lazarus, we cannot presume that all people respond positively to Christ's invitation. Some may be concerned that a ruthless and murderous dictator may jump at the opportunity of a cheap confession at the moment of meeting Christ. However, we remember that just one thief, when dying with Jesus, asked for new, and eternal life. In the parable of the Rich Man and Lazarus, the rich man was too self-possessed to ask for forgiveness. He was far too self-conditioned to ask for something he could not personally live with. How dare we cheapen the judgment of God? Isn't He the God who knows the secrets of all hearts? (Rom. 2:16). He will not be mocked (Gal. 6:7). He is never surprised!

Saturday represents a part of the entire Easter moment. It bears witness to the fact that Christ's body was placed in a tomb from which He was also raised. But His body was stone-cold dead. This is the natural and ultimate fate of all humanity. It also represents a connection of all the Easter events. The connection is the redemption of time between the point of death and the restoration of time to new and everlasting beginnings of first-day Light.

There isn't much point in trying to work out an exact chronology of events to describe this awesome, history-changing moment of Easter. So we won't even try. To trace the moment by moment events of how Jesus was restored, descended to hell, and then appeared to His followers would be to miss the wholeness of the entire series of events. In terms of the whole Easter moment, an exact chronological approach is not the way to go.

However, the third day of new hope is vitally important. What we do know is that, while the lifeless body of the man Christ Jesus lay in the darkness of death, God was busy. And, on the third day, God brought forth the restored fruit of the earth: the first fruit of Eden's innocence. By grace alone, saints of all time are incorporated with Jesus into His resurrection.

But how? We shall see what the Bible says about some commonly held myths.

RESTORATION

CHAPTER 11

Eternal Life: Is It for Everyone?

*I*n the Easter moment of restoration, the Light of the first day once more burst upon the darkness of creation's disorder.

There are many people, some through ignorance or tradition, and others who are still in denial of the penalty of sin, who somehow believe that restoration to eternal life can be gained through natural means. Some say that we all live forever. If that is true, then what's the point of the resurrection? If they were right, then the most important event in the Christian calendar would be rendered meaningless.

We began our theological journey understanding that, by grace, it was always God's purpose for us to live forever. If natural means were not enough to secure that existence, then we really must consider why resurrection and miracle are connected. Miraculously, the day of resurrection ushers in the restored time of first-day Light.

Natural Immortality

Almost all the natural religions of the world hold to a belief that we naturally move from this life to another. Many in the Christian faith believe the same thing. But is that true? We are aware that the impressive pyramids of Giza in Egypt housed the remains of many pharaohs and other important dignitaries of the land. Graham Hancock suggests this wasn't the sole reason for their existence.[1] Similar examples of a common hope reside in many of the natural religions. The Egyptians spoke of the soul going to Amenti, Babylonians to Aralla, and Ethiopians to Si.ol.[2]

In Egypt, a pharaoh was laid in a sarcophagus and surrounded by food and various symbols of wealth. Sometimes servants were walled up in attendance and left to die. (Few people volunteered to be servants of an aged pharaoh!) All of these trappings symbolized the hope of a continuance, or even of an improvement on the state of life the pharaoh had left behind. Unfortunately, his servants were destined to spend an eternity serving their former master. For them, immortality wasn't much to which they would look forward.

The Egyptian Book of the Dead holds a view that after death, life continues in roughly the same way as it did before. It is simply a matter of continuation. In primitive and natural ways, Egypt conceived of some form of resurrection. The idea was massively underdeveloped. "Osiris, on the other hand, did come back. Although he was murdered by Set, soon after the completion of his worldwide mission to make men 'give up their savagery,' he won eternal life through his resurrection in the constellation of Orion as the all-powerful god of the dead."[3] A natural reward lived out among the stars!

Similarly, North American Indians speak of happy hunting grounds in the life beyond. Caribou may volunteer a second opinion!

What seems to be common in all natural religions is the wish for continuation of life, or the disbelief that this magnificent human creature could ever die. Didn't we notice something like this previously?

An Old Testament View of Death

Historically, in spite of the fact that the ancient Hebrews were surrounded by natural beliefs in immortality and had spent 430 years with the Egyptians, they most certainly did not emerge from Egypt with its developed and natural view of an afterlife. Maybe in the recesses of their collective memory, they recalled, "You are dust, and to dust you shall return" (Gen. 3:19).

During the larger part of Jewish history, resurrection to eternal life was not considered. Any rewards were in this life. Not surprisingly, the idea of reward for righteousness was not realized in an afterlife but, as we see in the Book of Job, in material prosperity (Job 42:10, 12). Therefore, we are not surprised to read of a very hazy Hebrew view of Sheol. It was sometimes described as "the pit." As a form of existence, it was ambiguously foggy and shadowy. Nevertheless, however vague the belief, some form of consciousness seemed understood to remain in order to experience the place.

Sheol represented a condition where, after death, all the physical senses are diminished to meaninglessness. Nothing was clear, possibly not even the clear awareness of self-consciousness. There was little or no ability to see, feel, smell, touch, or relate to anything. There was no light! (Job 10:21). Try proving your existence in total isolation from all other people. It's particularly hard to do so without senses that offer some sort of connection.

To all intents and purposes, every person is dead in Sheol. The existentialist philosopher Descartes, in considering proof of existence, concluded, "I think, therefore I am." That philosophy cannot easily lend itself to a belief in the continuation of life beyond the grave. For the Hebrews, there was no ability even to think in Sheol. Even God would not be able to find them.

> For I will soon lie down in the dust; you will search for me, but I will be no more. (Job. 7:21)

> For in death there is no remembrance of you; in Sheol who can give you praise? (Ps. 6:5)

> I am counted among those who go down to the Pit; I am like those who have no help, like those forsaken among the dead, like the slain that lie in the grave, like those who remember no more, for they are cut off from your hand. You have put me in the depths of the Pit, in the regions dark and deep . . . Do you work wonders

for the dead? Do the shades rise up to praise you? (Ps. 88:4-6,10)

By the sweat of your face you shall eat bread until you return to the ground, for out of it you were taken; you are dust, and to dust you shall return. (Gen. 3:19)

(See also Psa. 7:5; 22:15; 28:1; 103:14-16; 115:17; Eccl. 2:14-16; 3:19-21; 9:5.)

While most of us may consider that King David's celebrated psalm of the Lord as Shepherd, Psalm 23, suggests eternal life, most Hebrew scholars interpret what some translations render as "forever" (v. 6 NIV) as "long life" or "life long" (v. 6 NRSV). This view is reinforced elsewhere by the psalmist who writes, "With long life I will satisfy them and show them my salvation" (Ps. 91:16). In other words, God will show them salvation from long-lasting problems.

This sense of hopelessness in Sheol isn't restricted to Wisdom literature. Isaiah continues to use similar imagery (38:18-19). The ambiguity of belief in immortality may account for the philosophy we see in the Book of Job. This skeptical approach to eternal life may also explain the idea of a prosperity gospel that has emerged in some areas of Christian fundamentalism. It's very easy to see that Job, in being faithful to God through all his horrendous troubles, was rewarded with more wealth than he had at the beginning (Job 42:10). When there is no view of eternal life, it is easy to see why material wealth becomes the sole reward for righteousness. Besides a good family, what else is there?

The verses above may be contrasted with Psalm 139:8.

If I ascend to heaven, you are there;
If I make my bed in Sheol, you are there.

And, during the later period of Israel, nearer the time of Jesus, the Pharisees may have believed in some sort of hope beyond the grave. Whatever one's interpretations, a theology of eternal life emerged very, very slowly in Israel.

Near-Death Experiences (NDEs)

There have been a plethora of books in recent years that speak of life after *near-death experiences* (NDEs). They are often cited as natural proof of life beyond this present existence.

I am not denying that people have such experiences, nor do I question the reality of them. Some experiences are good, and some of them are very bad. As a result of these experiences, some people have lost their fear of death. Others are totally terrified, while still others see them as life-changing encounters with God.

Common testimonials of such brushes with death include rushing through a long tunnel, being enveloped in a soothing white light, or crossing over a bridge and meeting an inviting, white-clad figure. Others speak of a horrible blackness, or even a terrifying abyss of nothingness.

No, my difficulty with such experiences is the *interpretation* of what has happened. I suggest that all of the experiences take place within the context of natural time. However, for three reasons, I suggest that none of these experiences demonstrate that life continues after death. They are not proof of resurrection or immortality.

First, the experiences, as relayed, come from people who have lost consciousness and have stopped breathing for a relatively short time. Apart from younger people who have died in frigid or watery conditions, or those who have awakened from a comatose condition, none of the credible reports come from people who have lost total consciousness and stopped breathing for a significant length of time, such as a day or two.

Neurologists tell us that, when brain cells are deprived of nutrients and oxygen, hallucinations may occur that are triggered by endorphins. Although some vital signs may or may not remain at such a point, the person concerned would not be considered to be clinically dead. The brain is still in an active state. The person may still be revived. It's during this state, when consciousness is suspended, that the person seems able to experience what are often called "life after life" experiences. At some level, the brain is still functioning within the context of time. Natural time has not yet ceased to exist.

Second, the spiritual experiences relayed are normally consistent with the religious memory of the individual. For example, a recovering Buddhist rarely speaks of an encounter with Jesus Christ, any more than a Muslim speaks of an encounter with the Buddha. Memory seems to determine the nature of the religious experience. In moments of stress, it is understandable that a person raised in a Christian culture might cross a bridge and be met by a Christ-like figure. The religious experience takes place in the context of time as we know it. Brain cells are still alive and producing a religious experience consistent with a person's normal religious memory.

Third, neurologists are able to produce identical or similar experiences in volunteer patients. Under controlled conditions, a person may enter a hallucinatory state. Encounters that are recalled are often shown to be of the same nature spoken of by people in their supposed life after life or near-death experience. Hallucinatory drugs have also been known to produce comparable effects.[4]

Some researchers are now questioning whether all consciousness really does reside exclusively within the brain. "Consciousness could exist in the absence of a functioning brain . . . If that is so, then those cells still alive when someone is declared brain dead, may perceive events that are otherwise inexplicable. This hypothesis may lead us away from the interpretation of NDEs as evidence of an afterlife."[5] This recent area of research lends a measure of scientific credence to the hypothesis that, because some measure of consciousness is still present, possibly in some organ of the body, or other parts of the body, then revelations and decisions of some sort may continue to exist. For example, some people, having recovered from a serious operation during which clinical death occurred, recall events known only to the attending medical staff.

Wilder Penfield, a renowned pioneer of modern neurosurgery, is one who is now convinced that mind and brain are distinct from each other. He has concluded that human beings consist of both body and spirit.[6] Dr. J. P. Moreland, a nuclear chemist with a master's degree in theology, agrees that consciousness and the brain are distinct entities. When questioned concerning the proposition that consciousness and the soul are immaterial entities, Moreland agrees with Penfield's conclusion.

Nevertheless, we seem to be left with a theological assumption that immaterial must also mean immortal. For Moreland, the soul is made in the image of God, so it is immaterial. "While the human soul survives the death of its body, I don't think the animal soul outlives its body. I could be wrong . . ."[7]

There is another way of thinking concerning the nature of humanity as a whole. John Polkinghorne, a British physicist who is also a Christian, speaks of a certain complimentarity residing in the distinctions of the human condition. This is particularly evident when comparing the distinct nature of both mind and matter. "One could summarize this as dual-aspect monism. There is only one stuff in the world (not two—the material and the mental) but it can occur in two contrasting states (material and mental phases, a physicist would say) which explain our perception of the difference between mind and matter."[8]

He continues by quoting Thomas Nagel's dismissal of a dual aspect theory: "The strange truth seems to be that certain, complex, biologically generated physical systems, of which each of us is an example, have rich nonphysical properties. An integrated theory of reality must account for this, and I believe that if and when it arrives, probably not for centuries, it will alter our conception of the universe as radically as anything has to date."[9]

This idea of integrated reality is truly amazing; it has very interesting implications for the nature of the bodily resurrection of Jesus Christ.

Getting back to so-called proofs of natural immortality, no one wants to deny the extraordinary power or the reality of near-death experiences. However, I want to stress that, in a near-death experience, for some time, consciousness seems able to exist beyond our bodies. It is in this state that consciousness is able to experience so-called "heaven" experiences.

In reality therefore, consciousness continues to exist in time, as we know it. NDEs have had profound effects upon many of the persons concerned, and mostly for the good. But what we see here is that all the experiences mentioned occur within the context of natural time. As such, they are no proof whatsoever of life beyond the grave. These experiences do show that there may still be awareness, a consciousness of life, but always in the context of time that, in some natural way, continues to exist for the person. However, I suspect that Polkinghorne might agree that the two contrasting states would also be subject to natural decay.

What About Purgatory?

For our purposes and theological pursuit, we may apply questions of time to notions of both purgatory and universalism. Purgatory is, "… according to Roman Catholic teaching the place or state of temporal punishment, where those who have died in the grace of God expiate their unforgiven venial sins and undergo such punishment as is still due to forgiven sins, before being admitted to the Beatific vision."[10] Universalism is the doctrine "that hell is in essence purgative and therefore temporary and that all intelligent beings will therefore in the end be saved."[11] I want to suggest here that such notions of purgatory and universalism and of their purgative nature are, ultimately, unworkable.

For both of these situations, there is an assumption that beyond the grave there is a consistent procession of chronological time. Of course, if eternal life is of a spirit nature, then there is no reason for time. Be that as it may, this procession of time raises a serious problem. Presumably from the moment of death, the spirit would depart to a spiritualized state and prepare for some point of acceptance to heaven. We must remember that time, as a distinct and restored entity, requires material dimensions for it to be intact. For those selling indulgences in the sixteenth century (i.e., Johann Tetzel), time was certainly an important factor. Time is a factor, and spirit is another factor, but not both in the same context.

Once we consider the question of time, then we must of necessity consider the physical dimensions that make the time dimension a reality. We see from basic creation principles that a condition for both purgatory and universalism requires such physical dimensions, but not for entities belonging to the spirit world. So where is there a physical place we may call purgatory?

What we are suggesting in this thesis is that body, soul, and spirit— the constituents of a human being, as it was with Jesus—all die at the point of death. How may it be just a spirit undergoing expiation? In what kind of environment is this spirit? Somewhere in purgatorial thinking, essential elements of humanity are missing. But if a spirit can somehow exist in isolation, the parts of its humanity must surely come together again.

The difficulties of this introductory thesis should become clearer. However, we will see that judgment for all persons is in the context of time. Indeed, we may even say that NDEs furnish some clue as to how it will be possible.

A New Testament View of Death

To the question, "Is there life beyond the grave?", the Christian answer is yes and no.

The fact is that in a chronological sense, everyone who had ever lived is now dead and buried. As far as biblical revelation has taken us to this point, there is nothing more. Even the breath of God, which once gave eternal life, is now dead. Dust to dust!

When the apostle Paul speaks of all people being dead in Adam, he is not simply speaking analogously about some sort of spiritual darkness. Maybe, as Polkinghorne has suggested, we can't totally separate the spirit from the physical anyway. Wasn't it the *inbreathing* of God that separated humanity from all other creatures? Speaking to the Romans, Paul offered a simple polarity of existence versus nonexistence (Rom. 6:23).

Let me repeat: Everything that constitutes the human condition died on the day of Christ's death. And, in spite of attempts to explain away a real death, the fact remains that the death of Jesus is a matter of historical record. There are two vitally important factors implied in this effort to emphasize the complete death of Jesus.

There was absolutely nothing remaining in Jesus that gave him the ability to raise Himself from the dead. A dormant but dead spirit could not do it. Humanity was totally impotent. On that Good Friday, it didn't take very long for His body to become as cold as the tomb in which it was laid. Nicodemus and Joseph of Arimathea placed His dead body to rest. It was wrapped in linen cloths that were soaked in precious spices (John 19:38-40).

If the most wonderful and obedient person who ever lived died, and was then buried, what possible natural hope could there be for anyone else? This fact alone doesn't offer much to support the claims of other religions in their claims to secure natural immortality.

All die in Adam. (1 Cor. 15:22)

For the wages of sin is death. (Rom. 6:23)

These verses do not speak symbolically of a spirit dying. So the logical consequence we arrive at is that there really isn't any hope for humanity beyond the grave. That's it, folks!

But what about the promise Jesus gave to the repentant thief on his cross? What can it possibly mean for him to be in paradise with Jesus?

I cannot overstate the importance of returning to the statement that Jesus made from the cross. Nothing less than the sovereign purposes of God for creation are at stake here. Let me put my concern in the form of a question, and assuming the sovereignty of God's purposes. If God's purposes for Adam's eternal life were defeated, would not His original plan stand in need of revision? (See Gen.2:7)

Put very briefly, God's purposes really are sovereign. He created a material world. In it, He also placed within a signatory garden physical and inbreathed people. They were intended to live in it forever in blissful intimacy with God, and in an apostolic life of stewardship. If, at the end of this one story, all those elements are *not* in place, how can God's purposes be sovereign?

Before His crucifixion, Jesus had confused His disciples with a statement they failed to understand. (At least, they didn't understand it until after the resurrection). "In my Father's house there are many *places* [Greek *menai*: places remaining, or to settle]. If it were not so, would I have told you that I go to prepare a *place* for you? [Greek *topos*; dwelling]. And if I go and prepare a *place* for you, I will come again and will take you to myself, so that where I am, there you may be also" (John 14:2-3; italics and brackets mine).

We have to get back to that statement which Jesus made on the cross. In the moment of His identification with all who had formerly lived outside of the Calvary experience of time, Jesus led the procession of all the saints, including the penitent thief. He took them to the paradise of

God. It was a real place (just as it was in the beginning) accomplished by God in Christ's victory through the entire Easter moment: "today you will be with me in Paradise."

The Greek word *paradeisos* has its derivation in an oriental word meaning "park" or "garden." In the Greek version of the Old Testament, the Septuagint, the same word is also used to describe the garden of Eden. In the New Testament, the word is used when referring to a celestial paradise.[12] It is also the word used by Paul when describing his heavenly vision (2 Cor. 12:3). The same word is used again in the apocalyptic vision of John: "I will give permission to eat from the tree of life that is in the paradise of God" (Rev. 2:7).

With Jesus at the Head, the new creation is, therefore, a *better place* than that which fell into decay. But it is a real place? Not all scholars agree that Paradise is the ultimate destiny for those in Christ. The renowned English scholar, N. T. Wright, notes, "Paradise, in Jewish thought, wasn't necessarily the final resting place, but the place of rest and refreshment before the gift of life in the resurrection."[13] Some would also suggest that there is an intermediate paradise. "When we die, believers in Christ will not go to Heaven where we'll live forever. Instead, we'll go to an intermediate Heaven."[14] But a broader view of time, one not restricting God's activity in time to our chronological thought, or to millennial theories such as we have seen in science and in God's eternal nowness, plus the fact that we do meet Christ in resurrected life from the moment of death, means that we meet with Him in a completed paradise.

This paradise is absolutely consistent with the Eden that is restored because of Christ's resurrection. Therefore, a consistent view of creation, redemption, and restoration makes a strong biblical case for Christ's words to the penitent thief.

I don't want to spend any more time on matters of disembodied spirits moving on, or the fact that the Book of Hebrews reminds us, "And just as it is appointed for mortals to die once, and after that the judgment, so Christ, having been offered once to bear the sins of many, will appear a second time, not to deal with sin, but to save those who are eagerly waiting for him" (Heb. 9:27-28). Let us simply remind ourselves of four biblical realities.

First, there is no biblical evidence that the man, Christ Jesus, with the repentant thief, entered into an intermediate condition after death. It was in Christ's resurrected condition that He appeared to many in the fullness of His restored humanity (1 Cor. 15:3-8). Life never ends for those in Christ (Rom. 8:38; John 11:25). Connection to Christ's resurrection means connection to the fullness of Easter; this includes His ascension into heaven. We remember that the great saints of the Old Testament are *already* participating in Christ's resurrected life (Heb. 12:1).

Second, God's original purpose for humanity was for them to be stewards of the earth forever (Gen. 2:15-17). This means that material people were intended to live in a material world forever. And in paradise, they do! Originally, they were fashioned from clay. Spirits were not hanging around in a temporary, celestial existence. Are God's purposes not sovereign after all? Have His purposes failed? Have they been modified? As Isaiah says, God really does know the beginning from the end, and His purposes will not fail (46:10).

Third, the particular tradition of paradise to which N. T. Wright alludes is solely made possible within the confines of chronological time. It is a way of explaining a sequence of events in time as we know it. But God draws all time into Himself. Only in this way was the transfiguration made a reality. Moses and Elijah really did appear with Jesus. To inhabit, with Jesus, the paradise that God intended is to enter into the fullness of the Easter moment.

Fourth, we enter into a theologically impossible position when we introduce any condition that speaks of existence in an intermediary state. Existing in an incomplete condition beyond the grave is the major basis upon which the problems of purgatory and universalism appear. In all of these situations, we must be very hesitant to speculate about what may easily become the bizarre.

The above four points carry sufficient weight for us to think literally of the promise given to the thief on the cross. Near his last breath, he met the Christ who was able to offer entrance to the eternal banquet in paradise. We are back to our original thoughts about time being related to space and place. In other words, because of the resurrection of Jesus, time itself has been restored forever, as it was in the beginning.

The most unnatural implication is that this paradise is *unearned*. In the Christian story, it has been given by grace from above, and through the finished work of Jesus (Eph. 2:8-9). Isn't that an astounding miracle? Also, God's sovereign purposes are intact. Paradise, or the *place* Jesus prepares, is still a four-dimensional creation that, as at the beginning, has time that never ends. Quite possibly, with Jesus as the Head, the new community may once again be capable of exercising stewardship with enormous, Spirit-filled possibilities.

At the heart of the new creation, the one paradise of God, is the Holy City, the New Jerusalem that comes down from heaven (Rev. 21:1-2). This place is a brand-new creation, but is somehow connected to that which fell into decay. The same principle exists when we look for recognizable connections between the old and the resurrected body of Jesus. The connection is real, but is nevertheless a mystery. The apocalyptic writer records, "See, I am making all things new" (Rev. 21:5).

Is Total Annihilation Possible?

The question of total annihilation is an important one, and one that has divided scholarly-godly people throughout the ages. I suggest that, apart from a born-again miracle, continued life is impossible to new creation. Our final lack of self-awareness, somewhere beyond self-consciousness, is also the point of our total annihilation. It happened to Jesus!

Nothing can change that unless, at this point of helplessness, God takes the initiative to offer some sort of miraculous intervention; something that could not be offered by nature itself (John 1:12-13).

It is also important that we avoid notions of sentimentalism. Honoring the creation principle of free choice, the gospel is always offered by way of invitation. We are free to embrace or renounce it. The gospel order is very clear: God issues the invitation; we are called to respond. The process does not begin with our decision.

Hence, the question of eternal punishment in hell is raised. We are also forced to ask whether there really is a *place* called hell. According to

Jesus, we are certain that paradise is a place. If hell is really a place, then it consists of place, space, and time. It is a four-dimensional entity. The corollary to this thinking is that, if people are raised from the dead to go to this place of physical dimension, then they are eternally punished in this *place* called, hell.

The existence of an eternal hell would necessitate one or both of two images: First, it is spirit alone that continues after death. The idea of a spiritual existence beyond the grave is more easily traced to Plato, but certainly not to Jesus. In the resurrection of Jesus, we will see that time, with all its dimensions, has been restored in Christ. If there is time, then there must also be place and space. In Christ, we go to a real place! In Plato, a select group of egg-heads flit around in a spiritual existence; at least until this spirit gets absorbed. But that's another story.

What evidence do we have that time exists for those outside of Christ? We did not observe a thesis of restored time in the Old Testament. But Jesus did speak of the patriarchs by pointing out that they really are alive in connection to His finished work (Luke 20:37-38; see also 1 Cor. 15:20). However, it may well be that Daniel, when speaking of resurrection, refers to a future hope for the nation of Israel (12:2).

In the wonderful vision of Isaiah concerning new creation or a new created order, the language is of length of days, not everlasting days (65:17-20). In this passage there are infants and those considered to be accursed because they did not reach a hundred. Does not the New Testament resurrection promise of restored time extend *forever*, but to the redeemed? Did God raise Jesus in order to create a *place* called hell? Are there really two entirely different forms of existence beyond the grave? This would mean that there is a spiritual existence for those in hell, while a second and material order is for those in paradise. Two forms of existence do not have biblical warrant.

Second, if an eternal, spiritual place called hell really did exist, would it not mean that all persons possess a natural, spiritual state of immortality, regardless of where and how eternity is spent? People were not created by God as spiritual beings. They came out of the ground.

In this schema of thought, the creation theme of humanity's wholeness of body, soul, and spirit is clearly *changed*. We continue to be left with questions regarding God's sovereignty, particularly one of settling for a different life situation than that which was designed at the beginning. Human beings were never intended to be spirit-beings. We are all people with a nature consisting of body, soul, and spirit. Therefore, we would have to be recreated as spirit-beings in order to experience an eternal fire of hell. Meanwhile, because of the finished work of Christ, the redeemed would be whole people enjoying life in a new, physical creation.

If, as is strongly postulated here, we cannot accept the thesis that all people become spirit-beings after death, then we are left with one alternative: for all those choosing to live outside of the finished work of Christ, their destiny is one of *total annihilation*. Humanly, they cannot possibly fit into the purposes for which God intended in the restored creation. Can they humanly exist for any *other* purpose? (Gen.2:7)

There are many who are horrified by the thought that a loving God could consign people to everlasting torment simply because they rejected the choice God has given them. Maybe such people should consider the possibility that it is humans who consign themselves to their future condition.

Clark Pinnock offers a view of total annihilation, but it may not be for the best reasons. He says that a loving God wouldn't torture people forever for sins done in the context of finite life. For him, it doesn't make any sense to suppose that a lake of fire exists with souls burning in it forever.[15]

Pinnock may not have ventured into the arena of sentimentality, but a reminder is still appropriate: this question should not be debated on the basis of sentimentality, but on biblical substance, with an understanding of time.

We are speaking of free choices, all of which have their consequences. God's love is clearly unconditional, but it does not interfere with the natural *consequences* (for good or ill) that flow from our decisions. Hence, God's plan of salvation is to rescue us from natural consequences, not to accept, without any consequences, the decisions that are offensive to His awesome holiness. Remember: accountability equals worth.

Hugh Ross offers another theological view that, I believe, may also be flawed. He believes that the traditional approach of an eternal hell can still speak of a loving God. This God can consign people to hell because they are spirit beings and so they cannot be eradicated. Therefore, for spirit beings, "Hell is a place people choose. While the people in hell will despise their torment, they have demonstrated their preference for it over eternal fellowship with God and with all who love the Light."[16]

Obviously, I cannot concur with both of his assumptions. That is, I do not agree that future life is one of purely spiritual existence, nor can I hold the view that hell is a place. It seems strange that a scientist would speak of a spiritual existence in what seems to be a physical arena. Quite apart from this very serious difficulty, we see that Ross preserves God's character of love because "those who inhabit the lake of fire occupy the best possible realm for them. God expresses his love and compassion for hell's inhabitants by afflicting them with sufficient torment to prevent the place from being as bad as its inhabitants have the capacity to make it."[17] Where is there biblical evidence for this thought?

In this thinking, hell becomes an everlasting degree of torment relative to the present state of the individual. Unless Ross is prepared to define the lake of fire as simply a spiritual metaphor, then he is clearly speaking of a place called hell. Hell, as a metaphor, is a condition, not a place. We know that we can speak of a condition of hell while we continue to live on earth, but the question is whether there can be a material hell. Wouldn't this eternal continuance mean that God is continually involved in such a place of torment? Where do we find any evidence to support such a claim? It can't be that bad, because God seems to continue taking a hand in it. Fire, as we know it, is a form of energy. Who supplies this material substance of energy? Does or can Satan produce the energy for his own eternal torment? (Rev. 20:10).

If, on the other hand, hell really is a place, then it must possess dimension in order for eternal time to be experienced. Who created this hell with physical dimensions? Revelation 20 (see also 2 Pet. 2:4 and Jude 6) may allude to the possibility that God has reserved this condition for spirit-beings. But here (v. 10) they are named as the Devil, his angels, the beast, and the false prophet. These are spirit beings! Who can possibly know what eternal torment these spirit beings will experience at their judgment? Revelation 21 gives us a clue.

In this passage from Revelation, those three entities do not experience a second death, but as spirit beings, they are tormented forever. (Rev.20:10) However, people experience a second death, which is the lake of fire. (Rev.20:14-15) And death is death! Of course these scriptures raise further questions concerning the nature of life existing in such an unearthly state of hell. So we ask, where do we find solid evidence that the physical bodies we possess, as originally intended by God, suddenly become spiritual bodies with no connection to the physical? Isn't this really the thinking of Plato?

We must face the fact that the notion of an eternal punishment in a place called hell may possibly find some sort of biblical justification. For example, "They serve as an example of those who suffer the punishment of eternal fire" (Jude 7). This position may also be found as far back as the fourth century. Cyril of Jerusalem described the death of Jesus in this way: "For upon Christ death came in reality, for His soul was truly separated from His body, and His burial was true."[18] A century earlier, even Origen may have said the same thing. We must emphasize again the power of revelation. The Old Testament curse does *not* say, "Dust you are, and to spirit you shall return," but "you are dust, and to dust you shall return" (Gen. 3:19).

The position taken by Cyril of Jerusalem is shared today by many who are highly respected for their academic ability and Christ-centered spirituality. James Packer is one such person, whom I know to be a godly, gracious, and well-respected academic in the conservative evangelical tradition. He proposes, "Eternal punishment, then, as Jesus declares it, is departure into eternal fire."[19] John Blanchard, writing on questions of hell, has as his pivotal premise the idea that body and soul are two separate entities. They can be separated, one being physical and the other spiritual. Therefore, he concludes that death never means cessation, but separation, because Adam and Eve continued to live after eating the fruit.[20]

But the Bible does tell us that Adam and Eve really did die! It just took a little time. They continued in their God-given physical existence until the natural course of life returned them to dust and nothingness

(Gen. 3:19, 5:5). "For as all die in Adam, so all will be made alive in Christ" (1 Cor. 15:22).

Is there a place called hell? *No!*

Can we experience the fullness of hell? *Yes!*[21]

Consequences Do Exist for Those Who Are Annihilated

There are equally respected biblical scholars who hold the view that, apart from the possibility of a miraculous rebirth, the ultimate destiny of *all* people really is annihilation. For them, this approach is perfectly consistent with the Hebraic view that we are made from dust, and to dust we shall return. After ten years of study, the Church of England's Doctrine and Worship Committee concluded that "a fiery eternal hell speaks of a cruel sadistic God," and so it goes on, "if a person refuses God's offer of salvation, the consequence is ultimate non-being."[22] At least, this statement actually does speak of God's revealed nature as the criterion for final judgment.

The late John Stott, who was another generous and well-respected English evangelical, offered this thought: "But I do plead for frank dialogue among Evangelicals on the basis of Scripture. I also believe that the ultimate annihilation of the wicked should at least be accepted as a legitimate, biblically founded alternative to their eternal conscious torment."[23] In his dialogue with the esteemed liberal David Edwards, Stott agrees that, while a *weeping and gnashing of teeth* should be taken seriously, "The imagery which Jesus and his apostles used (the lake of fire, the outer darkness, the second death) is not meant to be interpreted literally. In any case it could not be, since fire and darkness exclude each other."[24] Further, "The most natural way to understand the reality behind the imagery is that ultimately all enmity and resistance to God will be destroyed. Therefore, both the language of destruction and the imagery of fire seem to point to annihilation. It would be easier to hold together the awful reality of hell and the universal reign of God if hell means destruction and the impenitent are no more."[25]

Although verses of Scripture may be bandied about on both sides, let me suggest that both Jesus and Paul were cognizant of the question of conditional immortality.

Do not fear those who kill the body but cannot kill the soul; rather fear him who can destroy both soul and body in hell. (Matt. 10:18)

To those who by patiently doing good seek for glory and honor and immortality, he will give eternal life; while for those who are self-seeking and who obey not truth but wickedness, there will be wrath and fury. (Rom. 2:7-8)

Note Paul's contrast of "eternal life" with "wrath and fury," which is not the lot of those experiencing eternal life.

In the second letter to Thessalonica, the Apostle Paul continues:

He will punish those who do not know God and do not obey the gospel of our Lord Jesus. He will be punished with everlasting destruction and shut out from the presence of the Lord. (2 Thess. 1:8-9)

In this last passage, we note that the Greek word *ollumi* is interpreted in Moulton's lexicon as "to destroy" or "fatal." (The Analytical Greek Lexicon, 1978 Edition, Zondervan, Grand Rapids, MI 49506) This means the "destruction" is not of a temporary nature. Destruction is Paul's belief; not eternal "somethingness."

Further Thoughts on Annihilation

I have to look at the question of how eternal time (i.e., time that never ends) may not secure the justice that some feel must ultimately be attained by everlasting torment. Clearly, for those who believe in universal immortality, the underlying principle of hell's eternal existence means that no amount of time will bring about the required punishment. So we are faced with a difficult contradiction. If one hundred or one hundred million years is not enough—and remember that any measurement of time also requires the dimensions of place and space—then justice seems to tread a very difficult path.

There are legitimate ways that honor the required principles of God's justice and of the consequences that flow from it. They reside both in the realms of the nature of time and in the nature of God's love.

God's justice is connected with the free decisions that people make. The *consequences* of those decisions require the involvement of His justice. On several occasions we have noted that the righteousness of God is always the determining factor tempering the nature of His justice. The Bible nearly always connects the two. When a person has chosen to live outside the character of God's revealed righteousness (not their own perceptions of righteousness), then he or she chooses to live outside the nature of God and, therefore, of His kingdom.(Surely God's judgment would take into account the fact that, for some, life in the new creation would be a hellish experience; it would be a compulsion to live in denial of the very nature the unrepentant had clothed his ego and sense of security).

But the Bible continually speaks of a logical corollary. The choice is life or death. What is the opposite of life? "The wages of sin is death, but the free gift of God is eternal life in Christ Jesus our Lord" (Rom. 6:23).

In another context, not one of eternal life, Moses urged Israel to follow God's commands. In that context, He challenged them to choose life (Deut. 30:13, 19). Here, Moses was speaking of choices relating to consequences.

I believe the Bible consistently looks at these questions without confusing agape with eros. Throughout this entire book I have spoken of a God who honors the dignity of human decision, whether He likes the decision or not.

We remember that Jesus, with loving disappointment, accepted the rejection of His penetrating challenge to the rich man. But Jesus didn't change the relational conditions in order to include him (Mark 10:17-22).

Nor did Jesus change kingdom standards in order to satisfy those who didn't accept its high ideals (Matt. 5:48). It would be the grace of God alone that would enable people to cross those insurmountable hurdles.

The freedom to decide for this relationship with God is vitally important. But responsibility is required in making that decision. The rich ruler knew that he would have experienced great difficulty in following Jesus. To take on a new life, putting God's kingdom first, was too much for him.

Jesus rose above sentimentalism by connecting love for Him with obedience to His commands (John 14:15). God knows best how relationships work. And there are eternal consequences in not living them.

Is there then, as Hugh Ross suggests, some sort of spiritual existence for spirit bodies to endure eternal torment? Or, as John Stott suggests, is the New Testament's four-dimensional imagery of hell simply an allegorical picture? One that enables us to understand that all those who blaspheme the work of the Spirit will experience the pain of hell? (Matt. 12:31). Then, for humanity, are we really thinking of hell as an experience of destruction and not as an eternal, material place?

When God raised Jesus from the dead, everything that constituted His humanity was raised: body, soul and spirit. That is the *miracle* of God's raising the lifeless body of Jesus from the grave of nothingness to a restored time. (See Acts 2:24 and 3:15; and 1 Pet. 1:3.)

And we shall be like Him. The ascended body of Jesus is evidence of how we are to think of our eternal bodies. "He . . . will come in the same way as you saw him go into heaven" (Acts 1:11).

It should also be noted that the feet of Jesus do not again touch the ground of the old order. Those in Christ, who are alive and remain, are raised as an act from above. They meet Jesus *above* the old order, as He leads the procession toward the order of the new (1 Cor. 15:52-53; 1 Thess. 4:16-17).

We see then that as far as humans are concerned, the fire of hell is the torment of knowing that life is rushing to absolute nothingness. Such torment is accompanied by an unbelievable agony of aloneness. It is a tormenting experience of knowing the total loss of all relationships, and the horrific terror of separation from life itself. The unrepentant face the consequences of living a self-focused life that is mocking to the just

Creator, while the horrors of hell's vicious and rapacious fury become telescoped into one moment of unimaginable fear.

It would appear that Jesus is quite deliberately taking this approach in several of His parables. For example, we see it in His metaphors of weeds and goats (Matt. 13:30; 25:33) and of one in the field and the one left at the mill (Matt. 24:40-41). The parable of separation of wheat from tares is particularly useful.

The kingdom of heaven is not simply about wheat and weeds; it is about God's reign among His people. In this analogy, He speaks of weeds being *burned up*. The Greek word that is employed is *katakaio* (though *katakausai*, the aorist infinitive, is the form of the verb that is used). The verb means "to burn up" or "to consume with fire."

In this present-tense sentence, the deliberate use of the aorist infinitive denotes a completed action. Otherwise, the writer would have utilized an imperfect verb. In other words, the action is complete; it is sealed. There is no longer any ability for personal control. The parable is illustrative of a personal awareness of *a great separation from life*.

What About the Rich Man and Lazarus?

Certainly, it is in the context of time that we may consider certain implications in the story of the rich man and Lazarus (Luke 16:19-31). For some, this story furnishes proof of everlasting torment. I don't think so! It is really about eternal separation from the Source of life itself (e.g., 1 John 5:12-13).

By choice, that separation is permanently ingrained in the character of the unrepentant person. In this story, the rich man was experiencing his judgment; Lazarus had received his. The rich man received a moment that was neither a good nor a lasting experience. The rich man was totally unrepentant concerning his ingrained lust for riches, or the actions and character which fulfilled them. Therefore, he:

+ Saw what he had missed and would never, by habit of choice, possess.
+ Was already in the throes of hell's aloneness.

+ Experienced unbearable agony and torment. In his agony, he encountered Abraham, not as judge, but as forerunner of all those accounted righteous before God (Rom. 5:1-2; Heb. 11:39-40).
+ Could do nothing to change the course of what their inherited nature had set for his family. Yet, even this did not, or could not, draw him to repentance.
+ Experienced the fullness of hell's moment.
+ Realized the Word of God always gives warning about the consequences of decisions and actions (Amos 3:7).

The redemptive work of Christ takes place within the context of time, and must be appropriated within the context of time.

The rich man, in his self-centered lifestyle, had made *his decision*. It was a decision to gain wealth and maintain it at the expense of the poor. It was an attitude indelibly imbedded into his self-sufficient character. Satan himself does not repent, even though he knows his eternal and future torment.

The rich man fears that his family has inherited his attitudes. Their characters had been formed by the rewards of injustice and family environment. In those closing moments of time, by experiencing the torment of what his decision had cost him, the rich man called out—not for salvation or forgiveness, but for comfort from the torment of knowing what was ahead.

Maybe, in this moment of judgment, it was possible for the rich man to be repentant. Yet he was already experiencing hell because he was able to see what it would cost in his ingrained, self-successful style of thinking.

What about others who feel they can leave such important decisions to the very last moment? God, who knows the secrets of all hearts, cannot be mocked. God is looking for the desire to change in heart and nature. He is looking for people whose hearts' desires and hopes are to be servants in God's kingdom. Jesus calls this change of heart and nature "conversion" (Matt. 18:3). In Greek manuscripts, the aorist subjunctive is used for this verb, *strepho*; e.g., the change should take place as a complete and permanent action.

The self-sufficient nature of the rich man remained dominant; it elicited a negative choice in the man (see also Luke 13:24-29). In Matthew 24:30, we see that there is absolutely no thought that mourning will produce salvation. (Is this the meaning of Revelation 9:20-21?) Somehow, the rich man chooses, or is so conditioned by his chosen lifestyle, that he will not make decisions that could lead him to such a drastic change of heart. Jesus suggests that this self-centered condition dominates over the need for penitence. "If they do not listen to Moses and the prophets, neither will they be convinced even if someone rises from the dead" (Luke 16:31).

"There is a way that seems right to a person, but its end is the way to death" (Prov. 14:12).

Jesus once said, "Those who believe in him are not condemned; but those who do not believe are condemned already" (John 3:18). Is Jesus speaking of those who have already condemned themselves because of life-conditioning that does not allow for a change in heart? If so, then we can understand that not all people meeting with Jesus in judgment will genuinely repent of the past.

There is often a great deal of sentimentality associated with biblical understandings of the rich and the poor. It would be correct to say that Jesus was always on the side of the oppressed, and that attitude mostly included the poor. However, He did not say that it was *impossible* for a rich person to enter the kingdom of heaven (see Luke 19:1-10). Also, He did not say that we could get to heaven so long as we are materially poor. What He was saying was that the attitudes and style of life that produced lust for wealth made it very difficult for the consumer-minded person to accept the character of God's kingdom. Achieving wealth, to the cost of others, is not a kingdom principle.

Jesus did applaud honest enterprise. We see this in his teaching on stewardship in Matthew 25:14-30.

We all receive the consequences of the decisions we have made in response to God's gracious invitation. The consequences are life in God's grace, or death in oneself.

The larger meaning of the story of the rich man and Lazarus is about the fate of Israel at the time of Jesus. Abraham, the patriarch of God's chosen people, explains that the story of Israel points toward the salvation they, as a nation, had rejected. Like the story of the Prodigal, this is also an analogy of the choices that had been made by Israel.

So let's eat, drink, and be merry! Some may consider annihilation to be a reasonable alternative. Why not? At least, if that is all our decisions will cost. Annihilation may be all right so long as I get what I want in this life. That's especially true if I can do it "my way!"

But it's not at all about God zapping us if we don't do what He wants. The fact is that we were created to live lives in relation to Him and His purposes for creation. To do otherwise simply opens us up for the consequences of disharmony of relationships. We bring our own judgment upon ourselves.

For such people, heaven itself would be a hellish experience. They wouldn't fit!

The me-focused life is clearly not the position taken by Jesus. And so, in the context of consequence and judgment, He refers to a conscious experience of "weeping and gnashing of teeth" (Matt. 13:42, 50). In this sense, I want to compare the closing moments of self-consciousness with the terror of hell. It really doesn't matter what amount of time we consider. A moment comes when life and time ceases to exist for those outside of Christ's restoration.

However, the moment *before* that occurs, the torment and terror of hell are experienced in their fullness during that awful moment of personal accountability.

We see that the rich man experienced a devastating degree of horror. This moment contained all the experience that was necessary for him to comprehend the torment and terror of hell's meaning. A view of chronos (successive, natural time) is telescoped to reveal the fullness of hell's experience.

Whether we prefer to think in terms of seconds or millions of years, it really doesn't matter. It's irrelevant! Nothing more of hell can be experienced beyond that moment. It is an eternal moment of aloneness. The ultimate result is unchanged, and is truly horrific to those experiencing it. The fury of hell's torment is therefore fully revealed in the closing moments of time.

Having said this, I must also note that a case may be made (as Ross suggests) for the possibility that the degree of torment and terror may well be more severe for some than it is for others. Jesus intimated this in Mark 12:40, and Matthew reminds us, "Do not fear those who kill the body but cannot kill the soul; rather fear him who can destroy both body and soul in hell" (Matt. 10:28).

The writer of Matthew, penning the words of Jesus, does not make use of the future tense, but of the aorist infinitive as a completed act of destruction. *Apolesai* is very clear, *(to destroy utterly-The Analytical Greek Lexicon)*. Coupled with its association to the condition of hell, it is even more terrifying.

The cruelest irony in the question of evil's existence is that, in the end, there is no one there to reward its adherents for their faithfulness to its perversions. It is easy to understand why ancient Hebrew writers of the Old Testament could only grasp at a description of Sheol. As we have noted, Hell is an awareness of the aloneness of nothingness.

Clearly, God's offer is one of life or no life at all. "God gave us eternal life, and this life is in his Son. He who has the Son has life; he who has not the Son has not life" (1 John 5:11-12). This verse doesn't speak of some Gnostic spiritualization of the separation of body from spirit. It speaks of the wholeness of life as God originally intended: of body, soul, and spirit living in the fullness of God's essential relationships of new creation.

God is the Lord of life, and the offer of eternal life must be seen completely in terms of response to His generous invitation.

In the resurrection of Jesus we see that once more, and through our personal connection to Christ's resurrection, we have been gifted with a Life that never ends. Having said all of this, for me the physical resurrection of Jesus Christ is still a mystery. Let's see why. It may well be a mystery for everyone.

CHAPTER 12

The Mystery of Time Restored

*I*n Adam, all die! (1 Cor. 15:22). That's the terrifying reality of life *unless* some sort of God-given miracle takes place. When you're dead, you're really dead. The Light of the world had been plunged into the terrifying abyss of darkness and oblivion.

But it was the dawn of first day; a miraculous moment of new creation was about to occur. The fact of His death is a matter of historical record. It is found, not simply in the gospels, but also, for example, in a commentary of the writings of the Jewish historian, Josephus.[1]

> Serious historical research, however, now indicates strongly that the gospels do indeed belong to the genre "biography." Of course they are not just that. They contain a good deal besides. But they are not less than biographies . . . There is now, therefore, no reason to say that the writers of the gospels, and their very first readers did not expect them to be taken as accounts of things that actually happened within history . . . We must not forget that the gospels would have appeared to a first-century reader, whether Jewish or non-Jewish, as books

which told the story of an actual person who had lived and died in recent memory.[2]

There is a resurrection! Surely, that would have to be a miracle. The idea of natural immortality had proven to be a noble but vain hope. Resurrection would have to be a supernatural accomplishment from above. And God did it where the man, Christ Jesus, could not. In death, He suffered the same separation from life as did every other person. He identified with death itself!

At some undetermined but chronological moment, and at some specific point in the kairos of first-day Light, God breathed into the lifeless body of Jesus. The man, Christ Jesus, was born again to lead a regenerate community into the unfettered joys of God's eternal life. It was to be in a new order of existence and purpose. In signature to all humanity, the real Adam was reborn. He was gifted as the first fruits from the dead into the everlasting time of new creation (Rev. 21:5).

Jesus is "the first fruits of those who have died, For since death came through a human being, the resurrection of the dead has also come through a human being" (1 Cor. 15:20-21).

In other words, no one before Jesus had been resurrected to the fullness of the new order of life. No one! The great cloud of witnesses (Heb. 12:1) were incorporated into Christ's Easter moment. The Easter moment incorporates all time into its victory.

For one more momentous time, the passive verb is used in relation to the finished work of Christ. God had said, "Let there be" in Genesis, and now God spoke again into the chaos of humanity's darkness. "Christ died for our sins in accordance with the scriptures, and *that he was buried*, and *that he was raised* on the third day in accordance with the scriptures, and that he appeared to Cephas, then to the twelve. Then he appeared to more than five hundred brothers and sisters at one time, most of whom are still alive" (1 Cor. 15:3-6; italics mine).

But Some Did Not Believe

Before we go on, we must consider, as the verse above indicates, that the resurrection of Jesus is not a spiritual symbol, but *a fact of history.*

Paul, who had Luke as a companion, may have considered Peter (Cephas) the first to see Jesus. However, it is more likely that his list of those who had seen the resurrected Christ was not so much chronologically exact as one that lent social credence to the fact of the resurrection (1 Cor. 15:5-8). The names he gives are those holding a recognizable place of leadership in the Christian community.

In Matthew's gospel, the women see Him first. Both in the longer ending of Mark, and also in John's gospel, it is specifically Mary Magdalene. In Luke's gospel it is difficult to discern who was first. Was it Peter, or was it the two who walked with Jesus on the road to Emmaus? (Paul may well have given social credence to Peter when he refers to him as the first to see Jesus. 1Cor.15:5. Nevertheless, that account, in terms of the Bible being one story, is significant.

When attempting to reveal who He was, Jesus chose to quote Old Testament Scripture. "Then beginning with Moses and all the prophets, he interpreted to them the things about himself in all the scriptures" (Luke 24:27). And later, to the eleven, ""These are my words that I spoke to you while I was still with you—that everything written about me in the law of Moses, the prophets, and the psalms must be fulfilled. Then he opened their minds to understand the scriptures'" (Luke 24:44-45).

When we read the resurrection narratives in the gospels, it is apparent that there may be ambiguity, maybe even discrepancy, concerning some of the precise details. Paul mentions the Twelve, representing the apostolic leadership and including Matthias (Acts 1:20-26). He knew, quite clearly, that Judas had not been present to witness the event. It was an exciting, surprising, and traumatic time in the experience of all those mentioned.

Maybe the differences in written traditions may be compared with the testimony of witnesses to a car accident. Individually, as they recall the event, they do it from the perspective in which they saw the accident. Some of the details may not always dovetail exactly. However, listeners to the stories would not doubt that the witnesses all agreed an accident had occurred.

One thing is empirically clear in the Bible: all those who bore witness to the fact that they had seen the risen Christ spoke objectively of the experience as a tangible and historical event.

To them, the event was not a matter of subjective experience, or an allegory, or a poem. The gospel accounts are real-life descriptions of what they saw. Any fuzziness in details may have produced skeptics, but the witnesses were convinced of the historical reality of the event. After all, they had witnessed a real-life miracle. No wonder, in human terms, it was difficult to swallow.

There are presently Christian skeptics who want to interpret the resurrection in ways that are something less than empirical or miraculous. In John Hick's controversial book, *The Myth of God Incarnate*, a number of contributors add weight to this "Thomas" approach. For example, Michael Goulder offers a psychological explanation. For him, Christ's disciples had a desperate need to keep the memory of Jesus alive, even if it meant having to conjure up an apparition that became part of a future tradition.[3]

At most, this type of psychological explanation would last for no longer than one generation. Realistically, if the subsequent experience of the risen Christ was not in common with those who claimed to have seen Him, the story would not even last for one generation. Goulder should try explaining how people of the twenty-first century can speak of sometimes surprising but always transforming encounters with the real Person of Jesus! How would Goulder explain how these contemporary experiences of Jesus square up so easily with those of apostolic age believers?

Others join the fray by suggesting that the meaning of resurrection is confined to some sort of spiritualized interpretation, such as the triumph of good over evil, or the valor of self-sacrifice, or the victory of hope over despair. It is quite probable that the writer of 2 Timothy was concerned that a Gnostic approach to interpretation was already being considered by some (2:17-18). This mode of interpretation is becoming, unfortunately, too common in many of our contemporary mainline churches. It really wouldn't make any difference for those people if someone claimed to have dug up the bones of Jesus from the sands of the Middle East.

Apart from Judas, all of Christ's apostles had a firsthand experience of their resurrected Lord. Symbolic, spiritual language or a psychological apparition had absolutely no meaning for them. In fact they would have laughed at such natural suggestions. Together, the apostles had the same experience of the resurrected Christ. Their relationship with Jesus had been restored through the reality of an historical event, and it is a fact to which they were all witness. This historical reality was very important for them; they realized that the very heart of their message could never be simply about the good words, teaching, and deeds of a dead carpenter.

The teachings of Jesus may live on throughout the ages, but they cannot bring with them a personal and intimate relationship with the resurrected Christ. Such a present-day and personal encounter with Jesus occurs on the pathway of faith.

In order to be numbered among the chosen foundations of the new Israel, the twelfth person who replaced Judas had to have "accompanied us during all the time that the Lord Jesus went in and out among us, beginning from the baptism of John until the day he was taken from us—one of these must become a witness with us to his resurrection" (Acts 1:21-22).

The resurrection is clearly at the very center and heart of the Christian gospel. That's because the experience of the Christian story is embodied in a Person much more than in an "ism," such as Buddhism, or even Christianity.

No wonder Paul said "If Christ has not been raised, your faith is futile and you are still in your sins" (1 Cor. 15:17).

The reality of faith is that, for nearly two thousand years, those Christians who know God, in terms of a personal relationship, have experienced the intimacy of numerous encounters with the risen Christ. For example, we may observe from the call of Abraham (Gen. 12:1-9) that the way of the faith walk, in which God sets the goal and the agenda, is a complete reversal of the normal and natural way of experiencing its knowledge.

Here we see that the normal process is one in which knowledge precedes faith. The truth of Christian experience is the very opposite:

faith precedes knowledge. The apostle Paul wrote, "For I know the one in whom I have put my trust" (2 Tim. 1:12). It's all about relationships!

Apart from subjective experience, empirical data is also of the utmost importance. The wholeness of the resurrected body is the most important sign in vindicating the sovereignty of God's purposes for a restored creation. It is the one, tangible sign of the bridge between the old order, leading to death, and the new, which is a guarantee of eternal life for all those in Christ.

From the very moment of Christ's resurrection, the miracle of new creation became the inheritance of a newborn community. The observance of that unique, new-creation body is the most astounding and miraculous sign that has ever happened.

In Christ, a reversal of the curse in Eden has taken place. It is in this sign, lauded for two thousand years, that the entire Christian community has rejoiced in the hope of death's reversal. God's purposes do not reside in the vague hope of natural immortality, but His sovereign miracle of resurrection. It is in this historical sign we all possess the hope that, five minutes after we die, we are already in the fullness of a newly created order for humanity. Christ has paved the way. Achieved from above, the newborn community falls behind Christ, the first fruit of new creation.

A miraculous, *physical* resurrection is, indeed, the *only* hope there is. Without it, there isn't a story. A miracle from above was absolutely necessary to make the one story credible.

With deference to those who are indifferent concerning the body of Jesus, I nevertheless state categorically that *it is absolutely necessary for the world to be granted this one physical sign of resurrection.* And this body must be the living, physical body of Jesus Christ, the real Adam and first fruits of those who have died.

If the physical resurrection of Jesus were not a reality, then there couldn't have been a resurrection at all. When Christ was raised, the *whole* of His humanity was restored. Only God could do that. And He did!

The promise of never-ending life was fully signed and restored in the real Adam. It is precisely for this reason Paul noted, "If there is no resurrection of the dead, then Christ has not been raised; and if Christ has not been raised, then our proclamation has been in vain and your faith has been in vain. We are even found to be misrepresenting God" (1 Cor. 15:13-15).

Enough of this! It all seems a far cry from the heart desire of Paul, "that I may know him and the power of his resurrection" (Phil. 3:10).

Resurrection and Ascension Are One Moment

"When he ascended on high he made captivity itself a captive" (Eph. 4:8).

The ascension, itself an integral part of the resurrection moment, speaks of the hope of all those in Christ following in the train of His triumph to the new Eden. We may say that the ascension includes the moment of being caught up with Jesus in the train of His victory. In other words, for all who are engaged in consciousness with Christ, the Light of the world, and for those, "who are alive, who are left" (1 Thess. 4:17), they shall be caught up in that procession, with Jesus leading the way to Zion.

What we see here is the absolute necessity of equating the meaning of Christ's ascension with the entire picture of Christ's resurrection. The victory of Christ's resurrection and ascension speak of the victory of God's restoration.

It all sounds very well, but is there any biblical evidence that people once dead are now alive? What I am going to suggest may be a little perplexing. Aren't we all somewhat restricted by the parameters of our four-dimensional ways of thinking?

What I am proposing, in very positive terms, is that, in the nature of God, the continuing procession that Jesus leads to Zion consists of all the saints of old who responded to their moments of Light, and of all those who are yet to receive the Light and Life of the world. In this sense, past and future are in God's eternal present. I'm convinced that there are several very powerful images in the New Testament that bear out this thinking.

The writer to the Hebrews wrestles with the meaning of restoration for those who have walked by faith (chapters 11-12). In reading this account, we may glean some theological sense of the strange passage in Matthew that speaks of bodies rising to enter the holy city (Matt. 27:52-53). Peter also attempts to describe the restoration of those from the past (1 Pet. 3:19-20). The major difference in Peter is not that Christ's redemption cannot reach back to the past, but that, indeed, Christ's invitation is also extended to those who have ever longed after God. Peter sees Christ's finished work extending to all people of all time.

But it must be made perfectly clear that the invitation for all is given *in the context of time*, and not in some afterlife of natural immortality.

With a modern view of time's restoration, there is no biblical precedent for a belief in purgatory or for some further, universalist opportunity. What we learn from New Testament thinking is that judgment takes place within the context of time for all peoples from all ages (John 3:18).

For example, the writer to the Hebrews really does invite us to examine questions concerning the theological and scientific meaning of time. He invites us to join with an awesome community of saints in worship. We are told that, through the finished work of Christ, our worship is presently in communion with live saints of all ages. In chapter 11, the writer mentions some of the great saints who have trusted God in faith, not by sight. Then he goes on to tell us that they worship the God they formerly trusted, *now*! (Heb. 12:1). The writer makes use of two participles, and in the present tense. Together, they translate to mean, "we are having around us."

Clearly, the ancients of faith are *now* in this present condition, but only in connection with the perfection and completion of Christ's finished work. The Beatitudes may also be understood in this light (Matt. 5:48). The ancient saints are not waiting in a grave for a future moment of resurrection.

"Therefore, since we *are* surrounded by so great a cloud of witnesses . . . looking to Jesus the pioneer and perfecter of our faith, who for the sake of the joy that was set before him endured the cross, disregarding its shame, and *has* taken his seat at the right hand of the throne of God" (Heb. 12:1-2; italics mine).

Of course, the question must be asked, "Where is it that the saints of old are now worshipping God?" In 1957, the American physicist Hugh

Everett may have attempted to answer such a question with his original quantum physics thesis of parallel universes. The correct answer may well be even more complex. But it is clearly associated with God's almighty power to control the awesome mysteries of time. Obviously, if all time has been restored through the resurrection of Christ from the dead, then God *has* completed His work of restoration. He *has* furnished all believers with a *place* in the fullness of new creation. In the miracle and mystery of time's restoration, the newly recreated saints of old are in the new creation, *now*!

The writer is informing us that this "cloud of witnesses," meaning Old Testament saints, had died in faith, not having received the benefit of God's promises. Yet they had seen these promises from a distance (Heb. 11:13). In fact, they could not possibly receive the fullness of what God's promises meant apart from the finished work of Christ.

The apostle Peter offers this magnificent summary: "By his great mercy he has given us a new birth into a living hope through the resurrection of Jesus Christ from the dead" (1 Pet. 1:3). To Peter and the writer to the Hebrews, Jesus Christ, in the fullness of His humanity, though totally dead, was raised to new life by God. He is, therefore, the first human being to be born again. Christ is perfectly reborn in reversal of the calamity of Eden.

Only the One who is the first fruits from the dead could lead the procession of death into the realms of new life (John 11:2; 1 Cor. 15:20; Heb. 12:2). He had to die and be raised in faith in order to invite people of all time into the procession and power of God's miraculous work of resurrection.

"Yet all these, though they were commended for their faith, did not receive what was promised, since God had provided *something better* so that they would not, *apart from us*, be made perfect" (Heb. 11:39-40; italics mine).

Why could they not receive this grace, apart from the context in which the writer speaks?

When the scrolls of the Bible were written, the separation of chapters didn't exist. So the writer of Hebrews simply continues his thoughts from chapter 11 into chapter 12 and connects them with the conjunction "therefore" in 12:1. What was *promised*, which they did not receive in their day, were the benefits of eternal kingdom life that were gained by the finished work of Jesus. Just because they had not lived in the chronological time frame of Jesus (or after, as is also the case with us today) did not mean that they were not able to receive the fruit of His finished work.

There had to be a first fruits of the dead, One who is, therefore, the Pioneer and Perfecter of faith. The writer says that Jesus completed His work at His ascension, which is evidenced by His being seated at the right hand of God, and is therefore efficacious for all time. All that the ancient saints had hoped for was now possible through Christ's finished work and through God in raising Him from the dead. The passage then speaks of the writer's generation by saying that, apart from us, meaning those who had witnessed and entered into the benefits of Christ's completed work, those saints of old could not enter into glory.

The resurrection of Jesus from natural death is the most significant line of demarcation throughout all time. This line truly affects all people of all ages. As signs of kingdom righteousness, Enoch and Elijah were translated into the new order of eternal life, and were incorporated into Christ's first fruits work. There are no more translations to heaven recorded in the Bible once the finished work of Christ was completed in the death, resurrection, and ascension of His humanity. Indeed, there could not be any more of these occurrences after Christ's resurrection. Any claims in this regard would necessitate a diminishing, or an abolishing, of the power of Christ's resurrection.

An assumption into heaven is claimed by some for Mary, the mother of Jesus. But it has no biblical or historical justification. About six hundred years later, it is also claimed that Mohammed had an experience of bodily assumption into heaven. Any subsequent claims to assumption of the physical body must entail some lack of understanding of the completeness of the resurrection story. All of life beyond this is by incorporation into Christ's resurrection. Even Mary, who admitted her need of a Savior (Luke 1:47), could not have life of the new order apart from incorporation into Christ's resurrection. There is no need for so-called assumptions once we are in Christ and in the power of His resurrection (John 11:25-26).

The book of Hebrews speaks of a multitude of historical saints worshipping God, not sometime in the future, but *now!* As the psalmist reminds us, dead people cannot praise the Lord (Ps. 6:5). The cloud of witnesses are saints of old who presently exist in the power of Christ's perfect and finished work. They *are* living in the eternity of the new order, *now*. It is not that they *will be* raised—future-tense verbs are not used—but that they *are* raised with Christ, who is the first fruits from the dead. They *are* witness to His victory, *now!* They join with the thief on the cross and with all who reign with Christ in the consummated paradise of resurrection's eternal moment.

Jesus Taught It

Jesus taught that the resurrection means we may enter into life that never ends when it is connected to His risen life. That is because Jesus *is* the resurrection and the life. Life is now abundant with Him in the kingdom of God. Plainly, that is the reason why His disciples didn't speak much of an empty tomb, but of a risen Lord. For them, the resurrection signaled an end of death.

Speaking to Martha, in connection to the death of Lazarus, Jesus declared, "I am the resurrection and the life. Those who believe in me, even though they die, will live, and everyone who lives and believes in me will never die" (John 11:25-26).

It would seem to be a contradiction that people will never die even though, like Lazarus, they had died. But here, Jesus is speaking of a situation in which the *conscious presence of relationship with God* never ends for those living in resurrection power. Jesus also spoke of ancient saints in a similar manner: "Your ancestor Abraham rejoiced that he would see my day; he saw it and was glad" (John 8:56).

Speaking to Sadducees in the context of resurrection, Jesus quoted a passage referring to all the patriarchs in the same way: "I am the God of Abraham, the God of Isaac, and the God of Jacob. He is God not of the dead, but the living" (Mark 12:26-27).

And when some of the Sadducees spoke as if they believed in the resurrection, Jesus replied, "I tell you, anyone who hears my word and believes him who sent me *has* eternal life, and does not come under judgment, but has passed from death to life . . . the hour is coming, *and is now here*, when the dead will hear the voice of the Son of God, and those who hear will live" (John 5:24-25; italics mine).

Jesus is speaking of the *now*, or hour, in terms of His own finished work that was upon Him. It will be in the context of His finished work that those dying in time are able to hear His voice of invitation to eternal life.

In the much-celebrated passage where Jesus speaks of the destiny of those who believe, He goes on to say, "Those who believe in him are not condemned; but those who do not believe are condemned already, because they have not believed in the name of the only Son of God" (John 3:18).

We must also remember that there were two real people talking with Jesus on the Mount of Transfiguration. Moses and Elijah, through the sovereignty of God's involvement in time, are connected to the finished work of Christ. As the completed work of Jesus Christ reaches through time to the Old Testament saints, so God makes it possible for Moses and Elijah to meet with Jesus on the Mount of Transfiguration. They were not ghosts talking to a live man. As real human beings, they faded in comparison to the light of Jesus. Nevertheless, they were signs of life connected to Jesus.

Paul Believed It

We should consider that Paul, raised as a Pharisee, sometimes communicated the meaning of resurrection, particularly to Pharisees, in terms they understood, and as he had learned at the feet of Gamaliel (Acts 22:3). In his defense to the Roman governor Felix and Ananias the high priest, Paul said, "I have a hope in God, a hope that they themselves also accept, that there will be a resurrection of both the righteous and the unrighteous" (Acts 24:15). Here, Paul refers to a "day" of resurrection in the same way the term is used in Genesis 1. It is our moment, at death, when all are accountable to God. (Rom.14:12)

There is no contradiction of the case presented. Paul's statement may well be consistent with the approach we have previously considered. This moment is also the horrendously eternal occasion when some realize that they will be forever separated from the life of continued existence. And this moment is surely consistent with that mentioned by Jesus, "where there will be weeping and gnashing of teeth." (Matt.25:30) However, it doesn't seem that Paul possesses a sense of ambiguity concerning those outside of Christ. Maybe we can clarify this problem in the light of resurrection implications.

It is true that the Pharisees believed in a literal resurrection of a dead body. This event applied to all people, both the just and the unjust. We see this exclusively chronological view again in the Book of Revelation, chapter 20. Before the judgment seat of God, some will be raised to go to heaven, while others will be raised for a destiny in hell. However, in both those cases, resurrection is definitely connected to judgment. The apocalyptic writer speaks of this latter destiny as the "second death." (Rev.20:14) This is a view literally interpreted by some who need to see resurrection in chronological terms rather than in terms of the wholeness of the judgment picture of resurrection (Rev. 20:15).

Viewed in the light of restoration through Christ's resurrection, a chronological time sequence involving a literal second death would be difficult to reconcile with John's gospel. Maybe this is one reason why some scholars believe it was a different John who wrote the Book of Revelation. Possibly, we may relate this first death of the Christian in the light of Paul's teaching in Romans 6:4: "Therefore we have been buried with him by baptism into death, so that, just as Christ was raised from the dead by the glory of the Father, so we too might walk in newness of life."

There is no doubt that those who experience the life-giving power of Christ's resurrection would certainly testify to a death of the "old self." Again, we must see this imagery in Revelation in the light of the entire broad picture of the Easter moment. Here, death, resurrection, and judgment are all included. As we have seen already, this language problem may be resolved when we understand that death, resurrection, and accountability takes place for all in Christ, within the context of receding consciousness.

People from all ages are held to account for the stewardship of their lives.

As we have seen, the great cloud of witnesses and all saints of the past experience the resurrected Christ at the final moment of receding consciousness. Individually, they all meet the resurrected Christ, because He is not circumscribed by the limitations of chronological events. God sees every moment in His life of eternal nowness.

In the light of other things Paul says, we may well see that the resurrection perspectives he holds have moved far beyond those he learned in his Pharisaic training. Paul's major apologetic for his defense is his complete assurance in the reality, experience, and meaning of the resurrection. It is literally the miracle of being raised to new life with a new body. This is a point that would make quick inroads with some of his Jewish listeners.

A deeper explanation, in those volatile circumstances, may have raised unnecessary complications. In contexts where he addresses Christians in particular, we see that Paul is more ready to deal with the question of the restored time of the new order, precisely because of his belief in the end of death (Rom. 8:38-39). We must remember that Paul had a real and life-changing encounter with the resurrected Christ, the Light of new creation. This was the Light that caused the self-sufficient Paul to be reduced to blindness. It would seem that his view on time is really dominated by this encounter.

On the one hand, he appears to speak of suspended time (Acts 26:5-6; 1 Cor. 15:52) or a falling asleep until there is a resurrection of the body. But here we must caution that the phrase "we shall not all fall asleep" (1 Cor. 15:51) is used in the King James and the Revised Standard versions. However, in later translations using earlier manuscripts, including the NRSV, a much different interpretation is expressed: "we will not all die." (And this thought is thoroughly consistent with the teaching of Jesus in John 11:25).

Here, it is highly possible that Paul is also thinking of the imminent return of Christ. However, some will most certainly die; and it is in this context that he speaks of "eternal destruction" (2 Thess. 1:9). On the other hand, we must recognize that Paul cannot possibly imagine a time, *not any time*, when he may be separated from his beloved Jesus. Just look at a few examples:

> For I am convinced that neither *death*, nor life . . . nor things present, nor things to come, nor anything else in all creation, will be able to separate us from the love of God in Christ Jesus our Lord. (Rom. 8:38-39; italics mine)

> For to me, living is Christ and dying is gain . . . my desire is to depart and be with Christ, for that is far better, but to remain in the flesh is more necessary for you. (Phil. 1:21, 23-24)

Paul expresses an almost identical thought when writing to the Corinthian church (2 Cor. 5:6-8).

How Could Nicodemus Be Born Again?

Nicodemus was obviously a very religious man; in fact, he also appears to have been a member of the highest court in Judaism (John 3:1). Subsequently, he became a follower of Jesus (John 7:50; 19:39). He was a man who had received the visible signs of the Old Covenant and, amid the pluralistic society of his day, was one of an entire community that believed exclusively in the one and only God. The encounter with Jesus that John describes took place long before Christ's death and resurrection, so the question of how Nicodemus could be born again is a good one.

His conversation with Jesus didn't begin with a question, but a word of affirmation: "Rabbi, we know that you are a teacher come from God; for no one can do these signs that you do apart from the presence of God" (John 3:2).

Jesus could be addressed (unofficially, in terms of the Jewish institution) as a rabbi, because He had met two Hebrew requirements:

He was more than thirty years old, and had garnered twelve male disciples. This constituted the basis for a formal synagogue.

Jesus took the opportunity to respond with a puzzling reply: "Very truly, I tell you, no one can see the kingdom of God without being born from above . . . no one can enter the kingdom of God without being born of water and Spirit" (John 3:3, 5). And again, "You must be born from above" (John 3:7).

No wonder Nicodemus was puzzled. He couldn't imagine putting his mother through all that again, not at his age! This language is perfectly consistent with that used by John in his prologue. So first of all, what about that language?

The Greek word that is sometimes legitimately translated "born again" (NIV) is *anothen*. Its prefix *ano*—means "above." In its qualifying form, the word literally means "from above." The consistency of this meaning is heralded when John says, "Who were born, not of blood, or the will of the flesh, or of the will of man, but of God" (John 1:13).

In other words, there is absolutely no natural way that a person is able to enter the kingdom of God. Here comes that word "miracle" again.

As God miraculously raised Jesus to new life, so we have to be born again from above. In other words, Nicodemus was to undergo a re-creation, and God alone, as on the day of Christ's resurrection, would accomplish this work.

Basil the Great put it this way: "First, it is necessary that the old way of life be terminated, and this is impossible unless a man is born again, as the Lord has said. Regeneration, as its very name reveals, is a beginning of a second life."[4]

In some parts of the early church in Africa, the baptismal liturgy included words such as "I kill you." These words were spoken at the point when a person was submerged beneath the water (see 2 Cor. 5:17; Rom. 6:4-5). But now we are back to resurrection again. Jesus, Paul, and Peter connect resurrection with the born from above experience: "By his great mercy he has given us a new birth into a living hope through the resurrection of Jesus Christ from the dead" (1 Pet. 1:3). Continuing in chapter 3:21 Peter says: "And baptism, which this prefigured, now saves you-as an appeal to God for a good conscience, through the resurrection of Jesus Christ."

Does this mean that Nicodemus would be saved to new life by virtue of *his* decision for Christ? Most definitely not! Nicodemus would be rescued by God's decision for him, and by God's actions upon him (1 John 4:19; Rev. 17:8). The decision of Nicodemus is simply *a response* to God's call, "Where are you?"

Response is the human act. Maybe Nicodemus's responsive part can be described by the word "conversion." It speaks of a decision to face, or to move in, another direction (Matt. 18:3). In God's eternal nowness, that call for salvation is heard by God in all times and ages. Somewhere in the responsive process, God acts from above by the work of the Holy Spirit.

The term "born from above" is therefore related to time and God's part in it. Remember, Jesus had not even died at this point! Wouldn't it be wrong, and even lacking in integrity, if Jesus had impressed upon Nicodemus the need to be born from above when it wasn't yet possible? Christ had not died, and the resurrection had not yet taken place. Poor old Nicodemus could have turned up his toes the very next week. For some, that would have meant Nicodemus would have to wait until Pentecost before he could be "born from above." Now, we are back to the meaning of the resurrection moment and the restoration of time.

The saints of old are a cloud of witnesses who worship the Lord, *now*. Similarly, as Christ embraced and restored all time into Himself, then Nicodemus—along with Old Testament saints of Hebrews 11—represents all those who will and have responded to Christ's gracious invitation. The power of the resurrection extends to all people from all time. Jesus does not suffer, die, and then is raised again, and again, and again. It has all been done, *once and for all*. All of those who respond, who are or will be in Christ, are restored to an eternal relationship with God through the miracle of resurrection. They enter into one moment of resurrection.

Jesus was raised *anothen*, as an act of God from above. The new birth is achieved in and through Jesus, who is the first fruits of new creation.

It is through the work of the real Adam that humanity may live forever. Time in eternity has been restored through the resurrection of Jesus.

Those saints of old in Hebrews 11 most certainly know it. That's just what God intended in the first place; and, in the foreknowledge (*proegno*, Rom. 8:29) of God, the offer is extended in the context of time to all people in all times and in all places.

With What Kind of Body Do They Come?

"But each in his own order: Christ the first fruits, then at his coming those who belong to Christ . . . But someone will ask, 'How are the dead raised? With what kind of body do they come?'" (1 Cor. 15:23, 35).

The plural verb *erchontai* is in the present tense and may literally be translated, "With what kind of body are they coming?"

If we believe that Paul's dominant theology is one negating any separation from Christ, then we must conclude that his use of the adjectival term "spiritual body" is a description of the body that is equipped for life in the new creation.

As a pastor, I was sometimes asked about burial procedures. Some people are concerned that their loved ones will not be resurrected if their bodies are cremated. Others wonder how God can piece together all the ashes of a loved one that have been scattered over the ocean.

Is this really a problem? We remember that death, judgment, resurrection, and ascension are all a part of the Easter moment. In this light, the disposition of the mortal body does not affect the reality of resurrection power.

Those in Christ have passed from death to life (1 John 3:14). They do not meet Christ to enter judgment but to give accountability. In other words, their judgment takes place while they still possess a mortal body, i.e., in the context of time, in the past or receding moments of self-awareness. Their clothing of the *spiritual body* has taken place even before a funeral service has occurred. The connection between the old order and the new has already taken place in this Easter moment. Of course, like a sensitive service of Holy Communion, the bodily elements remaining are treated with reverence and dignity.

Paul said that he wanted to show his Corinthian Christians a mystery. The fact is, we really are faced with a mystery here, and the mystery both reveals and conceals our answers when we think of the resurrected body of Jesus and of our own.

Vladimir Lossky, the late, great Orthodox theologian, may offer some useful insight by connecting the meaning of resurrection with its completion in Christ's ascension. "In his resurrection there was, to be sure, the transition from a physical body to a spiritual body, but in the ascension there was not a further transition into a wholly spiritual entity."[5]

Further, Lossky says, "At His ascension, first of all He unites the earth to the heavenly spheres, that is to the sensible heaven; then He penetrates into the empyrean, passes through the angelic hierarchies and unites the spiritual heaven, the world of mind with the sensible world. Finally, like a new cosmic Adam He presents to the Father the totality of the universe restored to unity in Him, by uniting the created to the uncreated."[6]

Lossky may not have delineated the nature of this spiritual body, but he clearly identifies it as one, like that of the priestly Adam, who, in innocence, united earth to heaven. And so does Jesus, our real Adam.

Nevertheless, we really are confronted with an awesome sense of mystery. How do we glean a seamless answer from the post-resurrection appearances of Christ? The Book of Revelation speaks of Jesus reigning with His saints in a real place: it is the earth of the new order (Rev. 5:10; 11:15). But how *earthly* is this place, and in what way is it connected to the old?

Mystery in the Resurrected Body of Jesus

If we appreciate something of the mysterious body of Christ, we may know more about the body intended for a new humanity in the new creation. Indeed, we may also know more of the nature of the new creation itself. There is no doubt that the resurrection appearances elicit many questions. Interestingly, in the post-resurrection appearances, particularly recorded in John and Luke, Jesus, the resurrected man, speaks exclusively in terms of His humanity, not His incarnate divinity.

For example, in John 20:17, the disciples are now "brothers," and God is equally their God and Father as well as His.

Nevertheless, it really takes us into the realms of mystery when we attempt to define the *spiritual* nature of Christ's resurrected humanity. As a matter of fact, when we look at the written accounts, there appear to be contradictions in the way Christ's appearances are written. Probably they are paradoxical accounts that are deliberately presented so that we are forced to realize there is something mysterious about the body that is restored to new creation.

Apart from this body of Jesus, we've never seen anything like it before except briefly in the innocent Adam of Eden. In this body, we may be receiving a glimpse of what was once naturally real for the original Adam.

That is why we are left with just a partial understanding. We may appreciate both the mystery and the paradox in the following post-resurrection appearances:

+ *She knew Him, but she didn't recognize Him.* Mary Magdalene thought that Jesus was a gardener until He called her by name (John 20:15-17).
+ *There were grave clothes, but no body* (John 20:6-7). The one commonly understood sign of *death* had disappeared.
+ *Don't touch me!* (John 20:17). *Touch me!* (Luke 24:39). Surely, this paradox presents us with a mystery of the body we have yet to experience. Thomas recognized Him by the marks of crucifixion. We recognize Him by the glory of His resurrection.
+ *The doors were locked, but he got in anyway* (John 20:19). Will this possibility exist for a new humanity not restricted to four-dimensional activity? Does this seemingly unnatural encounter remind us of natural abilities once possessed by Adam?
+ *He knew where to find fish* (John 21:5-6). What does it really mean to have such an intimate knowledge of creation? This Jesus is really well connected with nature.

+ *They walked for two hours with Him, and still didn't recognize Him, until . . .* (Luke 24:30-31). The mystery of the Word becomes intimate at a banqueting table.

+ *After a whole week, Thomas could still feel the nail prints in Christ's hands* (John 20:27). The marks on this bruised and battered body of Jesus, which Thomas recognized, revealed Him to be the One distinctively displaying the connection with the body of new creation.

+ *Does a ghost have flesh and bones like I have?* (Luke 24:39). This *spiritual body* is knowable to the physical senses.

+ *Do ghosts eat fish?* (Luke 24:42-43; Acts 10:39-41). We shall eat familiar food (such as God provided in the original, physical creation) in a new creation only partially understood.

+ *The disciples knew Him, but they didn't recognize Him* (John 21:12). There is something intriguingly exciting about all of our new creation relationships: Puzzlingly, and excitingly new, but somehow and mysteriously connected to the old. "These are my words that I spoke to you while I was still with you" (Luke 24:44). The resurrected Jesus shared memories they understood.

+ *Do spirits drink wine in the new creation?* This Jesus was not a spirit re-incarnated in another form. The resurrected Jesus really was, in whole, *a man of memory!* (Luke 24:44). He brought into the new order common memories of life in the old order. The disciples who followed Him were able to recall, together, incidents to which Jesus related. "For I tell you that from now on I will not drink of the fruit of the vine until the kingdom of God comes" (Luke 22:18).

This emerging principle will be important when we consider the substantial relationship between the creation of the old order with that of the new.

In all the appearances of Jesus, the disciples were witness to the mystery of the spiritual body of new creation. But somehow, this body had recognizable elements of the physical, and also of the personality characteristics they had known in their beloved Jesus. This resurrected body was very puzzling. A spiritually physical body didn't seem to be subject to physical laws—at least, not as the disciples understood them.

For Hugh Ross, the idea that a body can walk through a door isn't a scientific improbability at all anymore. Other skeptics don't accept this account of His appearing. It's not because of an inability to think scientifically, but an inability to think with a *contemporary* knowledge of science.

Our knowledge of scientific laws has dramatically changed. Hugh Ross speaks of the multidimensional possibilities of the risen Christ. "Though it is impossible for three-dimensional physical objects to pass through the three-dimensional physical barriers without one or the other being damaged, Jesus would have no problem doing this in His extra dimensions. Six spatial dimensions would be adequate."[7]

Was this truly the real Adam with an inbreathed ability to manage the earth in Spirit-filled work of stewardship? Paul speaks of the body fitted for new creation in this manner: "It is sown a physical body, it is raised a spiritual body" (1 Cor. 15:44). He is simply trying to say that there is a mysterious *connection* between the person who is raised with Christ and the body that is fitted for new creation.

When connected to the risen Christ, there is no annihilation of the individual personality. In this spiritual body, the person will be recognizable to others possessing bodies fitted for new creation. As in the beginning, this is truly a *spiritual body*, consisting of body, soul, and spirit. It is equipped for life in a material world of the new order. These awesome teaching signs continued until the time of Christ's ascension (Acts 1:3). Whatever the new creation is, this *spiritual body* will work in it very well.

The Victory of God's Purposes

The cry of the Lover to the beloved (i.e., to those who have received Christ) is no longer, "Where are you?" for they have been found by Him. The Prodigal Israel has been invited to return to the forefront of their inheritance. But this intimacy of restored relationships has not come cheaply to anyone who now lives in it. We all have a little idea of what it cost God; we all know that this restoration came by His initiative, not ours. "We love because He first loved us" (1 John 4:19). We chose Him because He first decided for us.

The fact is that we cannot experience the life of Easter Sunday without a death of Good Friday.

> To rise again we must die. Die to our hampering selfishness, die to our fears, die to everything which makes the world so narrow, so cold, so poor, so cruel. Die so that our souls may live, may rejoice, may discover the spring of life. If we do this then the resurrection of Christ will have come down to us also. But without the death on the Cross there is no resurrection, the resurrection which is joy, the joy of life recovered, the joy of life that no one can take away from us anymore.[8]

The way of Christ's suffering will be always *before* those who love Him, but the hope of eternal life will always be *in* them (Rom. 6:4-5).

That which is being shouted from the rooftops is at the very heart and soul of the gospel. It is an affirmation that resurrection reality is the beacon sign: God has miraculously restored all creation's essential relationships.

This joyous affirmation is heralded by saints of all ages because of the intimate power of Christ's resurrection. The community of the resurrection is called to be an authentic sign of kingdom life that God instituted in Eden. But how may this be humanly possible?

CHAPTER 13

Pentecost: An Awesome Moment of Light

To this point, we have looked primarily at the "why" concerning the purpose of the church. To a greater extent, we now consider the "how." The story of both may be encapsulated in this way:

1. The church is called to be a model community or sign of Eden, the life and character of God's kingdom presented to the world.
2. By the power of the Holy Spirit, in proclamation and service, the church is called to invite the world to participate in the life of a restored Eden.

As It Was in the Beginning

The beginning was literally an awesome moment of light! We cannot think of the full meaning of restoration unless we include Pentecost in the restoration-Easter-ascension moment. As in the beginning, the power to accomplish the apostolic mandate, given to God's community in Eden, was restored. The anointed community of God was playing out the story of Eden's restoration while inviting the world to participate in its joyous dance.

The real Adam, the King of creation, sends His new Israel, His royal priesthood, on a universal mission. All the steps of the dance are in place and the pace has been quickened. The members of the church are active witnesses and sign-bearers of what they have seen and heard of the good news (Acts 1:8-11). They wait in Jerusalem, not fully understanding why.

And then the *fire came down!* It must have reminded them of Moses by the fire of the burning bush. Inexhaustible flames of glorious light seemed to touch their heads *without consuming them* (Ex. 3:2; Acts 2:1-4) There were about 120 gathered together, and all of them were filled with the Holy Spirit. They would never be the same again. The light of God's fire was an ancient sign that the awesome power of God's presence would illuminate them in all times of darkness (Ex. 13:21).

Surely, Pentecost was included in the Easter moment of light's restoration of new order! Irenaeus, one of the early church fathers, describes the scene in this way: "This Spirit . . . also, as St. Luke says, descended on the day of Pentecost upon the disciples after the Lord's ascension having power to admit all nations to the entrance of life and to the opening of the new covenant from whence also, with one accord in all languages, they uttered praise to God, the Spirit bringing distant tribes to unity, and offering to the Father the first-fruits of all nations."[1]

Luke, in his letter of Acts, records that signs and wonders of the kingdom (as Jesus had promised, John 14:12) were first manifested through the twelve apostles, the foundational community of the new Israel (Rev. 21:14). Paul considered signs and wonders a required proof of a person's apostolic credentials (2 Cor. 12:12). After all, the new community of Israel was intended to be a sign of what was once possible in Eden.

Peter spoke in the power of the Word, and with a new boldness about the power of Christ's resurrection (Acts 2:22-24). He and John pronounced healing in the name of Jesus, and a man, crippled from birth, walked for the first time (Acts 3:8). "Many signs and wonders were done through the apostles" (Acts 5:12).

There is a passage at the end of Mark's gospel, sometimes strange, which is often disputed concerning its time of origin. (Mark 16:9-20) For example, it speaks of picking up snakes, they will not die of poisoning, but also includes healings, speaking in tongues, and casting out demons.

Without including this passage, nevertheless the inescapable bond between Word and wonders is very dominant throughout the New Testament. By God's grace, the entire post-resurrection community had entered into a charismatic dimension signifying the recovery of creation's essentials. Besides the Spirit-enabling of signs and wonders, in character these spiritual realities also encompassed the masculine, feminine, the intuitive, the intellectual, and the sensual dimensions once experienced by the Adam community. With equal integrity, the non-cognitive experience moved naturally alongside the rational. They were experiencing signs of what it means to be truly human.

Great numbers of men and women were added to the Lord (Acts 5:12, 14). Peter had never preached like this before. The anointing touch of the Spirit created in this community the deep longing to bring the lost into the apostolic heart of God.

In Luke's gospel and in the Book of Acts, Luke does not acknowledge a hierarchy of apostolic leadership. Luke tended to emphasize equally that Peter *and* Paul (along with others) were enabled by the Holy Spirit to perform extraordinary signs and wonders. Certainly, Paul never attributed anyone as having ecclesial authority over him. (2Cor.12:11) Obviously, it was the twelve apostles who, as a community, were honored as the authority and deposit of New Testament revelation. However, apart from them, there was no honoring of a hierarchy in the apostolic era. There was an honoring of leadership, given by spiritual anointing.

The many works of the Spirit included healings, the raising of the dead, and the freeing of people from demonic bondage. Luke records that both Peter and Paul were miraculously freed from imprisonment. The ministry of the anointed servant (Isa. 61; Luke 4) was surely at work in the entire community of a new Israel.

Was the Anointing for Ordinary People?

I have often wondered why Ananias, who very fearfully laid hands upon Paul, is hardly ever acknowledged in historic churches (though one of these churches is the Church of St. Ananias in Damascus). For his obedience to God, the Holy Spirit was imparted to Paul, who also regained his sight. More importantly, Ananias received a word of knowledge that

Paul was to be the apostle to the Gentiles (Acts 9:15-19). Today, in most of the orthodox world, Ananias is thought of as a "layman." Most certainly, neither Peter nor Paul demonstrated signs of accepting the subsequent hierarchical thinking of the post-apostolic church.

The apostles were not the sole believers able to do mighty works through the Spirit (Acts 6:8). However, the Twelve, representing the continuation of Israel, were the focus of relational authority and unity for a new and empowered community of Israel. The faith and praxis of the Christian community would be apostolic and would come under the authority of the community of the Twelve. But the *work* of the Great Commission wasn't given to the Twelve exclusively. Philip is also a good example (Acts 8:6-8). The question is: What place did the Twelve hold in the implementation of the commission?

In John's gospel, on the first day, when the resurrected Jesus appeared to His apostles (probably privately, and to ten of them, John 20:22,24) He breathed upon them, and they received apostolic authority. We're back to creation again. It was an apostolic community given apostolic authority. This community had (a) accompanied Jesus from the time of His baptism to His ascension; and (b) become a witness to Christ's resurrection (Acts 1:22). As such, they each had firsthand experience of Christ's entire teaching and had seen how it played out in the signs of the kingdom. Truly, Jesus alone had represented the remnant of the community in Eden as it performed its apostolic purposes.

On the Mountain of Ascension, those assembled with Jesus as representatives of new Israel's tribes received their own commission in the context of the whole community of Israel. It was once given to Adam and was now repeated in the continued community of Abraham. There were only eleven of the apostles present for the Great Commission. A replacement for Judas had not yet been found. We were introduced to the Twelve, even though only eleven then existed as a community in authority. (Mark 16:14) It was eleven that actually heard the Great Commission from the lips of Jesus.

> All authority in heaven and earth has been given to me.
> Go therefore and make disciples of all nations, baptizing

them in the name of the Father and of the Son and of the
Holy Spirit, and teaching them to obey everything that
I have commanded you. (Matt. 28:19-20)

Go into all the world and proclaim the good news to the
whole creation. (Mark 16:15)

To those who have problems with the authenticity of those texts,
there has to be a recognition that all the synoptic writers are in agreement
with Christ's purpose.

Repentance and forgiveness of sins is to be proclaimed in
his name to all nations, beginning from Jerusalem. You
are witnesses of these things. (Luke 24:47-48)

You will be my witnesses in Jerusalem, in all Judea and
Samaria, and to the ends of the earth. (Acts 1:8)

And, in the high-priestly prayer of Jesus, John records, "I ask not
only on their behalf, but also on behalf of those who will believe in me
through their word . . . so that the world may believe that you have sent
me" (John 17:20-21).

God's purposes were to be heralded and signed by them, as a
community, for the sake of the entire world. Jerusalem, the Old Testament
replacement symbol for Eden, provides the starting point of this universal
mission. A new community is born in Jerusalem, formed and enabled
by the Holy Spirit. Although one was absent (Judas) nevertheless, the
authority for this commission was given to the entire community of the
Twelve.

Authority of the Apostolic Community

According to John's gospel, ten received the inbreathed gift of
authority for mission. The text, *on them*, certainly refers to a community;
the method, individually or collectively, is less clear.

Neither Thomas nor Judas was in the room on that occasion. However,
both Thomas and the later-appointed Matthias were numbered among
the Twelve as having been included with those of apostolic authority.

There is no biblical evidence to show that Jesus breathed upon Thomas on a separate occasion, and it certainly did not happen to Matthias. But had the conveyance of *individual* authority been of significance, John would most certainly have made record of it. Otherwise, there would have been no need for the casting of lots (Acts 1:26). The Ascension took place before Matthias was included into the Twelve (Acts 1:20-26). Apart from Pentecost, which he shared with the 120, there is no record of distinct inbreathing of authority upon Matthias. If individual authority had been bestowed upon Peter, surely this was the time for it to happen, and for it to have been recorded.

This occasion again raises serious questions concerning communal or individual authority. For example, after Jesus had breathed on the ten, He said, "Receive the Holy Spirit. If you forgive the sins of any, they are forgiven them, if you retain the sins of any, they are retained" (John 20:22-23). In other words, no individual apostle had authority to forgive or retain sins that were not agreed upon by the whole apostolic leadership. One apostle could not offer or prevent reconciliation unless it was agreeable to the apostolic leadership and, therefore, consistent with the teaching and ministry of Jesus.

We see in the example of James, the leader (*archon*, as described by Eusebius) of the church in Jerusalem, that he would not have been empowered to pronounce reconciliation to certain believers in Antioch (who insisted that circumcision was a rite of membership) if it had not been agreed upon by the other apostles and elders in council (see Acts 15:13-28). We also note that the *deacons and other so-called laypeople in Jerusalem played no part in this theological decision.* In other words, the authority to grant reconciliation came through the community teachings of those who had witnessed the ministry and teaching of Jesus. James, in his letter to Antioch, makes it clear that he is speaking on behalf of the apostles and elders who had just debated the issue (Acts 15:28).

This is an unimpeachable principle employed when the apostle Paul instructs Titus to appoint *"elders"* in certain towns of Crete. Of course, in its diversity, the Pauline order was not exactly the same as that in Jerusalem. Paul urges that these *"bishops"* should possess an affirmed list of leadership characteristics, including "sound doctrine" (Titus

1:5-9) These elders were receiving their authority from a person who had received it from Paul. In other words, the corpus of Christ's teaching still had firsthand authority in the community of believers.

A democratic vote (mentioned in Acts 15) on what was acceptable was clearly *not* acceptable. The opinion of one of the apostles was not acceptable if it was not in agreement with the entire corpus of apostolic experience in the apostolic community.

In defiance of this principle, we note that many contemporary bishops of seemingly orthodox churches act in defiance to this process. Claiming to have individual apostolic authority, some bishops do not act in this collegial way when they promote issues as interpreted by the contemporary culture. Indeed, some bishops in my own part of the church have told me how they have fruitlessly opposed the majority of the house of bishops, who desire to change theology by the method of democracy.

Can such individuals really claim to have individual and apostolic authority? When the apostle Paul recites his apostolic credentials to the Corinthian church (2 Cor. 12:12), how many of our modern bishops, elected democratically, would meet this criteria? How many of them exercise charismatic gifting, such as was demonstrated by Peter and Paul?

On one occasion, the apostle Peter exercised a remarkable charismatic gift of knowledge and discernment when he challenged Ananias and Sapphira concerning their stewardship of financial gifts. Peter, discerning their deceit, also correctly predicted that each of them would die quickly. They did! (Acts 5:1-11).

This would sound like a very strange story had we not realized that Peter and other apostles had witnessed the remarkable and life-changing encounter that Jesus had with the woman at the well (John 4:1-30). Jesus exercised gifts of knowledge and discernment that resulted in changed lives and the advancement of kingdom life beyond that of the Jews. The apostles were connected, as a community with authority, to the teaching and ministry of Jesus—not by ritual or title, but by apostolic anointing.

The authority of the *episkopos* (bishop, overseer, watchman) today lies, not in the opinion or institutional position of the individual, but in the anointed community of apostolic leadership, appointed and affirmed by a Spirit-guided community.

Of course, that assumes that the people who do the affirming were put in positions of decision-making because of their personal relationships to Jesus, their prayer-soaked lives, and their ability to move and act in the power of the Spirit.

Deliberately, we arrived at that point at St. James's Church, Calgary, when no one could be in a leadership position unless they had taken a "Growing in Christ" course. This was a course that I had designed precisely for that purpose. What an amazing difference!

We see, then, on the awesome day of Pentecost, the *power* to carry out the apostolic commission was given to all 120 assembled believers, and subsequently to all others baptized in the power of the Spirit. The authority for this universal commission was in the keeping of the apostolic leadership (Luke 24:33,49; Acts 1:8, 15; 2:1-4; see also Jude 3).

Consistent with this view, the early church most certainly honored the apostolic authority of the Twelve. Indeed, Luke notes that Peter, with the eleven, stood before some Jewish pilgrims to make the first Christian apology (Acts 2:14).

Clearly, the power of an apostolic ministry resided in the *entire community* and was historically focused in the commissioned authority of the Twelve. Individual authority, apart from the power and purpose of the entire community, was meaningless. Not to mention the fact that such individual authority contradicted the very nature of the Trinity. There is no subordination of Persons in the Godhead.

This is not to say that the early church did not believe in or honor leadership within the community. Most certainly they did, but that is not the same as institutionalism determining order and faith by setting up a particular individual in monarchical authority (1 Pet. 5:1-5; Heb. 13:7).

Others Ministered Under Pentecostal Authority

Stephen, the first martyr, was not an apostle but did great wonders and signs among the people (Acts 6:8). Equally, Philip cast out unclean spirits, healed the sick, and was miraculously transported to Azotus (Acts

8:6-8, 39-40). Was this strange occurrence of unrestricted movement yet another sign of what had once been possible in Eden?

Philip made it a family affair. He had four daughters who had affirmed, prophetic ministries (Acts 21:9). In this vein, Peter's quotation of Joel also includes women in the priesthood of proclamation (Acts 2:17-18; Joel 2:28-29). Truly, greater things were being done, not necessarily in quality, but in the quantity of a new community voluntarily dispersed on its apostolic mission (John 14:12).

It is as if we are hearing God say, "I breathed into you once (the first Adam community), then I breathed into you again (the real Adam—and the individual Head of the new community, Eph. 1:22, 4:15), and now I am also breathing into you (the community of the real Adam)."

Here, we see a major difference between the old and new covenants. In the old, we see *individuals* such as Moses, Joshua, Elijah, and Elisha, obviously scattered over the pages of Israel's history, but nevertheless demonstrating signs and wonders of the kingdom. In the new covenant, in this awesome moment of light, we see an entire real-Adam community baptized into kingdom power. A real-Adam community was reborn to reflect God's ability and purpose into His creation.

The newly empowered community of Jesus was enabled to continue, for all time, in demonstrating signs of kingdom restoration. No wonder Peter and John (but also Paul) made certain that well-meaning and repentant converts had received more than an outward sign of the intent to live a repentant life (e.g., the baptism of John in Acts 19:3). They were all called to be disciples and to live it out in the anointed power of the Spirit. At times, there were apostles who encountered people baptized with water for repentance, but not for the Holy Spirit's power (John 3:5; Acts 19:1-6). Through the laying on of hands and effective discipleship, these apostles ensured that Word-centered converts also became Spirit-filled disciples (Acts 8:14-16).

However, this was not the only way the Spirit came upon believers (see Acts 10:44-47). The time had come for an anointed community to demonstrate once more what God had intended for His creation.

The purpose of this community would be the same as it had been in the very beginning: to bring the world into harmonious relationship with

God, others, and creation, and also live a life in communal signature of God's kingdom.

Baptism in the Spirit

In order to provide a framework for questions surrounding Spirit-baptism, it is important that a thread be woven into the context of Pentecost.

First, we realize that absolutely nothing of gospel importance occurred unless the Jewish story embraced it, for "salvation is of the Jews" (John 4:22; Rom. 1:16). "Surely the Lord does nothing without revealing his secret to his servants the prophets" (Amos 3:6).

Although Peter's ministry was primarily to the Jews, while that of Paul was to the Gentiles (Gal. 2:7), Peter is the first to declare the invitation to the Gentiles. Formerly, they had not been included in the lineage of the sons of God. Of course, Paul recognized that all, in Christ, were children of Abraham (Gal. 3:14, 29). So was revived the universal commission that God intended at the beginning. It was from Jerusalem, the symbolic Eden, that Peter was the first to sign the community's apostolic ministry. When he was at his best, King Solomon saw the holy city, with its temple, in the same way (1 Kings 8:43). We should not be surprised to read that Jesus gave a universal commission that was to begin from Jerusalem (Acts 1:8). We remember that the Holy City stood on Mount Moriah.

Second, through Peter, it was to a celebrating Jewish community that the promise of the event was first delivered (Acts 2: 1-4). Pentecost was originally a Jewish celebration of the first wheat harvest. It was called the Feast of Weeks. This was a time when, *as in Eden*, the Jewish people acted out their priesthood by offering to God the fruits of creation.

This feast was not one of blood sacrifice. Pentecost could not have occurred until Christ had finished His work of reconciliation on Calvary. Nor could it have occurred until Jesus had rightfully taken His sole position of authority—that is, the ascension (John 16:7).

In Christian terms, the Feast of Weeks was further transformed to be the offering of an entire community made innocent. Little did Moses know that, by instituting a celebration of the Feast of Weeks, he was presenting a sign of a future priesthood focused in Jesus, offering the fruit of a restored creation.

Third, the gospel invitation proclaimed by Jewish apostles at Pentecost received its first and positive response from Jewish people (Acts 2:41, 47). As a nation, the Jews did not accept Jesus as their Messiah. But it was from the Jews that God would offer His blessing upon people of all nations (Gen. 12:3;17:4-5; John 4:22).

When speaking to his Jewish listeners on that astounding day of Pentecost, Peter reminded his ethnic kin that God's apostolic purpose was their own inheritance and purpose, as it was prophesied in Joel 2:28-32. From the stock of David, Jesus was, in person, their long-expected Lord and Messiah (Acts 2:36).

Fourth, a new community of Eden's line was empowered by the Spirit for the express purpose of proclaiming and signing kingdom life to the ends of the earth (Acts 1:8). It was a baptism of fire for a universal proclamation.

Fifth, the first thing that the Holy Spirit did was to send the anointed believers out into the street—to marketplace ministry (Acts 2:5-6). They were primarily an apostolic community: sent out. The mandate that had been given to Jesus (Luke 4:18-19) was to be exercised primarily in marketplace proclamation and in signal demonstration of life in the Spirit. The year of Jubilee had arrived.

Sixth, upon receiving the gift of the Holy Spirit, the immediate reaction of the followers of Jesus was to praise God (Acts 2:11). We are back to a community of worship, prior to Babel. Particularly after the destruction of Jerusalem, Eden is now the New Jerusalem that is above and free (Gal. 4:30).

The Holy Spirit touched the 120 who were gathered together; they spoke their praises in about sixteen known languages. Pilgrims to Jerusalem easily recognized the languages that were spoken. The implication is very clear: Pentecost is a signal demonstration of a universal unity that reverses the catastrophe of Babel. "In our own languages we hear them speaking about God's deeds of power" (Acts 2:8-12).

Seventh, we see that all of the believers now spoke in personal and intimate terms of the risen Lord. Through signs and wonders of the Spirit, they were given the power to witness in the medium of proclamation and service (Acts 2:24-26). They weren't thanking God for the memory of a dead rabbi. Jesus was alive, and they knew it. Jesus' words proved to be correct; the Spirit's work is to glorify Him (John 16:13).

Essential Relationships Restored

The first principle of essential relationships, relationship with God, was now possible because the real Adam had risen and ascended in power. Through His finished offering at Calvary, He had secured humanity's reconciliation with God (2 Cor. 5:17-19).

The second principle, relationships in community, were possible because the living Lord, through the Spirit, had become the focus and source of their communal relationship (John 14:18). They had entered into the family of the sons and daughters of God (1 John 1:7). "...this is the moment of the new creation, when a new humanity comes into being through the finished work of the second Adam."[2]

The third principle, relationship with creation, was that He resided in their hearts in a power and character originally given to the community of Eden. The community was charged with the authority and also the power to bring creation into harmonious relationship with God. They were now supernaturally commissioned to be a royal priesthood, specifically a priesthood of creation. As a communal priesthood, they were called to bring a groaning and rebellious creation into loving worship with their Source of being (Rom. 8:21).

The fourth principle, relationship with oneself, was possible since they were now filled with the harmonious Light of His presence. If the inner harmony of individual salvation had not been secured, then harmony with the community would also be in peril. Inner harmony had been gifted to them as a result of their concord with God, with others, and with creation. By the power of the Holy Spirit, the devolution of their Eden humanness was being influenced into the glory of their Jesus anointing. They were poised to live in signature of kingdom relationships intended for the entire world.

Catholic, Charismatic, and Evangelical—Do We Choose?

I suggest as strongly as possible that, in order for us to understand the meaning of baptism in the Spirit, we think of it in the context described in the aforementioned seven points about Pentecost. Today's evangelical thinker may describe "baptism in Spirit" in the way in which David Edwards summarizes John Stott's thinking. Stott is concerned about charismatic-minded people, who speak of something extra in baptismal initiation. He grants that growth in Christ is important—in other words, sanctification—but not a so-called "baptism of the Spirit" subsequent to conversion.

To Edwards, Stott seems eager simply to "associate the gift of the Spirit with conversion to Christ."[3] Personally, I think John Stott did move beyond that particular position. Clearly on the day of Pentecost, Peter expected the respondents to grow in the fullness of life in the Spirit.

The charismatic-minded undoubtedly acknowledge the Spirit's activity in the conversion process. However, he or she may try to avoid dispute by speaking of a further experience as a *process*, a process of the release of the Spirit's intent. Or, in Orthodox terminology, a further releasing of what was already promised at baptism. That release is often associated with speaking in tongues or delivering prophetic utterances (see Acts 19:6). Some consider it to be the entering into a sanctification of a *second blessing*, which is often associated with the ministry of John Wesley.[4]

Some Pentecostal churches state that certain signs are the evidence of a baptism with the Holy Spirit. For example, at a Pentecostal rally in the Albert Hall, London, I once heard a lady testify that she now knew God loved her because she had just been gifted with speaking in tongues. Hopefully, amid a thunderous applause, some of the leaders at that conference were a little embarrassed. Personally, although I appreciate that the respondents to Paul in Ephesus spoke in tongues and prophesied, (Acts 19:6) I find it very difficult to apply it as sole proof of the Spirit's anointing. I have had the great privilege of laying hands on many people who did speak in tongues, but many didn't. There are nine charismatic gifts listed by Paul (1Cor.12:4-10). I know people who are anointed in the Spirit and who exercise some of these gifts yet don't speak in tongues. So the exercise of this one particular gift should never be construed as proof that God loves us. The cross of Christ is more than enough proof that God loves us! However, I do understand why Paul wishes all of his Corinthian readers to speak in tongues. (1Cor.14:5) We'll get to that later.

What we may observe here is that, in general, quite regardless of when conversion takes place, the charismatic-minded tend to emphasize *power*, while evangelicals tend toward conversion as the beginning of sanctification. However, the character *and* the power of the Real Adam are both necessary elements in the entire meaning of Spirit-baptism. Both the character, i.e., the nature of God, seen especially in Jesus (Gal. 5:22-23), and the power of God (Luke 24:49) are essential marks of the inbreathing of the Spirit.

Conversion is not simply a matter of inner spirituality, but the beginning of an outward-focused heart. Nevertheless, leaning on one particular side of that term is a gross understatement of all that it means, at least when we associate it with God's original intent for creation. We must cease our choosing among individual gospel elements. It is very difficult to be poised on a one-legged stool when it has been designed to function with three!

We are called to be catholic (i.e., of one body and faith), charismatic, *and* evangelical. Why is that? Because the gospel is catholic, charismatic, and evangelical. The implication of this statement is that we are all called to grow in all these gospel essentials. We have never arrived in that process.

A Baptism of the Spirit's Power and Character

We have seen that a true experience of Easter means we have a personal encounter with the risen Christ. Jesus told His disciples, "I am coming to you." (John 14:18), and they clearly knew the intimacy and power of His presence. What this means is not only the *power*, but the *character* of Jesus grows in those who receive Him. The power of the Spirit and the graces of the Spirit are growing in us as the Spirit is forming Christ in us (Gal. 4:19).

Therefore, it isn't necessary to choose what Scriptures should be most important to us. "These texts and others like them lead us to one conclusion: any model of the fullness of the Spirit which attempts to make empowering for service relatively separate from growth in holiness inevitably collides with the truth represented in the very title *Holy Spirit*."[5]

An expansion of this principle may be found in historic Orthodoxy. Although he makes no direct allusion to signs and wonders, or to an inward empowering for mission, the fourth-century St. Cyril of Jerusalem speaks of baptism this way: "Great indeed is the baptism which is offered you. It is a ransom to captives; the remission of offences; the death of sin; the regeneration of the soul; the garment of light; the holy seal indissoluble; the chariot to heaven; the luxury of paradise; a procuring of the kingdom; the gift of adoption."[6]

We must see that the fullness of life in the Spirit has to be *appropriated*. The promise of the Paraclete needs no further additions.

When introducing a work of the esteemed tenth-century St. Symeon, George Maloney tells us that Symeon is solidly rooted in the theology of the Fathers, "but he accentuates with great originality the need of a stage in the Christian life beyond the mere Baptism of water, which Symeon calls the Baptism in the Holy Spirit."[7] The stage of which Maloney speaks is not of a further theological enlightenment, but the *growing appropriation* of all that is promised in the born-again, Spirit-filled life that is promised in baptism.

"The important question that Symeon poses to his readers is not whether the Holy Spirit lives within them, but whether they are consciously aware of this presence within them through a continued penitential conversion."[8] Straddling the tension between apophatic and kataphatic experience, it would seem that Symeon would not be impressed by a person simply waving a baptismal certificate of Christian authenticity. What would a certificate mean if the person knew little of a substantive difference in his or her life? What would that mean if the person could not testify to an intense, mystical intimacy with Christ enabled by a heart-desire to live in obedience to Him?

What we observe here is that, whether a person is baptized as a professing adult or a babe in arms, to be baptized into Christ means that, in the initiative of God, we are called to and promised the ability to embrace, to sign, and, through the community of Christ, to grow as heirs of the complete story of restoration—a story originally embraced in the dance of Eden.

The Word-Spirit Dynamic

A prophet, when hired and dependent upon the ecclesiastical institution, becomes an oxymoron. He or she cannot speak prophetically within the restricted parameters and permission of institutional order. This is particularly apparent once the ecclesiastical institution has become negligent in its primary apostolic purpose.

Surely, those church leaders who believe in and experience spiritual gifting can never be satisfied with the limitations of life restricted to natural abilities. They can never be satisfied with what is, only with what is possible through the new wine of the Spirit. They rejoice in the fact that God holds the future in His hands, and that profoundly affects the way they do things today.

Sometimes the character of the crowd or the fickle moods of the culture take on too much importance in an institution. Consequently, the community appears to be unrecognizable, not being distinctively different from the culture itself. The embarrassing prophetic voice becomes a lonely voice in the wilderness (see Jer. 23:9-11, 18, 22). This has profound implications for an empowered community of believers.

An old gospel hymn echoes the naive sentiment, "This world is not my home, I'm just a passin' through." Clearly, in our present context, this world *is* our home; it's our Canaan, but it is not our paradise of the new order. In Christ, we are called to win it for God. The challenging authority of the Word, demonstrated by the enormous, life-changing power of the Spirit, is the normal way through which the Church exercises its invitational plea.

Whenever the Word speaks, things begin to happen.

We remember that in the written word of God, particularly when spoken by Jesus, we see the nature of God best revealed. "Whoever has seen me has seen the Father" (John 14:9). It is in accord with God's revealed nature and command that contemporary issues should be addressed. On the other hand, the Scriptures should be a major corrective for flakey expressions of charismatic life.

The written word stands as a beacon illuminating the real nature and character of the kingdom of God (Ps. 119:105), However, it is also vitally important to move beyond current revisionist theories of Scripture in order that the power in the one story is not lost.

If we still have to move beyond such theories, then allow me, very quickly, to identify those characteristics. They go something like this:

- The Bible, according to many revisionists, simply records God's revelation in the context of a particular culture at a specific time. Therefore, we may ignore or reinterpret it in the light of current cultural principles. In reality, as we have previously suggested, the fundamentals of present revisionists have *not kept pace* with the implications of contemporary scientific and philosophical progress. Consequently, this position has produced chaplains to the culture rather than prophets within it.

- It's a bigger story now. But for them, it is a much smaller story. The fact is: Most revisionists persist in answering Enlightenment-type questions in an Enlightenment manner. Yet, the Enlightenment manner has now been superseded by the global Tele-Communication age, and is therefore now a much bigger story. For them, the awesome breadth of the one story is brought down to a reductionist experience of the much-diminished testimony of individual commentators, or indeed, in relativistic style, of any individual in his own time or context. The exclusivity of Jesus is denied. "There are many ways to God," they say. So the power of individual opinion overrides any claim of absolutes.

- They tend to view the Bible through the lens of their own cultural perceptions, rather than evaluating changing cultural conditions through the filters of biblical revelation. Theology, like social Darwinism, evolves through the culture, and so their God also *changes* with the varieties of evolving culture.

+ Revisionists are generally disinterested in debating on the basis of biblical revelation. "It was probably true for them, in their day," they say. And so informed biblical substance, often through the reinterpretation of biblical symbols of language, has exited the arena of much Christian debate. Very often, substance gives way to sentimentality. Easily manipulated democracy becomes the vehicle to truth, as historical and biblical authority is ignored.

We should note again, as strongly as is possible, that Jesus presented a gospel that was catholic (one universal body and one apostolic faith), charismatic (focused in the giving of the Spirit's character and power), and evangelical (an outward focus in restoring others to essential relationships through Christ).

Unfortunately, for a variety of reasons, and because of particular denominational priorities, church communities and individuals have tended to emphasize one aspect over another. We can't do that! Jesus didn't, nor should His community.

In the Word-Spirit dynamic, we must caution against those who display an imbalanced perspective regarding the Bible. There are those who hold tenaciously to the authority of Word while playing down the extraordinary power of the Spirit. The reverse may also occur.

Signs and wonders of the Spirit give contemporary and practical credibility to God's spoken revelation (Heb. 2:2-4; Acts 14:3). Jesus emphasized both Word and Spirit with equal force.

Personal Encounters with Historical Experience

I hope you will forgive me for injecting into this section a short, personal, and admittedly subjective contribution concerning life in the Spirit. Ever since my conversion to Christ, in Liverpool at the age of eighteen, I have found myself mixing with evangelical people. They were very helpful in embracing and encouraging me. My language, style, and intellectual curiosity became one with theirs.

By the time I entered theological college, the Lord had graciously used me to bring hundreds of people to Christ. A singular-focused message of conversion almost consumed my entire ministry. However, after about eight years of ordination and ministry in Canada, there came a point when I realized that there just had to be more than the persuasion of a well-constructed apologetic.

I was tired of delving further and further into the meaning of justification by faith. In groups, some who would effuse their own intellect while hiding themselves behind their Bibles disturbed me. As persons in need, they rarely raised their heads. I was also disturbed to hear people talk of the dynamic things that Jesus *once did*, but not see those things happening in my own ministry. In some situations I was tired of struggling with the propositional and often forensic approach to sanctification while missing out on the joy and power of New Testament apostolicity. I was a boring and bored Christian. There just had to be more.

I knew one or two people who had spoken of charismatic experience, but I never took them seriously. I felt I had a theological and intellectual perspective that didn't need that sort of thing. It was in the midst of this arrogance and conceit that *God surprised me*. He baptized me in the Spirit. It was wonderful, and I couldn't explain it. But I knew there was something different in me. Once again, someone had to explain to me what I was experiencing.

A few days later, around midnight, I was called to a Calgary hospital on an emergency. The next thing I knew was that God was using me in the miraculous healing of Bill. I had visited him many times in the hospital. However, after about five years of heart problems, the hospital doctor had called for his family in order to warn them of his impending death. "I don't expect him to last through the night," said his doctor.

Fully respecting that view, after praying with Bill's family, I entered the intensive care unit. Strangely, as soon as I entered the room, I had an unusual confidence that Bill was going to live. On my part, I had never prayed before with such *expectancy and thanksgiving*. It was a very short prayer, but I sensed that I was praying with an authority I had not previously known. I couldn't think of anything else to say, so

I said, "Amen." I left the semiconscious Bill to sleep. In four days he was discharged, and three months later he was dancing—something he hadn't done for more than five years!

That was just the beginning of a ministry laced with God's surprises. There are many times when I don't appear to see answers to prayer. Indeed, I have known patients to die ten minutes after I prayed for them. (Not many families call for me in such a crisis). However, I do know that when I stop praying in faith, I rarely find myself surprised by God. And that's how I define the meaning of being charismatic: someone who is given the ability to be surprised by God.

I remember when, on one occasion, I was ministering in a CSI church in Madras, South India. At the end of the service, the pastor was first in line for prayer—a line that extended right into the street. He simply asked for prayers for his back problem.

About three months later, he wrote to me in Calgary. He was very excited to tell me of the happenings subsequent to my departure. I didn't know it, but this pastor had suffered from spinal problems for many years and had been due for surgery two days after I prayed for him. First of all, he told me that his pain had immediately disappeared; then, after his insistence on further X-rays, doctors discovered there was now nothing wrong with his spine. He went on to speak of many other miracles that had occurred that day.

Quite possibly, in his excitement, there may have been exaggeration, but I do know that I have prayed about back problems many times in Western situations with results that are rarely so dramatic.

On another occasion, I was speaking at a service in Trivandrum, Kerala. After the service, I was ministering in prayer to those in need. Through a translator, one man had come with a very common request. "Please pray for a blessing on me and my family."

I was about to do so when, suddenly, I felt restrained. I faced the translator and said, "Please tell this man that God cannot bless him." He looked back at me with amazement etched all over his face. "Tell him that God cannot bless him for two reasons." I didn't have the foggiest idea what the first reason would be! I had to speak by shutting off my usual cognitive processes and trusting that God would reveal both reasons.

"Tell him that God cannot bless him because he is playing games with God. He is refusing to be a priest to his wife and family. The second reason is that this man has a violent temper and takes out his anger on his wife and children." I was amazed! I didn't know what to do. I was embarrassed. Fancy saying such an awful thing to someone I had never even met.

A little sheepishly, I asked the translator to ask the man if that was correct. I was prepared to apologize. The man ashamedly looked at the ground and told the translator, "That is perfectly correct in both instances." After about ten minutes of discussion, the result was, with tears rolling down his face, he accepted Jesus Christ into his heart. Instead of leaving with an impotent blessing, the man left the church with Jesus. He was determined to begin a new life with his wife and children.

For that occasion, I had experienced a *gift of knowledge*, and realized even more that spiritual gifts are for encouragement, but also, and primarily, for the apostolic purposes of signing the life of Eden.

I use these stories, simply to illustrate the following:

> For the kingdom of God depends not on talk but on power. (1 Cor. 4:20)

> My speech and my proclamation were not with plausible words of wisdom, but with a demonstration of the Spirit and of power, so that your faith might rest not on human wisdom but on the power of God. (1 Cor. 2:4)

By God's grace, I have been extraordinarily privileged to see my ministry transformed in the expectation that God is able to do whatever He wants in me; that is, if I don't get in His way. Along with many others in these days of joy in persecution, I am amazed to witness real signs of the kingdom in our contemporary world. And that, very naturally, gets us back to our apostolic focus.

Interestingly, the writer of Matthew's gospel uses the Greek word *mathaeteusate*, which literally means "be a disciple-maker" (Matt, 28:19-20). This word is an imperative, active, and aorist verb. As we have noted, the aorist tense, particularly when used in the context of a sentence employing present-tense verbs, means that the command is complete. It is sealed. There is no further debate when the Head of the church gives the command.

Coupled with the aorist participle *poreuthentes*, which means "to go," or "going from one place to another," we cannot avoid the charge that the primary task of Christ's community is that of engaging in a universal, apostolic mission. It is non-debatable! It's a command by the Head of the church!

In other words, each community of God's church is commissioned to be in the business of making disciples, wherever they are.

There are many church congregations that know what it means to attract lots of converts to their community but do their leaders know how to equip the membership to make disciples?

I'm afraid this is a serious problem in a great many Western churches. When conducting conferences in the past, these two questions have motivated me to challenge churches about Christ's imperative command:

- In practical terms, how does your own church engage in a continued process of making disciples? (Deut. 7:6, 1 Pet. 2:9; Ex. 18:24-27; Matt. 28:19-20).
- Is the primary, apostolic focus of your church congregation outward, in terms of service and proclamation, or is most of your energy and resources spent for the benefit of church members? (Gen. 1:28; Acts 13:1-3).

Appropriation of Spiritual Gifting

The story of the Prodigal Son is a good example of someone (or the nation of Israel) that returned to a relationship that was *already his*. In the long term, this means a cognitive and willing appropriation upon further appropriation, not a baptism upon baptism. ("One Lord, one faith, one baptism," Eph. 4:5.) The human decision is always a response to the initiative of the power-giving Holy Spirit. Genuine Christian experience is truly sacramental in terms of direction; that is, in the repentant human response to the gracious invitations of the Holy Spirit's actions from above.

Without minimizing the theological significance of the initial Pentecost, the Holy Spirit *continued* to touch the disciples in very special ways (see Acts 4:31). The gathered community was filled with the Holy Spirit *again*.

These situations must always be seen in terms of response to the "more" of what God promises. Likewise, decisions to appeal to the infilling power of Christ are always ongoing. Spirit-motivated decisions to be conformed to the image of Christ are always ongoing (John 16:13-14).

Many people know little of the Spirit's power until they experience emptiness in their own lives. It is at this point of *divine dissatisfaction* that they abandon the futility of self-effort; they risk new possibilities in the Spirit.

Theologies of how much we "possess the Holy Spirit" are really quite ridiculous. The real issue, which becomes a lifelong question, is not so much, "How much do I have of the Holy Spirit?" but "How much does the Holy Spirit have of me?"

Again, it is a *decision of faith* to risk life in the fullness of God's promises. The Holy Spirit, as the motivator and enabler of all such decisions, makes possible all that was promised at Pentecost.

The early church period was characterized by the relation of charismatic gifting with that of function and order (1 Cor. 14:40). In the apostolic period, the church was not very interested in institutional titles. They were more interested in the entire priesthood being gifted by the Spirit for ministries of His choosing (1 Cor. 12:4-11). The closing verses of Acts 2 show the apostles to be in a process of making disciples. It was a deliberate process.

What emerges from this Word-Spirit training is that the royal priesthood becomes *affirmed and authorized* in its individual gifting. Biblical titles of ministry are associated with spiritual gifting. Offices held in the church did not relate to institutional position, but tended to be consistent with spiritual gifting.[9] Ignatius was certainly a prophet-bishop.[10] A little later, Irenaeus (c. AD 180) speaks of gifts in the church that include casting out demons, knowledge, visions, prophecy, healing, and raising the dead.[11] He also wrote of people who "through the Spirit do speak all kinds of languages and bring to light, for the general benefit the hidden things of men and declare the mystery of God."[12]

Some time later, Tertullian, a Latin scholar, challenged a sect called the Marcionites to produce tongue speakers from among them as a test of orthodox experience.[13] However, by the time we get to the fifth century, John Chrysostom, of the Antiochene tradition, admitted personal ignorance of the charismatic gifts listed by Paul (e.g., 1 Cor. 12).[14]

Science has often been in the vanguard of explaining mysteries. This was particularly true in the simpler scientific age of the Enlightenment. However, in the ever-broadening complexity of modern science, there is a new humility in scientific responses. It is not contemporary clergy who are today's priests of mystery, but the scientific community. Nevertheless, in relation to spiritual gifting, we see that the gift of faith provides an avenue on which to tread the road of non-rational experience. It is a way to embrace gifting, which was once normal to the Adam community. Faith and science really are distinct avenues, but each one offers its own integrity and gifting to matters of mystery.

Speaking in Tongues

Most Christians would have little difficulty with spiritual gifts such as those listed by Paul in 1 Corinthians 12. However, speaking in tongues is a problem for many. Again, it is a gift that absolutely requires faith for enabling. The negative reasons are mainly psychological, e.g., intellectual (moving into an area of the non-rational can be petrifying), fear of emotionalism, loss of control, and maybe even theological positions adopted by particular denominations.

Morton Kelsey, a Christian psychologist, describes the phenomenon of tongues as a "supernatural gift of a foreign or non-human language given at the time of the breakthrough of the Holy Spirit into an individual life. Once this experience has been known, one can enter into it at will, and he finds an immediate way of relating to God and the Holy Spirit."[15]

From another perspective, Kallistos Ware, a theologian of the Greek Orthodox church, notes, "When it is genuinely spiritual, 'speaking with tongues' seems to represent an act of 'letting go'—the crucial moment in the breaking down of our sinful self-trust, and its replacement by a willingness to allow God to act within us."[16] Personally, I identify very well with this position. I have found the gift to be very powerful in private prayers of adoration and intercession. But it has also helped to loosen up the worship of congregations in which I have been the pastor.

Many of those who speak in tongues describe it as a *key* that seems to open up a whole variety of charismatic gifting. Possibly it is for this reason that Paul (who spoke in tongues more than all of them—1 Cor. 14:18) wished that all of his Corinthian readers could speak in tongues. (14:5) However, he never did insist that *the evidence* for having received the Spirit was the gift of tongues. Obviously, he didn't want them all to speak in a church gathering at the same time. He made it clear that *gifts of revelation* should be a matter of order (14: 40). And they should be tested (1 Thess. 5:19-21). God is not honored by confusion.

Baptism in the Spirit for All Traditions

Easter, ascension, and Pentecost are mutually interlocking facets of creation's restoration.

It is in this context that the aforementioned seven-point exposition becomes our common focus. Eden has now taken on more dimensions than we first imagined, but nevertheless, from a theological point of view, we are taken right back to the *purposes* of creation.

The tenth-century Symeon sums up baptism with the Spirit in this manner: "The soul through the fire of the Holy Spirit now becomes totally immersed in a conscious way in Jesus Christ. United with Jesus Christ in total conscious surrender of his whole being, the Christian mystic experiences the fire of the Holy Spirit spreading over the human body. Man has returned to the Garden of Eden, integrated in body and soul with God as his center, revealed constantly more and more in the light and fire that is the Holy Spirit of the Father and the Son."[17]

The life of the early church community was so attractive that even priests of the old covenant joined it (Acts 6:7). In a very short time, the community grew from 120 to 3,000, and then was added another 5,000 (Acts 2:41; 4:4). Or, as Cardinal Suenens once put it, "Thus we see beyond any shadow of doubt, how the early Church lived by and expressed its faith in the Holy Spirit."[18]

Not surprisingly, the apostle Paul considered that significant marks of apostolic leadership should be evidenced by demonstrations of signs and wonders of the Spirit (2 Cor. 12:12). But is that it, folks? Was all this intended for an age long gone? Does it mean we shouldn't even look for such signs of the kingdom anymore?

Ongoing Signs in the Community

The early community of believers experienced kingdom life in a number of ways. They are surely the very same ways we may observe emerging in the meta churches of today.

First, the lifestyle of the community changed from that day on. In great measure, the Year of Jubilee had arrived. It was not so much about changed systems, but changed lives that enabled individual and social change. In their way of dealing with one another, they wanted to be a sign of kingdom relationships. With the risen Christ as Lord and focus, they desired to demonstrate to the world signs of Eden restored. They really did care for one another. If anyone was in need, then they could rely on the community for help (Acts 2:45; 4:34; 1 John 3:16-18). This love for one another spilled out. They were not simply a sign of God's justice and righteousness, but longed for it in the life of the world.

Robert Webber tells us of a revival of this broader view of mission and style among what he describes as today's "Younger Evangelicals."[19] Is not this sense of mission consistent with the lifestyle advocated by the writer of 1 John?

Second, they didn't separate a spiritual from a social gospel. In other words, they did not separate spirit from body and soul. The power of the Spirit-filled gospel stretched out to the whole person. We see in people of this mind-set a loving methodology of evangelism. People are met at the point of their greatest and most immediate need. And so we see today that the saving of the soul is more and more accompanied by a passion for justice and righteousness toward the poor and oppressed.

What we observe is an equal concern for John 3:7 (being born again) as there is for Matthew 25:40 ("as you did it to the least of these"). Clearly, the effective outworking of both these emphases required spiritual gifting we see in 1 Cor. 14:12. If this is not a priority of disciple-making today, then we are left with nothing more than a humanistic desire for self-survival, or a spiritualized gospel with little incarnational value.

Third, their apostolic focus was nurtured by practical methods of discipleship. Most of the process of disciple-making did not take place in a classroom, but in real-life situations with their training leaders present. In the West, how much do we see leadership demonstrating what they are teaching? Where this is happening, we can be sure that some sort of classroom evaluation takes place before events of service and also afterward.

They loved to fellowship together, pray together, learn together, worship together, break bread together, work together, and praise God together (Acts 2:42-47). Not surprisingly, the quality of their life attracted a surprisingly large following (Acts 5:12-13). In many countries of the southern globe, the Christian church is also growing at a very fast pace. One Anglican bishop, answering my question on how such rapid growth was occurring in Africa, simply replied, "Through signs and wonders of the Spirit." Admittedly, effective discipleship for leadership has to keep up with the pace of growth over there. They are aware of their own problems of keeping things together in kingdom fashion. But they are far better problems than we have in the West. We are in serious decline.

Fourth, they leaned heavily on making disciples who were consciously dependent upon a need for the anointed power of the Spirit. Where this is happening today, we are likely to observe congregations where a "waiting in Jerusalem"—in other words, where basic courses on training and life in the Holy Spirit are offered—is very important (Luke 24:49). An opportunity is then given for the expectant learner to receive the laying-on of hands. For many contemporary churches, of a meta mind-set, the structures of their affiliations become less important than the discovery of ways in which the kingdom may be served more effectively, and primarily at the local level. This sense of diversity was certainly true of the church in the apostolic age.

The attempt to address the renewal of structure, form, and purpose in mainline churches found some authenticity as far back as the early days of Methodism. John Wesley (1703-91) had enormous difficulty in being acceptable to his Anglican establishment. No doubt the main problem was his challenging the institution about its impotence and stagnation.

He challenged his own denomination about the need for balance of the institution with the evangelistic and charismatic life of its membership. Forced outside of the established structures, he was moved to create new ways of developing effective disciples for the gospel. We learn some very important principles in the Methodist zeal to present an unchanging gospel within new paradigms of a changed methodology.

- A wholehearted acceptance of traditional Christian doctrine coupled with the conviction that such doctrine is useless unless verified in life and experience.
- A strong emphasis on the personal relationship of the believer with Jesus Christ as Lord and Savior.
- An equally strong emphasis on the work of the Holy Spirit.
- A serious attempt to embody life in small groups and with other communities of committed men and women.
- A desire for the proclamation of the gospel to all humanity.
- A concern for material well-being, as well as the spiritual needs of the poor.
- A tendency to bring together laypeople and the ordained in new structures of shared life and ministry.[20]

What was true for Wesley's day is equally true for ours. The form and structures of the church community become secondary to the purposes of the historic and universal community. Jesus had appropriated the character of all that it meant to be the servant of Isaiah 61 (Luke 4:18-19). By the anointed power of the Spirit, the community of Jesus is also enabled to be a servant church. Or, as we have noted from the very beginning of this book, the community of God has an apostolic mandate to be the servant community *for the sake* of the world, but not the servant *of* the world. The world has its own agendas!

The kingdom has not arrived through the church, nor will it. Indeed, the church, in its remaining time, will not win the battle over injustice and suffering. The signature of Eden, sometimes seen through God's ancient community, was renewed on the face of the earth from the day of Pentecost to the present.

Nevertheless, Jesus prophesied that the days of struggle would not continue forever. God has appointed an end. And, in doing so, He warns us of signs that will accompany the end. I think there is a way of looking at these signs in ways that are consistent with the principles God instituted in His creation. Let's take a brief look at the meaning of latter days.

CHAPTER 14

From Latter Days to the New Eden

A Natural End

Creation's principles are restored! The one story of the gospel is magnificently consistent in its procession throughout the chronicles of history.

In the beginning, the glory and the Light of God shone upon a raw creation; it was further crowned in an Adam-Eve community charged with an apostolic mission. In its entirety, it was a mission of kingdom signature that invited people to join the story. A pattern of harmonious relationships was in place in a paradise where all syntheses of relationships had their focus and source in God.

When things went wrong, God did not give up on His purposes or His principles. His purposes are sovereign, even if individuals choose to reject them. The methodology of God is one of total freedom; it is always an invitation to accept or reject participation in His eternal purposes. Clearly, God never compromises His creation principle of freedom of choice. It is at the very heart of His purposes, which, in His Omniscience, are secure. "My purpose shall stand, and I will fulfill my intention" (Isa. 46:10).

We have come a very long way from a creation of which God said, "It is very good," to the commentary of the apostle Paul. He reminds us of the pain of our present creation, which is groaning in travail (Rom. 8:18-23). Jesus went beyond this comment by predicting that *creation will move toward a much-worsened state*. His prediction reminds us of a condition of darkness existing before the Spirit breathed on the embryonic creation. Confusion and disorder appears to reign without check. Jesus is really telling us that the natural consequences, through chronological time, must be *worked out* in the desperate and suicidal course of nature's pain and fury.

What this means in terms of chronological time is that the entire creation continues to experience the pain and consequences of its own impotence and self-centeredness. Kingdom-governed relationships are becoming more and more at odds with creation's actual purposes.

"And this end must not simply be equated with a cosmic catastrophe and the sudden end of human history. What is old, transient, imperfect and evil will indeed be ended: but this end must be understood as ultimate completion and fulfillment."[1] Hans Kung offers a broad and natural view of what this ending may mean. Clearly, we must not lose sight of the fact that the Bible provides striking evidence that the *old order* will most certainly pass away; and so this present order will surely come to a *natural end*.

However, Isaiah had spoken of a chaotic end many hundreds of years before Jesus.

> The earth shall be utterly laid waste and utterly despoiled; for the Lord has spoken this word . . . The earth lies polluted under its inhabitants; for they have transgressed laws, violated the statutes, broken the everlasting covenant. Therefore a curse devours the earth, and its inhabitants suffer for their guilt . . . The earth staggers like a drunkard, it sways like a hut . . . and it falls and will not rise again. On that day the Lord will punish the host of heaven, in heaven, and on earth the kings of the earth. (Isaiah 24:3, 5, 6, 20-21)

Amid such chaos, we are to see that lights of the inbreathed community are being rejected by a world inevitably plunging itself into nihilistic darkness. There are many who venture to predict the actual time when God allows the chaos to fulfill its natural course. Jesus isn't counted among the foretellers of that day: "But about that day and hour no one knows, neither the angels of heaven, nor the Son, but only the Father" (Matt. 24:36).

However, Jesus does predict the *signs* of the end. They are consistent with the breakdown of essential relationships from early moments of creation. When inbreathed, humanity appeared as stewards of creation's godly harmony. God described the scene as being "very good." Most certainly, Jesus did not predict that existence in this world would get better, or that human effort would ever be capable of reversing this nihilistic direction. The dream of modern revisionists that humanity could rebuild a world of justice won't happen. Their early twentieth-century predecessors also became silent in 1914.

Hope Amid Chaos

Latter day disorder signifies the total breakdown of all four elements of essential relationships. The chaos in the chronological process is irreversible as it moves relentlessly toward its ultimate demise. Like the totally helpless body of Jesus in the stone-cold tomb, all nature and all human effort cannot reverse its inevitable descent to nihilistic nothingness. Certainly, the point in time will emerge when the Spirit will no longer hover in protection over a rebellious creation.

Haven't we seen a picture like this before? Doesn't it resemble the apparent chaos of raw creation prior to its ordering and shaping by the holy Breath of God? Doesn't it remind us of the similar chaos working out its inevitable destruction at the time of Noah?

The major difference here is that one scenario represents the first day of new creation, while the latter is a description of the erosion of God's divine processes. What is abundantly clear is that revisionist hopes for the creation of a better world are nothing more than naive dreams. Everything will get considerably worse.

At some point, the sustaining power of God is removed from a creation that has run its self-destructive course. It will fall prey to the inevitable law of consequence. Indeed, it would appear that at this very present, as in no other time in history, we are feeling the effects of our neglect and plunder of the environment to which we were initially called in stewardship. It is now possible for us to venture predictions concerning what those ultimate consequences will be in this world. At some time, many will be shocked to realize that the sustaining Light of God is not shining upon the face of the old order (Matt. 24:22; 25:8-13). We have seen this scenario on humanity's behalf, prefaced in the death and resurrection of Jesus (Matt. 27:46).

Apart from Jesus, the first-fruits of restoration, all things do pass away. But does that really mean that the planet Earth will disappear from existence?

We have cause to believe that the old order of the world will certainly pass away—see 1 John 2:17 and 2 Corinthians 5:17—but there are other biblical allusions that suggest the physical earth may also be restored to a new order (Gen. 8:21; Rev. 11:15; Eph. 3:21). The most significant fact of history, which is the resurrection, leads us to believe that there will always be a tangible relationship with a physical world of first creation. Christ's resurrected body was certainly surrounded in mystery, but there was a *recognizable physical connection* of the old body with that of the new.

In the same way, the new creation will hold a certain sense of mystery. But connections with the old world will be apparent. Interestingly, the very verse that appears to deny this is precisely one that also affirms it. "Then I saw a new heaven and a new earth; for the first heaven and the first earth had passed away, and the sea was no more" (Rev. 21:1). *Kainos*, "new," is defined in Moulton's 1978 *Lectionary* as "new in species, character, or mode." The Greek word *ouranus* is used equally for "sky" as it is for "heaven."

If a brand-new earth were intended to appear from above, we would expect that the writer of Revelation would employ the common Greek word for new: *neon*. He doesn't! Rather, he employs the word *kainon* in order to ensure that a very real *connection* is made between the old and the new.

This word speaks of renewal or refreshment. It may also be seen in Romans 12:2, where the apostle Paul speaks of the "renewing of your minds." The word is also used in Mark's gospel where Jesus speaks of new wineskins: "but one puts new [*neon*] wine into fresh [*kainos*] wineskins" (Mark 2:22; brackets mine).

In other words, there is clearly a physical connection between the world of the old order and that of the new order. Therefore, it is not easy to say that new creation is entirely created ex nihilo. It has some recognizable connections with the old.

Accepting that it is virtually impossible for us to comprehend a complete picture of the chronological process of decay of the old order, nevertheless we may more easily understand the final *result* from the perspective of time's restoration. What we are about to postulate in this area is truly remarkable. It is certainly God's mystery of time's victory. For those who will die tomorrow in Christ, the old order of creation will *completely pass away* as they enter into the fullness of new creation.

Along with other passages of Scripture, we have seen that the ancient saints of Hebrews 11-12 have clearly demonstrated the point that this mystery of everlasting time in Christ continues to be enjoyed from the very last moment of consciousness in the old order. Nevertheless, the accounts of Christ's resurrection have left us with paradoxical elements of familiarity tinged with elusive images of mystery. That is the way we must think of the restoration of all things of the new creation; of the new heaven and earth coming down *from above* (John 3:3, 7; Rev. 21:2). The gift of being born again from above, through the resurrection, and after a death to the old order (1 Pet. 1:3) is precisely the manner in which restoration takes place. Creation itself is born again!

"And the one who was seated on the throne said, 'See, I am making all things new'" (Rev. 21:5; *kainos* is used once more).

In some sense, there will be recognition of what once was, but also unfamiliarity with the restoration of what was originally intended and was once experienced by the first Adam. New creation is always seen to be in the context of *anothen*, "from above." When Jesus comes again, "in the same way as you saw him go into heaven" (Acts 1:11), His feet will not touch the earth of the old order. Whatever Zechariah intimates (14:3), Luke intends to emphasize an irreversible separation of the old order from the new. Those of the new order will be connected to Jesus forever.

Jesus, basing His teaching in the natural calamities of Eden, also depicts a more natural process of events than what may be gleaned from events in symbolic biblical literature.

A Way of Looking at Last Things

I want to share some thoughts emphasizing the chronological process of viewing latter days from a synoptic perspective. We cannot begin our thinking built on foundations that are primarily of a symbolic nature, such as we see in the books of Daniel, Ezekiel, and Revelation. We cannot ignore such books, but we look at them as supports for the bigger story, as told by Jesus.

The synoptic gospels record the words of the Word concerning events of latter days. So the teaching of Jesus must take precedence, while symbolic literature is evaluated on the basis of Christ's more direct teaching. What we don't understand in symbolic literature, we allow to percolate in the light of the teaching of Jesus.

Formerly, we observed a prophetic principle that the future may unfold a picture bigger than the original context.[2] If we believe we have determined who the beast is of Revelation, we should also take note that he has been specifically identified in different ways throughout several periods of history.

In the early church, the beast was the power of Caesar sitting on the seven hills of Rome.[3] At the time of the Reformation, the beast was identified as the Bishop of Rome.[4] In much of the contemporary world of fundamentalist Christianity, he has been identified as the power of a European Union or the world of a united Islam. These are theories that remind us to be careful not to develop a biblical theology based on the moods and politics of one particular age. In determining the process of latter days, it's not a good idea to interpret Scripture with a Bible in one hand and the daily newspaper in the other.

Although . . . ! The chronology of the Book of Revelation does not always move successively from one moment or age to the next. The book invites us to view a big picture depicted in symbolic imagery. It's like being in a dance hall where a light shines on a revolving glass ball. The ball has to turn 360 degrees in order for the entire picture to be observed. In this way, we would note that the whole picture is quite consistent with the one story of the Bible. It is difficult to be tied to one view of chronological events.

John Robinson beautifully illustrates the problem. He picks up on the difficulty of strict, chronological time sequences in Revelation by addressing the question of the "second death" in chapter 20. He has difficulty with the idea that everyone will experience a resurrection, then, after a millennial reign, will experience a judgment, then a further resurrection. The destiny of all those raised in this resurrection will be either, to an eternal reign with Christ, or to a second death in hell (Rev. 20:14).

> The idea of two kingdoms and two resurrections . . . does not appear in the Gospels. It is best viewed as an attempt to harmonize, under the form of successive events, the two elements of the myth emphasized by the prophets and the apocalyptists respectively, namely, that the meaning of history must be vindicated within history and yet that the complete purpose of God must transcend history. The representation of this tension as two stages leads to error if taken literally. For us, the resurrection of the body (an essential element in the total eschatological myth) must be related to the whole doctrine of resurrection which does justice to both these emphases.[5]

At least I can identify with Robinson's point in seeing the whole doctrine as one big picture.

Possibly, we may liken this Revelation picture to Jesus' teaching in Luke. "For you will be repaid at the resurrection of the righteous"

(Luke 14:14). We note that, in its fuller context, Jesus is not referring to a judgment of acceptance or rejection to the banqueting table. All those of all time who meet Jesus in His righteousness are not judged here, at least concerning their eternal disposition. That is not a question to be raised. They are experiencing the resurrection of those born again (1 Pet. 1:3; John 11:25-26; 1 John 5:12-13). So it is a judgment concerning *where* they are privileged to operate in the kingdom (Luke 14:10). It is a judgment concerning the stewardship of God's time and gifts. Of course, those who have rejected Christ's gracious invitation never get this far. In the context of receding time, they meet Christ's eternal judgment of death at the point of death.

Whether we meet the Lord before or after the Parousia, the fullness of resurrection judgment is declared for all: either to the banqueting table or to the grave of total annihilation (Luke 14:24).

I may be wrong in building upon this comparison of Christ's teaching with that of the author of Revelation; however, the comparison may be made. At least this comparison does honor Robinson's desire to see two resurrections in one holistic picture.

We must also consider that a literal position in Revelation is also a contradiction of others, such as Hebrews 9:27, where death is experienced but once. Maybe it is only in this way (e.g., Heb. 12:1) that we can reconcile passages such as that which speaks of the tombs in Jerusalem being opened: "and many bodies of the saints who had fallen asleep were raised. After his resurrection they came out of the tombs and entered the holy city and appeared to many" (Matt. 27:52-53).

Surely, this is also what the writer to the Hebrews had in mind! (11:39-12:2)

We may appreciate Robinson's conclusion, but we must also insist on the *historical process* that made the conclusion possible. Apart from his strangely unsubstantiated view of universalism, I believe that Robinson quite rightly places the *resurrection* at the heart of restored time.

That is paramount when we try to settle the very difficult task of harmonizing Scriptures dealing with questions of latter days. It's probably not a good idea to insist on a chronological schema in the Book of Revelation.

The chronological schema of latter day events in Revelation is difficult to harmonize with John's gospel unless we view Revelation as part of the whole eschatological picture, and one that is not always interpreted in literal terms. Because of this difficulty, we will view all latter-day literature in the light of how real events in time are illuminated through the light of the Synoptic Gospels. After all, the word of Jesus *must be the criterion* by which we evaluate all literature that speaks of latter days—or anything! Jesus is the Living Word. In view of the tension between theological order and chronological events, it is not surprising that many scholars conclude there are two different writers involved in authoring the books of Revelation and John.[6]

In keeping with our creation schema, we realize the importance of taking a similar course in relation to latter days. One way of viewing biblical passages is to recognize that Jesus speaks of a growing chaos and decay from four different perspectives: religious, social, environmental and cosmic.

If we view such passages from these perspectives, we will note that the process aligns itself quite naturally with the unfolding deterioration of the essential principles of creation.

What we are seeing throughout a horrific period of irreversible chaos and decay is a frenetic unraveling of the harmony of those relationships. In the latter stages, creation seems to reflect ever-diminishing signs of God's light and glory. But there are still signs of hope. In the closing stages, creation itself seems to join with the disconsolate train of Adam and Eve departing the gates of Eden. Therefore, with the priestly residents of Eden, a fallen creation has taken its natural chaotic course.

A Possible Synoptic Approach to Latter Events

We must be conversant with the essential principles of creation's relationships in order to understand the meaning of events related to latter days. What we are to observe are events that signal the *climactic disharmony* of the relationship among religious, social, environmental, and cosmic elements.

To consider something of the chronology of latter days, we will look at the processes of decay in the light of those characteristics. Without identifying the process too tightly, we will easily observe that Jesus' view of latter-day events really does signify an immense deterioration of the aforementioned characteristics.

Religious

1. False claims to Messiahship: (Matt. 24:5; Mark 13:6) Never in all of history have we experienced so many claims to final revelation and messiahship. These signs often seem to appear alongside natural occurrences of upheaval. But there has also never been a time when the world has not experienced such natural and social disturbances. Jesus tells us they are just *the beginning of birth pangs.*

The rise of individual claims to truth, accompanying the diverse style of a globalized village, has not nor ever could have been quite as intense or achievable as it is now. Religion is fine; absolute truth is not. Much of our present worldwide media is very effective in presenting this attitude.

Paradoxically, and in reality, this uniquely globalized attitude has actually provided avenues for absolute claims of revelation. Sometimes, the tyranny that is being left behind has led to ruthless pressure for religious conversions, such as has been rarely seen at a global level. Nevertheless, the upholding of individualized religion, has indeed given rise to claims that messiahs of *final truth* have now emerged upon the stage of history. Such repercussions may produce a global desire to do more and more things with a one-world view. The motivation for this desire would not be focused in discovering absolute truth, but in the quest for human survival. Desperation will set in.

2. Fear amid wars and rumors of wars: (Matt. 24:6; Mark 13:7; Luke 21:9) and

3. Nations rise against nations, earthquakes, famines, plagues: (Matt. 24:7; Mark 13:8; 21:11)

Rumors of wars, earthquakes, famines, and plagues are nothing new, nor were they at the time of Jesus. Indeed, seismologists tell us that earthquakes are very natural, and that they must happen. These signs of nature at work were also present during the time of the temple's destruction. Jesus knew that; He had prophesied it.

However, contemporary events are having astounding effects *on increasing numbers of people*. In our complex communication age, we are not just simply more aware of these happenings. The fact is that they affect considerably more people than ever before.

Our essential relationship with creation is in the throes of chaotic disorder. Should we be surprised by the results? They produce a chain reaction.

The last century saw two worldwide wars involving the death of untold millions of people, including six million Jews in the Holocaust. Two earthquakes, one on December 26, 2003, in Bam, Iran, and the other exactly twelve months later in Southeast Asia, exacted a combined toll of more than 250,000 lives. Later, after the turn of the millennium, the force of tsunami waves and fierce hurricane winds almost completely decimated Haiti, the coastal regions of Thailand, and immense regions of Japan. The toll in loss of life was horrific. Nature is truly groaning! (Rom. 8:19-21).

These astounding events challenge us not to dismiss the warning words of Jesus. They are a call for the church to reawaken its sense of urgency to the prophetic and evangelistic purposes of the gospel.

4. Jesus predicts the total destruction of the temple: (Matt. 24:2).

This prediction of Jesus proved to be historically correct, but Jesus never intimated it would occur near the end of days (Matt. 24:8). Indeed, in AD 70, the Roman forces of occupation, determined to stamp out the guerilla forces of Israel, demolished much of the city of Jerusalem. But there proved to be a further and final dispersion. In AD 135, a Second Revolt took place under Simon Bar-Kochba.[7] Not only did these dispersions signal the end of the monarchy and priestly orders, but the Jews, as a people, were not to return to Israel for another 1800 years or more.

5. From that time onward, Jerusalem will be in the hands of the Gentiles, until their time is fulfilled: (Luke 21:24; Rom. 11:25)

There is abundant evidence in the Old Testament of a dispersion that will take the Jewish people to the *furthest regions of the world* (Jer. 9:16; 25:33; Ezek. 36:22). Indeed, such a worldwide dispersion did take place. But its beginnings took place when the Assyrian occupation of the northern kingdoms began. That is, 721 BC to Judah's dispersal in 586 BC and from AD 70 to 135.

However, there are many biblical allusions concerning Israel's return to its homeland (Jer. 12:15; 23:3; 31:8; Ezek. 28:26; 36:24; 37:21-22). After more than 1,800 years, in 1948, a Jewish state of Israel was once more established. It was made possible through the guilt of the United Nations (then called The League of Nations) and its impotence in protecting the Jews from the horrendous persecution of the Second World War.

This event appears to be a major event through which ancient prophets saw the race of Israel coming to some sense of spiritual unity (Hosea 1:10-11). To this point, we may say that the unity of the nation is much more of a political, than of a spiritual nature. As a nation, Israel now takes its place among the major influences in the world. Undoubtedly, 1948 was a breathtaking breakthrough in prophetic understandings. All the guesswork should have given way to a tangible reality that Israel's formal return signaled a procession of tangible latter-day events. Much of the historic and prophetic guesswork is now taking on a secondary place.

Social and Environmental

1. For the elect, there will be persecution, torture, prison, and death. They will be a people hated by all nations (Matt. 24:9; Mark 13:9; Luke 21:12).

2. These conditions will give cause for a great falling away from the faith. There will be betrayal by family members, and false prophets will also lead many astray (Matt. 24:10-11; Mark 13:12; Luke 21:16).

3. The despair caused by an increase in lawlessness will be further occasion for a falling away from the faith (Matt. 24:12).

1-3: A time emerges when the gospel of Jesus has traveled around the world in order for the accomplishment of the condition He predicted.

Much of this persecution has already occurred in some parts of the world. And it is growing in intensity in the Western hemisphere, particularly in the falling away from the faith. In these days of political correctness, the rejection of absolutes by a postmodern generation rebelling against the values of their parents, the rise of New Age religions, acceptable, economically driven worldwide values, and privatized religion over absolute truth, all will make for an easy passage of changes in loyalties.

The honoring of absolute social values in a globalized economy would cause great embarrassment; it may well prove to be a deterrent to the universal goals of an ever—widening economy. *Absolutes values cannot be tolerated; individual spirituality can.* And, paradoxically, in much of the Western world, legal individual and minority rights may silence a majority of the populous whose generous values now become an instrument for their own persecution.

The idea that Christians escape persecution has no substance in fact (1 Pet. 4:12). In a Christianity Today webpage, Ted Olsen posted a statistic stating that every day approximately 270 Christians die for their faith.[8] It is commonly understood that more Christians were martyred in the twentieth century than in the entire previous history of the Christian church

In the Western world, its obsession with individual rights over collective responsibility is causing frustration among enforcers of law. There is an enormous contradiction of values and considerable lack of confidence in systems of justice. Violence, a daily delight of the media, is now a paralyzing and sense-deadening reality in the West after September 11, 2001. This historical turning point has anaesthetized the sensitivities of a generation now absorbed with the perverse thrill of violence.

As we move a little further into latter days, we observe a measure of intense suffering such as the world has ever known. It isn't difficult to understand. In our contemporary world, and without discussing the astounding frequency of terrorism abroad, the chaos has easily discernible roots—that is, when individual want is lauded over communal right, responsibility, and enterprise (see Matt. 25:14-30).

This me-centered focus is destined to result in indignant petulance when the right to possess whatever a nation or individual desires is denied. Already, we are witnessing a lawlessness emerging in the sphere of the entire world. It takes on a disturbing proportion of terror and fear.

Terrorism, with religious motivation, now springs up in all quarters of our world. Indeed, 2 Thessalonians 2:3-4 certainly looks possible from our present perspectives. When religious fanaticism gives credence to horrific slaughter, the stability of informed conscience becomes seriously threatened. In our Gnostic and stoic culture, where suffering and horror are more to be expected, it isn't difficult to imagine what would happen in the Western world. In sheer desperation, with anger toward God, and in pained disillusionment, many will turn away from the God of Jesus. They will look for another "savior" who will promise peace and order, even if there is a price to pay for it!

The values lauded in a globalized economy, in which all absolutes, such as the Lordship of Christ, and religious values are *privatized* and rendered devoid of social context, may easily contribute to well-meaning family members opposing Christian kin (Mark 13:12-13). This opposition will occur in the name of the maintenance of universally accepted values. The Baby Boomer generation were bombarded with it, and have passed a right of entitlement down to their children.

It is also possible that the present failure of historic mainline churches to reject the syncretistic influences of our fickle and ever-changing culture will also be a contributory factor in this falling away. Such a utilitarian approach may also contribute to the offering of a friendly nod toward other benevolent "saviors." Whether or not this scenario becomes a reality, it must be admitted that in this techno-communication age, such possibilities now loom much larger than at any other time in history.

4. There is an injunction that the end will not come until the good news is universally proclaimed (Matt. 24:14; Mark 13:10). The commission to the Adam community has been revived. This surge in evangelism is seen

to be a major sign close to the end of the ages. The universal commission of Jesus to His community is to be played out in greater measure than at the time of the apostles.

The universal spread of the gospel is now technically more feasible in our age of global communication. It is part of the historic apostolic commission that a Christ-centered global community be created from all nations of the earth. The sons of God are intended to be primary agents in facilitating blessings toward such a universal community (Gen. 12:3; Isa. 49:6, John 1:13). We note that the same technology may also be used by the powers of evil.

It is certainly more possible to brainwash the masses than ever before. The purpose of those forces opposing the gospel will be to deceive the nations. Many of these goals are accomplished by producing false signs and values. After all, so much can now be accomplished through an edit-crazed media and satellite-aided computers. Nevertheless, although there is presently a great *falling away* in the West, the church of the global south experiences breathtaking growth throughout most of its regions. It will not be surprising when we see the churches of the global south rise up to aid the renewal of their former missioners.

Remarkably, the primary method of sharing the gospel in these poorer regions is through the basic and unsophisticated mediums of developing personal relationships, clear biblical teaching, and signs and wonders of the Spirit.

5. The desolating sacrilege standing in the *holy place* will cause those in Judea to flee to the mountains (Matt. 24:15-16; Mark 13:14).

It would *appear* that Jerusalem, as the material focus of God's dwelling among His people, is also to be the focus of a *spiritual conflict* having global ramifications. The idea that the *holy place* is severely insulted, as in the days of Antiochus Epiphanes, 168 BC, gives us the impression that the saints of God are now a *globalized networking community*. Their primary messianic focus has enraged the universal and controlling powers of the world. These powers demand a capitulation to their own sets of values. Who would have thought that the little city of Jerusalem could ever have stood at the center of a worldwide conflict!

Some Orthodox Jews and evangelical Christians believe that this sacrilege is the Dome of the Rock, completed in AD 691 by the Muslim invaders. It now stands on the site of the former Jewish temple. Consequently, it may well represent a focal point for global armed conflict.

However, for most Christians and many Jews, the idea that another temple should be built in this place makes little sense. Most Christians see a spiritual temple in a different light. Jesus is the temple in a Jerusalem that is above and free (Gal. 4:26). He is the focus, now and forever! (Rev. 21:22).

6. At this time there will be suffering and chaos comparable to *the beginning of the world*, and nothing may be compared with it (Matt. 24:21; Mark 13:19).

7. For the sake of the elect, those days of suffering will be cut short (Matt. 24:22; Mark 13:20). In other words, the elect will be involved in considerable suffering. (Quite possibly, the *cutting short* may be accomplished by the Parousia.)

8. Also at that time, as people look for a messiah or a savior from their difficulties, false messiahs and prophets will be capable of producing enticingly false signs and wonders. Even many of the elect will be deceived, or induced by a politically acceptable religious diversity of belief (Matt. 24:23-24; Mark 13:21).

6-8: In the synoptic gospels and in John 16:33, the people of God who remain are not spared the pain of persecution, suffering, and death. Isaiah may also have prefigured this suffering to include the elect (2:21). We see similar allusions in Daniel 12:1, where it is recorded that *this distress is immeasurably greater than at any time in history*. In Revelation 13, we also see that there are faithful saints who refuse to buy into the world's new and universal values. As a result, they suffer untold distress.

However, as in the gospels, where Jesus speaks of this unparalleled time of suffering, He intimates that, for the sake of the elect, the time will be cut short. This is quite possibly consistent with the *one hour* (in relative terms) of suffering recorded in Revelation 17:12 and 18:10. Here, the unbearable pain of the saints will be ended by an Enoch-like separation and meeting with Jesus. Parousia speaks of separation.

The situation described above may not be too dissimilar from our contemporary situation. What we are witnessing today is that established historic and mainline churches are falling apart through apostasy and cultural accommodation. Conversely, we note that churches of the global south are growing at an extraordinary rate. They are no longer intimidated by the heavy-handed and controlling schemes of their founding mainline churches of the West.

Clearly, an uncompromising faith has given birth to a powerful mission in evangelism. While the church of the south is burgeoning in numbers, in many quarters it is also facing suffering and untold persecution for the sake of the gospel. This is a quality of discipleship rarely seen in the West today. What will we trade in the West to secure the absence of suffering? Suffering is the norm for those who walk the way of the cross.

It would appear that the only hope for the dry bones of the West is to be found in the recovery of its apostolic roots, made possible by the universal, outpouring power of the Spirit. It will be in the Holy Spirit's power that the church may stand like a mighty army (Ezek. 37:9-10). The Latter Days are clearly fraught in a globalized spiritual conflict. And it may come quickly, motivated not so much by an increase of evangelism, but a sudden manifestation of the Holy Spirit—to Jews and Gentiles! It would appear that the slow pace of evangelism amongst the Jews would not be sufficient for what God requires of them.

My very strong feeling is that God will miraculously manifest Himself to the nation of Israel, and in a very quick and imminent sense. Somewhere around that period, rather than a military contest in the Middle East, Armageddon may well be a metaphor for a short-lived epoch of global and *spiritual* conflict.

Possibly, in the latter days, all these former events will motivate a remnant to a universal mission of evangelism. Surely the time is right for a Western remnant to shake off the shackles of the old order and to recover the mission of Jesus, "to seek out and to save the lost" (Luke

19:10). Such a return to basics of purpose would constitute an apostolic focus recovering the servant heart for the whole world.

And so surely the most significant sign of Christ's return will be a time when His own Jewish people no longer reject Him (John 1:11; Luke 21:24; Rom. 11:21,23).

Environmental and Social Stewardship:

Speaking from perspectives beyond that of a faithless church, why should we be surprised that our apathy and lack of regard for God's creation results in environmental havoc? This me-focused attitude among nations and individuals is presently resulting in thousands upon thousands dying of starvation every year. Doesn't God provide all that is necessary to feed His creation? (Ps. 145:16). Our greed for more and for immediate satisfaction has produced anti-nature attitudes in the world, but also in the church itself. The major problems here are not those of God's provision, but humanity's unwillingness for fair distribution.

Social conditions in these days appear to be so abysmal that sheer desperation will be the motivation for many people to look for a global savior. Possibly an idolatry of modern technology may produce false and enticing promises. They lure away a self-centered and apathetic Western Christianity from the costly pathway of Calvary.

In our time, we note that there are consequences of a fragile and apathetic democracy that is pitted against the lawlessness of lustful terrorism. It is not difficult to see why a worsening situation would call for the rise of desperate solutions. *A supposed savior* may well be some sort of charismatic figure, or a universally acceptable political system, or even a religious ideology. Any or all of these will gain global acceptance for its chameleon benevolence and miraculous ability to ensure a universal political order.

A rise in violence should not come as a surprise. This alluring "savior" would promise to give order amid chaos, but also an attractive means of survival (Rev. 13:16-18). Even saints, people of goodwill, will be deceived by this pretender's promises.

Interestingly and already, former members of Christian churches are adopting once-shunned New Age religions. In the self-perceived notions of justice, the cry, "Peace, peace," when there is no peace is being widely lauded from pulpits today (Jer. 6:14).

Having brought about an apparent condition of stability, *possibly by enforcing submission to universal values*, this figure or system may well replace individual freedom of choice with a further submission to his dictatorial agenda. Is this the false prophet of Revelation 16:13--14 and 19:20? Whether beast or the false prophet, the writer of Revelation has them working together!

Signs in the Cosmos and the Decaying Earth

After that time of suffering, there will be chaos in the heavens and in the seas. There will be chaotic intrusions originating in the world and in the cosmos.

It would appear that, despite the advances in technology, humanity is not able to control the chaotic forces from the heavens above and the earth below. Amazingly, the old order undergoes chaotic situations such as we read of in Genesis 1:1-2. In creation, order came about when the Spirit breathed upon the disorder. No such thing is promised to sustain the old order. It will be allowed to continue on its suicidal course.

The disordered movement of nature is beyond any human power to control. Along with the natural cyclical changes, which no one can control, some such destructive directions may also occur as a result of human failure in its stewardship of the environment. Already, alarming signs of environmental decay are being experienced.

In a recent newspaper article, Margaret Munro cites reputable sources when warning of the massive escape of methane gases at the top of our planet. "Polar ice has been shrinking at a rate of 74,000 square kilometers annually for the past 30 years . . . The Arctic ice is withdrawing so fast . . . that by 2050 it may be nonexistent in the summer . . . But there is little anyone can do for the animals and other life forms that will be stranded as temperatures climb and the Arctic's icy cloak lifts. If you live on the sea ice, like the polar bear, you are in big trouble; your habitat is disappearing."[9] Meanwhile, agents of big business in energy and communicators of environmental values pit themselves against each other in their quest to lay blame.

Natural catastrophes may well effect changes in the sun, moon, and stars (Matt. 24:29; Mark 13:24-25; Luke 21:25—see also Joel 2:31). In other words, no matter how environmentally conscious we may be, there is nothing humanly possible to prevent the natural and catastrophic courses, particularly of the heavens. Indeed, few contemporary astrophysicists will guarantee that the planet Earth will be spared harm from the large number of asteroids that head this way.

On the day of Pentecost, quoting from the prophet Joel, Peter reminded his Jewish audience, "The sun will be turned to darkness and the moon to blood, before the coming of the Lord's great and glorious day" (Acts 2:20).

We have become much more aware that solar flares can affect the earth, and with disastrous effects. For example, in March 1989, a solar storm caused a major blackout in much of Quebec, Canada, and also the entire James Bay network. Later, in August, another storm disrupted radio signals and forced the closure of the Toronto Stock Exchange. In some parts of the world, it is already difficult to see the sun.

When we consider the results of the rape of the Brazilian rain forests, the polluted air emanating from the industrial world, and the terrifying results of what some consider to be a natural global warming, including Antarctica, things look to be quite perilous. On the other hand, some scientists are actually convinced that we are headed for another ice age. We may also observe the stark consequences of humanity's tardy efforts to live in harmony with God's creation. That's not all!

There is a major problem looming that, for a variety of reasons, is not receiving its deserved attention. "Water is not a renewable resource." Mark de Villiers, the commentator in this Discovery Channel program goes on to say that about two million children die every year from water that is unfit to drink.[10] Massive famine will be and has been the result of lack of water. There are other factors beyond our control. But, in some cases, certain cosmic actions may well be the consequences of humanity's failure to maintain its creation charge.

1. *Then*, the Son of Man will appear in the heavens:

With His angels, He will gather the elect who remain on the earth (Matt. 24:30; Mark 13:26; Luke 21:27). Does not this remind us of the *translation* of Enoch and Elijah? We noted in an earlier chapter that, at the Parousia, the feet of Jesus did not even touch the ground of the old order. However, the saints who are alive on earth do meet with the Lord in the context of chronological time. (Of course, their judgment for salvation has already taken place; see John 3:18.)

This moment of translation will be a moment of great separation. Theirs will be an experience similar to the translation experienced by Enoch and Elijah. "We will not all die, but we will all be changed, in a moment, in the twinkling of an eye . . . and we will be changed" (1 Cor. 15:51-52). Since the finished historical event of the resurrection, the dead in Christ are changed already (1 Thess. 4:15-17; Heb. 12:1). Possibly all of this will occur when the time of persecution and suffering has been cut short. But none of this will occur until there has been a massive grafting of Israel into the vine of Jesus (John 15:1; Rom. 11:11-13, 23). This will surely be an astounding and swift movement of the Spirit. It will rank as the most startlingly swift sign of how the Spirit miraculously touched the people of Israel, as a nation. For those acquainted with the prophetic teaching of Jesus, it will surely mean that the Parousia is very near. For example, Jesus speaks of the time of the Gentiles being fulfilled (Luke 21:24). When the day of Gentiles ends, it will be the saints of Israel in the vanguard (as it was in the beginning) leading the procession to Zion. (Isa.35:8-10)

Regardless of interpretation, one thing is certain. As the destinies of the two thieves on their crosses signify, there will be some determining point of eternal separation between those who are alive in the relationships of the new order of creation and those who are not (Matt. 13:30).

Probably, this separation will be near the moment of the final conflict, as recorded in the symbolic literature of Ezekiel 38-39; Zechariah 12:9 and 14:3, and Revelation 16:14-16. Here, the powers of the earth have, together, been seduced.

2. As in the days of Noah, much of the earth's population will revel in an orgy of self-centered abandonment and drunkenness:

They will live as if nothing could go wrong. On that day, as it was in those days and those of the rich man and Lazarus, the people who choose to remain outside of Christ are those who will see and will mourn (Matt. 24:30, 37). There will be weeping and gnashing of teeth (Matt. 25:30).

3. Each of the synoptic gospels includes a severe warning in its commentary:

It is a call to be ready, because Christ's coming will appear like a thief in the night. We will all be taken by surprise. And those who are not ready *will not be included* in the life of the new creation (Matt. 24:36-44; 25:10-12; Mark 13:32-36; Luke 21:34-36).

4. In each of the synoptic gospels, Jesus gives a sense of urgency in warning:

This generation will not pass away until all things are fulfilled. Heaven and earth, the old order of fallen creation, will pass away, but God's word will remain forever (Matt. 24:34-35; Mark 13:30; Luke 21:32—see also Isa. 40:8; 55:11).

5. Before the final cataclysmal chaos, the times of the Gentiles will be fulfilled:

Many of the natural, cosmic calamities appear to extend beyond the control or even the cause of human endeavor. They will cause terror on the earth. However, the disasters are fully representative of the fact that nature itself will turn in on itself, comparable to the end of the self-destructive Judas, and it will take down our known, natural world with it. This principle of consequence and subsequent impotence was established by God in the Old Testament, e.g., in Leviticus 18:24-25.

2-4 Warnings; Be Ready:

The ascension of Jesus (the real Adam) signaled the discernible end of the old order, but the chronological race to destruction has not yet played itself out. In the present, evil has not yet come to the conclusion of its inevitable futility. Clearly, the resurrection of Jesus' ascension and of Pentecost should be seen together as part of the whole eschatological picture. Together, they present to the world an astounding moment of light.

Armageddon may well be a metaphor for the climax of this global and spiritual conflict between good and evil. In this context, it may best be understood in the context of a moment of struggle rather than one physical battle of armed conflict. Nevertheless, this may not discount the possibility that there may be a major conflict between Israel and a gathering of allied forces that are focused in Iran. (See Hitchcock, Mark, *Iran and Israel*, Harvest House Publishers, Eugene, Oregon, 2011.)

In this latter metaphorical imagery, the elect of God are pitted against opposing forces in armed battle. The idea of winning spiritual battles for Truth by the means of force of arms is not consistent with the eschatological (or any) teaching of Jesus (Matt. 5:43-44). Paul agrees in 2 Corinthians 10:3-4. We may discern how the nature of this battle is played out in both the Old and New Testaments.

In the Book of Daniel 12:1-3, the haughty arrogance of the oppressor is quashed, not by the armies of the elect, but by the forces of heaven. In the *passive* mood, it is revealed to Daniel that "your people shall be delivered, everyone who is found written in the book." We should note here that, in a later part of Daniel, the final battle is connected to some form of resurrection. Maybe it represented a later hope for the revival of Israel's autonomy. Clearly, the battle is the Lord's. It has been won on the cross and is consummated in Christ's resurrection and ascension, "the first fruits of those who have died" (1 Cor. 15:20).

In 2 Corinthians 10:3, the apostle Paul speaks of the nature of our warfare: "We do not wage war according to human standards; for the weapons of our warfare are not merely human, but they have divine power to destroy strongholds."

Nowhere in the New Testament are we told that the purpose and nature of God's kingdom is won by employing the same destructive tools as the enemy. The final battle is the Lord's, and He has won it in the resurrection of Jesus.

In Revelation 20:9, we observe a picture of those opposing God's purposes and who are also attempting to overcome the saints of God.

But they are thoroughly consumed; not by superior armaments of the saints, but by the light and fire of God's glory. Apart from the disposition of the Gentiles, this may be the most significant moment of light of latter days. As in the beginning, the light of God shines upon creation, but in cleansing and restorative power. Possibly, this may be the time for a much-needed response to the Spirit's revival in the West.

5. Decline of the Old Order:

"They will fall by the edge of the sword and be taken away as captives among all nations; and Jerusalem will be trampled upon by the Gentiles, until the times of the Gentiles are fulfilled" (Luke 21:24).

A time will come when the Gentiles will no longer be a controlling force in the history of Israel or in the world. This saying of Jesus may well dovetail into the sentiment of Paul when writing to the Romans. He speaks of Israel being grafted back into the vine. God also miraculously made it possible for them to renew their bigger covenant with God (Rom. 11:23). And that is "until the full number of the Gentiles has come in. And so all Israel will be saved . . . for the gifts and the calling of God [to the Jews] are irrevocable" (Rom. 11:25, 26, 29; brackets mine).

In relation to Jewish control over the land of Israel, that has already taken place!

It would appear that the Lord, who knows all time, has made provision in history for just the right number of people, both Jews and Gentiles, to take their place in the new creation. There'll be no overpopulation there. The kingdom belongs to the sovereign God!

God's purposes are sovereign over creation's chaos.

This moment of God's sovereign triumph has been seen to have an extraordinary parallel in the Old Testament. As Enoch and Elijah are translated (Gen. 5:24; 2 Kings 2:11), so the *faithful on earth* are raised to meet Jesus in the translation from the old order to that of the new (1 Thess. 4:17).

The gathering of the remnant from a decaying earth will not go by unnoticed. Again, this teaching of Jesus most certainly denotes some noticeable form of *separation*. When some people are no longer around there will be great consternation. The whole world will notice this great separation and consequently, many will mourn over. At this time, those of His elect in a bed and one goes missing, that will be noticed. The whole world will see His sign and, consequently, many will mourn over the decayed nature that apathetically accepted such loss. At this time, those of His elect who are remaining, like Enoch and Elijah, will be caught up to meet Him into the new order of creation's restoration.

In this big picture, we see that Jesus has taken all His people who are alive and who have lived in the old order of time. They have gone to the new creation that He won at Easter. *So the meaning of being caught up in the air is clearly connected to the fullness of the new order of restoration.* At some moment in the dying embers of a decadent order, the victory of Easter Sunday is fully experienced by those who remain *in Christ* (Matt. 24:13).

The event clearly emphasizes that, for all those in this moment, *there is no ending of time for all who are in Christ*. What remains of the old order will be left to suffer the fate of its inevitable demise. How could it possibly endure once the Light and Breath of God's sustaining love has been withdrawn? Those, now impotent, of the old order will not remain active as if nothing has happened. And they will have no power to sustain themselves.

The word "generation" (*genea*) is often used in a simple chronological sense, i.e., Matthew 1:1, but it is also used to describe the moral condition of an entire community at a particular period (Matt. 12:39). Here, Jesus describes a *generation* as being evil and adulterous. In the Matthew 24 passage, we see a clear identification with a generation of people who, in latter days, morally identify with the apostate at the time of Noah. However, those who are identified with the Word are those who will endure forever.

Not surprisingly, in Matthew's gospel, Jesus ends His discourse on latter days with the following warning: "Therefore you must also be ready, for the Son of Man is coming at an unexpected hour" (Matt. 24:44).

In His finished work, Jesus holds together the one story of a new creation that is moved in opposition to the course of destruction. The old order of creation will most surely pass into nihilistic meaninglessness (Rev. 21:1). Of course, as we have clearly seen, this does not mean there no longer remain some sort of physical connection between the old and the new order. Indeed, the mystery of the resurrected body of Jesus allows us to ponder such a mystery. Jesus also offers this connection by basing His teachings in the meaning and purpose of creation.

Not even for one moment does Jesus doubt that *God's sovereign purposes will be accomplished* (Isa. 55:11). God's purposes have surely triumphed while He has maintained a self-imposed vulnerability to His principle of free choice.

The power of evil is defeated. Yes, the Lord did speak of an eternity for certain creatures. It is these entities that would remain in an eternal state of torment (Matt. 25:41). But these particular entities were created *as spirit beings.* They are not creatures consisting of the elements comprised of body, soul, and spirit. (1Thess.5:23) As such, they are not constrained by the dimensional elements that constitute the existence of time. *As spirit beings,* the beast, his angels, and also the false prophet remain in an eternal state of fiery torment (Rev. 20:10). Whatever existence is destined for the devil and his angels, we understand that he is permanently bound by an inability to roam the new creation. (Job.2:1-12, Rev.20:10)

Hell, for these creatures of a spirit nature, is forever and ever living with beings having the same perverted nature. However, we hasten to note that the God who created life in a spirit condition can also destroy it. The *destructive power* of the same fire, in which death itself is destroyed (Rev. 20:14), is promised for all whose names are *not* found in the book of life (Matt.10:28; Rev. 20:15; 21:7-8; 2 Thess. 1:9; 2:3, 8).

The old order of creation is clearly over. What we glean from the highly symbolic character of Revelation is that fire is the appropriate metaphor for both total destruction and eternal torment. However, as we have seen, fire may be experienced one way or the other. It represents extinction for mortal beings, which possibly may also mean cessation for some spirit beings.

What about the Jews? Where do they fit into this eschatological picture?

Quite honestly, there isn't a gospel story unless it includes the Jewish people at the beginning and at the end. The mandate given to Abraham demands that the Jews, near the end, play a significant part in the entire story (Rom. 11:23). Their purpose is to *unite* both Jew and Gentile in God. It may not be politically correct to emphasize the leadership of one particular race, but the one story of the Bible compels us to seek wholeness and consistency in the telling.

"One New Humanity"

Wasn't a universal community God's purpose from the very beginning? (Gen. 1:28). When Jesus spoke of the times of Gentile fulfillment, quite probably He had in mind a period when significant events of history would not revolve around the Jewish people. Not, at least, until the Gentiles had enjoyed their day in the sun. Both Jesus and Paul pick up this theme with the phrase, "until the full number of the Gentiles has come in" (Luke 21:24; Rom. 11:25).

What does "full number" mean? Is it the right number of people for the new creation? Is it the right number of Gentiles being led by Jews into and beyond the days of the old order? For some, the full number means the end of the leading influence by the Gentile church, this apostolic role being once more headed by a Jewish community, having recognized the promised messiah to be Jesus.

Apart from a small number of Orthodox Jews and some fundamentalist Christians, the hope that a temple will be rebuilt on Mount Zion is not widely held. The entire point of a temple would be the restitution of a blood sacrificial system, abhorrent to most Jews and totally obsolete in orthodox Christianity. For Christians, the work of redemption has been completed on the cross of Christ.

Therefore, the latter-day procession to Jerusalem, probably headed by Jewish people with Jesus at the head (Eph. 4:8), would not be for the purpose of offering sacrifices, but to enter into the worship of God in His awesome delight of a new order-with the New Jerusalem as the goal. (Gal.4:26)

The mighty work of the Spirit will have ended; the time of the Gentiles and the leadership of latter days might therefore be headed by

Jews eager to see their expected Messiah (see Isa. 35:8-10). Maybe the idea really does relate to the right number of people populating the new creation. Whatever it may mean, we may easily see that it will probably relate to a latter history of the Jewish people, who, as God's original community (sons of God), now provide an even clearer understanding of the joyous procession to Zion. Their royal king, Jesus, has already taken up the vanguard that has its singular focus on Him.

The most significant moments of latter-day history will be focused around the Jews *as a people*. Nations that do not know God will be attracted to them (Isa. 55:5; Zech. 8:22-23).

God had allowed for His chosen people to suffer the consequence of being scattered among the nations of the earth. They had lost their identity and possession of a land with Jerusalem as its focus. But through the prophets, God promised they would return to their homeland. Does not the promise go even beyond this to a New Jerusalem which is above, e.g., Micah 4:3-4 and 5:2, and repeating exactly Isaiah 2:4? This would not happen as a reward for anything they had done. The event would be signatory evidence of God's sovereignty upon the pages of human history. "It is not for your sake, O house of Israel, that I am about to act, but for the sake of my holy name" (Ezek. 36:22).

The apostle Paul does not see the aforementioned grafting in of the Jews to be the result of any human effort. It is a mighty work of the Spirit (Rom. 11:23). This miracle will require nothing less than the mighty and sovereign Breath of God sweeping over His ancient people.

Indeed, the entire sovereign plan of God is at stake here. Paul uses the Greek word *egkentridso*, "to be engrafted," in a future tense and in a passive mood. It is God who does this astounding work. It will likely be a massive and sudden move of the Holy Spirit upon His ancient people. It is worth repeating that *the most significant sign* of latter days will be when this miraculous work of God is accomplished.

One commentator bemoans the fact that very few Christians really have an understanding of God's plan for Israel. "It is also a fact that prior to 1948 hardly any of the mainline Christian denominations publicly stated or believed that God would raise Israel again in fulfillment of scripture."[11] Israel was intended, and understood that they were to be a people that would focus the world in unity under God's anointed One: "And he is named Wonderful Counselor, Mighty God, Everlasting Father, Prince of Peace. His authority shall grow continually, and there shall be endless peace for the throne of David and his kingdom" (Isa. 9:6-7).

However, the apostolic function entailed in this purpose was not well accomplished by the nation through their poor sense of a universal mission. Clearly, the fulfillment of all that is meant by restoration will not happen apart from Jesus. His place is at the head of the kingdom. Jesus made it clear to the Jews that He was the real David of prophetic fulfillment (Mark 12:35-37). Ezekiel, in his eschatological message of hope, believed that Israel could become an inbreathed people. Restored from their dry bones condition (chapter 37), they would look forward to a time when the real David is King: "My servant David will be king over them, and they will all have one shepherd" (Ezek. 37:24).

Of course, in the context of which Ezekiel speaks, this will not take place until Judah and Ephraim become *one stick* (Ezek. 37:19-22). How all this fits together in a neat, continuous fashion is something known only to God (Mark 13:32). It will most certainly not be fulfilled because of any human effort. It will be accomplished by the Spirit's gracious initiative. Ezekiel had spoken in agreement with the sentiments of Isaiah regarding God's sovereign purposes: "The zeal of the Lord of hosts will do this" (Isa. 9:7).

In other words, the restoration of the Jews, as one people and under the headship of Jesus, will be the major sign of the long-awaited Parousia. But hasn't this already happened? Returning to Israel from many nations, are they not now united as Jews (i.e., giving focus in Judah?) Jesus once said to His own disciples: "When the Spirit of truth comes, he will guide you into all the truth . . . He will glorify me" (John 16:13-14).

As an apostolic community, it may also be seen that the picture of consummation is *prefaced* in a united Jewish-Gentile mission that invites the world to unity in Jesus Christ (Gal. 2:8; 3:28-29). But, according to this one story, doesn't this mean that Jesus will be at the forefront of one Jewish and Gentile community? Yes, it does! He is the king of both Jew and Gentile. The Old Testament clearly points to one who will sit on the throne of David, and Jesus saw Himself in that picture of kingdom authority. We saw this bigger story when Jesus is shown to be the real Adam-King, and the one riding triumphantly *on a donkey* into Jerusalem. He now leads this universal community to Zion in a procession of praise. *The one story of the Bible really does come together in Jesus.*

How could any Christian, out of misplaced sentimentality, negate the biblical hope that the Jewish people will one day realize their own calling? Why exclude the Jews from evangelistically fervent prayer? It will be through *their* Jewish Son that *their* apostolic purpose, promised through *their* patriarch, Abraham, will find complete focus (Gen. 12:3). Paul, a Jew who saw completion of the nation's story in Jesus, also saw Jesus to be at the very center of its entire story. We should now have enough confidence in predictive prophecy to believe that, somehow, *God will achieve His stated original purposes* through His ancient people. When that occurs, the Jews may, once more, be at the latter-day vanguard of an apostolic mission to the world.

"For nearly 2,000 years the Promised Land lay desolate. Where once great forests stood, the hills were empty of trees and covered with rocks. 'The land was under Turkish control from 1517 to 1917, and Turkey destroyed this land thoroughly. The rulers enacted ridiculous laws; for example, one which required taxes to be paid for live trees. The people cut down the trees so they wouldn't have to pay taxes! This country, therefore, ended up in a truly wretched condition.'"[12]

However, God promised that, on the return of Israel, the deserts would once more blossom like a rose, and forests would return to their former glory (Isa. 35:1-2). With a charter of statehood in 1948, the astounding miracle of the Jewish return continued. Thousands of Jews were released from places like Russia, and came from other parts of Europe and North America. Upon arrival, they began the laborious work of restoring the land. In spite of continued conflicts, the country flourished. Massive amounts of money and expertise were exported to Israel from countries around the world.

Great waves of migration took place, and the miracle of restoration amazed an astonished world. Israel now sends agricultural experts to consult with leaders of the world's developing nations.

Yet there are distinctions of belief within the nation. For example, many are atheists, and a great number are agnostics. There are liberal Jews; also there is an influential segment of Orthodox Jews. *Their sense of commonality is ethnic, not religious.* They have become one stick in law, but not in heart. Of course, they are no longer separated into people of the north and south. They are all Jews, fulfilling the astounding prophecy of Jacob to Judah (Gen. 49:8-10).

"I am about to take the stick of Joseph (which is in the hand of Ephraim) and the tribes of Israel associated with it; and I will put the stick of Judah upon it, and make them one stick, in order that they may be one in my hand" (Ezek. 37:19).

Many years later, the writer to the Ephesians uses the language of a *commonwealth of Israel* (Eph. 2:12). Indeed, he may well have built upon a similar theme found in the book of Zechariah (12:10). Further, he goes on to speak of the breaking down of a wall of hostility that exists between Jew and Gentile. Then, he makes this most astounding statement: "He has abolished the law with its commandments and ordinances, that he might create in himself one new humanity in place of the two, thus making peace, and might reconcile both groups to God in one body through the cross" (Eph. 2:15-16).

However, this unity of Jew with Gentile could not happen until there was some form of unity within Israel itself.

The tribes of Israel are no longer separate. Intertribal marriage has formed Jacob's descendants into one group called the Jewish people, or Israel. The root of the name "Jew" is found in the proper noun "Judah." Today the names "children of Israel" and "Jewish people" are synonymous. This must surely be considered to be miraculous. Amazingly, the Holocaust, which was dastardly, and ruthlessly designed to cleanse the world of the Jewish race, became the very instrument to shame the United Nations into bringing Israel back to nationhood.

Israel now stands as a focal point of controversy and of conflict upon the stage of world history. There appears to be no enduring solution to the present conflict. But one thing is clear: it is perfectly legitimate to raise questions of justice to both sides of the present Jewish-Palestinian dispute.

At its roots, we realize that the main source of the problems in the Middle East may well be spiritual. Indeed, the Lord revealed to the Jewish patriarchs His desire for a benevolent relationship with other Semitic nations (Gen. 17:4-8). Has the hope of *one new humanity* become more possible now than in any previous age? Only God knows, and only God knows how that may be possible.

Surely such a union could not happen apart from some sort of divine involvement. And that would certainly be considered to be one more moment of light in the prophetic story of restoration.

The thought of Jewish and Gentile people coming together under the Lordship of Christ and sharing a common destiny does not sit well with present-day dispensationalists. (They are a faction arising from millennial thinking). Their idea is that Jews and Gentiles have two distinct destinies in latter days, *as well as in eternity*. As such, the church and Israel are not united in a common future.[13] Of course this entire reasoning does not fit into the one story at all. The first Adam was given an apostolic commission that was certainly passed on to Abraham, and all of his successors including Jesus, the kingly son of Judah.

One thing is very clear. From a theological perspective, it is inconceivable to think of a joyous and triumphant procession to a New Jerusalem that is not led by Jesus, the remnant servant-figure of Judaism. Nor would it be conceivable to think of that glorious procession bereft of great masses from among the Jewish people. Jesus must be at the head of this glorious procession because He is the real Adam. He is reclaiming, by resurrection, a better Eden. The old Jerusalem will not do. He is the One who leads from captivity *one new humanity* that is brought together in Him. "My kingdom is not from this world." (Jn.18:36)

Christ's victory was won at a cross. Maybe it isn't coincidental that Charles Ryre, an exponent of dispensationalism, in his summary of its major tenets, omits the crucial revelatory moment of all restoration history: the resurrection of Jesus Christ.[14]

A Better Eden?

Initially, there was nothing wrong with the old Eden; after all, God said that it was *very good*. The dance was a warm embrace of all essential relationships. However, in the light of God's redemption and restoration in Jesus, the question may well be posed. The new Eden is the focus for a redeemed community that once more is united with God. Its gates have been reopened by God through the victory of the resurrection.

The biblically consistent picture is one in which the Groom and the bride dance and fellowship together at the eternal wedding feast. The table is the very place where all eternal relationships are restored. Whatever difficulties we may have in interpreting symbolic, biblical literature, the common imagery of God's triumph is very apparent to one Jew of ancient antiquity: "For I am about to create new heavens and a new earth; the former things shall not be remembered or come to mind. But be glad and rejoice forever in what I am creating; for I am about to create Jerusalem as a joy, and its people as a delight" (Isa. 65:17-18).

From a scientific point of view, Hugh Ross tells us that God didn't just pick the best planet from all the space junk that existed; He fine-tuned His creation to make our planet a fit dwelling place. "The remoteness of the probability of finding a planet fit for life suggests that the Creator personally and specially designed and constructed our galaxy group . . . and Earth for life . . . While there is not the remotest chance that the natural conditions and physical laws of the universe will spawn a planet capable of sustaining physical life, there is nothing to stop the Creator of the universe from miraculously designing several planets, rather than just one planet, with the capacity to support life."[15]

"Then I saw a new heaven and a new earth; for the first heaven and the first earth had passed away, and the sea was no more. And I saw the holy city, the new Jerusalem, coming down from out of heaven from God, prepared as a bride adorned for her husband" (Rev. 21:1-2).

Much of the imagery in apocalyptic literature is highly symbolic; it is therefore open to a wide variety of interpretation. However, our primary purpose in examining such imagery is to glean from it a picture of how *the original purposes in creation* have been restored. Clearly, much of the imagery provides an impression of how the restoration may appear.

Our struggle is also one of discerning how such symbolism is consistent with the one story of the Bible. This imagery is often a poetic way in which to illustrate the reality that *God has secured His purposes.* The Lord is sovereign and His purposes have not failed. God has placed Jesus, the Lamb and the real Adam, in the central position of the restored creation. We will look briefly at eight biblical images of consummation.

First is Jesus, the real Adam, Who reigns with His saints in the new heaven and earth. His work is complete, and the victory has been won. The human community has been restored in order for it to take charge of a garden that will, once more, be the focus for innocent worshippers of a universal priesthood (Isa. 65:17-18; Dan. 7:13-14, 22; Zech. 14:4-5; 1 Cor. 15:24-25; Rev. 5:9-14; 11:15).

Clearly, its inhabitants are not spending eternity learning how to play harps. Once more they are embracing the dance of innocence in *worship,* i.e., the *work* of sustaining essential relationships. The apostolic mission is now complete, and the full number has been gathered in.

Interestingly, the *manner* in which final restoration is secured is the same as it was in the beginning. It is the power of the Word (Gen. 1:3; 1 Thess. 4:16; Rev. 19:11-16). Restored humanity returns to the open gates of a new Eden to delight in the *majesty of God's light and glory* (Zech. 14:7; Rev. 21:9-11).

As in the days of Eden, so, in the New Creation, there is no need for a temple: "And I saw no temple in the city, for its temple is the Lord God the Almighty and the Lamb" (Rev. 21:22). Truly, our New Jerusalem is above and is free. There is no longer need for the focus of God's presence to be centered in a building; it is there in the living *shekinah* presence of God and the Lamb who eternally dwells in His people.

No longer do we hear of moments of light; restoration heralds an eternity of Light!

First-day Light now saturates everything, including the people dwelling in God's restored creation. The sacrificed Lamb, the real Adam of creation, takes the seat of royal authority, and He reigns with God in the new creation. Where there were once four pillars of Israel, *there are now just two pillars of new creation.* The One Human Being, the One who has proven His submission to God, becomes Zion's assurance that God's haunting question of the old order, "Where are you?" will *never be posed again.*

As it was on the first day of creation, the Light of God's glory baptizes the everlasting dawn of creation's new day. The prophet Isaiah had already anticipated that there would be no longer need for natural light of the fourth day (60:19). Time would no longer be governed by fourth-day light, but by the first-day Light of God's glory. Somehow, the direct presence of God's reflected light and glory is all the energy needed to keep the new creation in Light forever.

In the vision recorded in the Apocalypse, there is also no more sea (Rev. 21:1). Disorder, resistance, and disobedience to God no longer dominate the passage ways of life. For Habakkuk, the waters of tranquility cover a troubled sea in a world that is filled with the knowledge of God's glory (Hab. 2:14). It is a picture of order. "And the city has no need of sun or moon to shine upon it, for the glory of God is its light, and its lamp is the Lamb" (Rev. 21:23; see also Isa. 60:19).

Second, where the sovereign Lord reigns, there is no place for tears, death, pain, or sorrow (Isa. 61:1-2; 1 Cor. 15:25; Rev. 7:15-17; 21:3-4). Although a theology of eternal life is underdeveloped in all of Isaiah, the third Isaiah receives a glimpse of some form of a New Jerusalem existing in a condition of exquisite concord (Isa. 65:20).

However, the New Testament shows us clearly that citizens of the kingdom live without sorrow forever. Time is no longer an enemy; it never ends. Its ability to spawn the terror of decay has been defeated. Humanity receives possession of the restored DNA of life in a dimension of time that is restored as an eternal friend.

Third, the dysfunctional humanity once driven from Eden is now repentant, redeemed, restored, and unified in a new order of community in the New Jerusalem. The dream of the psalmist has been realized. Even beyond the parameters of his vision, everyone will be in a unity, focused in Christ (Ps. 133:1; Rev. 21:22). Jesus, the royal judge as in days of Israel's kings (2 Sam. 15:2; 9:8), now reigns at the seat of justice (Ezek. 34:23). Clearly, there is no longer need for *a book*, for the everlasting Word and Way is ever in the presence of Zion's inhabitants.

The prophetic vision of Isaiah may well possess far more ramifications than he had envisaged:

> In days to come the mountain of the Lord's house shall be established as the highest of the mountains, and shall be raised above the hills. Many peoples shall come and say, 'Come, let us go to the mountain of the Lord. To the house of the God of Jacob; that he may teach us his ways, and that we may walk in his paths.' For out of Zion shall go forth instruction . . . He shall judge between the nations and shall arbitrate for many peoples; they shall beat their swords into ploughshares, and their spears into pruning hooks; nation shall not lift up sword against nation, neither shall they learn war anymore. (Isa. 2:2-4)

In order to enter the city of glory, the Royal Watchman has secured reconciliation and justice at its gate. This situation was secured besides a hill outside of Jerusalem; it was called Calvary. But imagine being in a situation where everyone you meet has a heart desire to serve you! And, even Jesus, *our Lord and Brother!* (John 13:14).

Maybe the great Arbiter of justice has very little to do. After all, the primitive impulse to settle disputes through warfare has now been abandoned (Isa. 2:4). The Lord reigns, and He sits as the focus and source of love and unity for His beloved bride.

As on the day of Pentecost, all the saints sing the songs of praise (Rev. 7:9-10). The songs focus on the Lamb of God. Jerusalem is truly above and is free. Its paths are trodden by the redeemed. There are no ravenous beasts of prey. The lion lies down with the lamb. Singing and everlasting joy reigns in the hearts of Zion's people (Isa. 35:8-10; 65:25; Rev. 21:27).

Fourth, the New Jerusalem has twelve apostolic foundations and twelve gates; they are inscribed with the names of Jacob's sons. Surely, the twelve by twelve (144 in Revelation 7:4 and 14:1) represent a perfect number of the new Israel, consisting of Jew and Gentile in one community. All the inhabitants have been redeemed by the blood of the Lamb (Rev. 14:3). Together, they are ready to lead a number *beyond count* (Rev. 7:8). "A great multitude . . . from every nation, from tribes and peoples and languages, standing before the throne and before the Lamb, robed in white with palm branches in their hands" (Rev. 7:9).

The pivotal foundations and the ever-open gates bear the name of Jew and Gentile as one, all being of the *sons of God*. New Jerusalem's gates of pearl indicate that the redeemed of Israel hold a place of glory, while connected to the city's foundations. Universal unity has been restored in a reconciled body of one humanity (Matt. 19:28; Jude 3; Rev. 21:12-14).

Through this body focused in Jesus, the real Adam, the apostolic commission of creation has been completed. Once more, we may hear God's triumphant shout of joy, "It is very good!"

Unwavering recognition of Christ as Lord is the premise upon which the *entire community* of the redeemed enjoys unity with God and with each other. Jesus, the Lamb of God, is indisputably the focus of mediatory unity in the new Eden.

Fifth, there is but one tree here: it is the Tree of Life, and it holds enormous significance for the universal community. Nobody is interested anymore in a tree that offers only natural ability and inferior glory. Mysteriously, the Tree of Life lies on both sides of the river. Its waters flow from the throne of God. This picture is an assurance that no one in God's Eden can be cut off from a life soaked in glory. As all have access to it, the river of life flows east, west, north, and south.

Jesus is the Tree of Life! "I am the vine, you are the branches . . . apart from me you can do nothing" (John 15:5). The purposes of the sovereign God are restored. The New Jerusalem really is the new Eden with healing streams of life flowing to every part of the new order. And every part of the new creation has its roots in this tree (Gen. 2:9; Rev. 22:2).

The Tree of Life produces twelve kinds of fruit—the entire year is filled with abundance for the whole community—and the leaves of the tree are for the healing of the nations. It represents the restored apostolic community that offers healing for all peoples. From this tree, all creation is nourished from its Source. All creation is dependent upon it!

Of course, this imagery belongs to the original Eden. Ezekiel sees this picture as that of a temple of hope for the people who are in diaspora (Ezek. 47:12). However, the apocalyptic vision of restoration in the New Testament shows the temple of Ezekiel to be neither ideal, nor yet complete.

Admittedly, and in hindsight, we realize that the Jerusalem that comes down from heaven really is free (Gal. 4:26). The restoration of the old Eden is deliberately incomplete in the vision of Ezekiel. Its primary purpose is to offer hope to a beleaguered people bereft of their focus in Zion. In the New Jerusalem, there is no need for a temple at all (Rev. 21:22-23). God and the Lamb become the temple, its light, and its glory (Rev. 22:5). We note that Ezekiel's temple of hope continues to require a priesthood offering now-obsolete sacrifices of redemption. Only in the obedient sacrificial work of Jesus may it be said, "It is finished!"

Sixth, an undivided river, a symbol of eternal unity, now flows through the New Jerusalem, replacing the imagery of old Eden's river of life (Ezek. 47:1-9). Zion's river of life has no streams branching from it, at least not in the new Eden. It is a single river providing everlasting sustenance and hope to a city that is at unity in itself (Gen. 2:10-14; Zech. 9:10; Rev. 22:1-2, 14). But this river flows out from the throne of God and through the streets of Zion. The purpose of the river is to feed the entire new creation stretching from east to west (Zech. 14:8). The worship of Jerusalem's citizenry is never exhausted because the worshippers possess an everlasting thirst for the inexhaustible riches of God (Rev. 7:15; Eph. 2:7).

Interestingly, Jesus waited until *the last day of the festival* to invite the celebrants to drink: "Let anyone who is thirsty come to me, and let the one who believes in me drink" (John 7:37-38). "But those who drink of the water that I will give them will never be thirsty. The water that I will

give will become in them a spring of water gushing up to eternal life"
(John 4:14).

Jesus is the River of Life! Basil the Great is surely correct in suggesting
that eternity will never be exhausted by our desire to know Him.

Seventh, in the original Paradise, Eve was presented to Adam as
his bride. Now, the real Adam is the Groom Who presents His bride,
the church, to God. Christ's offering is one of praise and thanksgiving
because He, with its citizens, in the priestly fashion of innocence, ever
presents a new creation back to the Source and Author of life (1 Cor.
15:23-24). Once again, a royal priesthood, fitted for the new creation,
walks in harmony with its Creator in the garden He has prepared for
them (John 14:2; 1 Cor. 15:44).

Eighth, God has restored a people to the realities of new creation. This
creation constitutes God's original meaning and purpose for humanity
(Rev. 5:10). Here, the citizenry of this new creation can touch, taste, see,
and smell. This is no Sheol!

The creation story tells of God creating physical beings (fashioned
from clay) who were originally intended to be at home in a *physical world*.
If the restoration of our humanity is something other than as physical
creatures, touching the earth of new creation, then God would surely
have failed to demonstrate His sovereign purposes. His involvement
upon the pages of history would not have achieved what He intended at
the beginning.

But, through the death and resurrection of Jesus, God has insisted
in playing out the entire duration of the dance. *He became the perfect
summary of the story.* God allowed Himself to become vulnerable to the
greatness and ego-motivation of human choices. But its joys and tragedies
had to be played out. Otherwise, the love required for perfect freedom to
exist, would merely have been a cruel joke on the part of God.

Once again, there is communal, environmental, cosmic, and personal
harmony. The inhabitants of the new creation are fully in step. In total
unity, they embrace the eternal dance of creation's innocence. Once

again, the essential relationships of creation are working together in an awesome dimension of praise and worship.

How can Jesus, the very heart and life of this one story, ever be compared with any other figure of any other religion? "They saw no one with them any more, but only Jesus" (Mark 9:8).

In the light of God's activity throughout this biblical view of time's theological seasons, Jesus Christ cannot simply be considered to be the best news on the block—He is the Good News for every block!

CONCLUSION

Eternity in First-Day Light

*T*he Lord reigns! His sovereign purposes for harmonious relationships in creation have been accomplished in Jesus Christ. This one story has not been a fairy tale. How dare we arrogantly compare it with a human construction such as Camelot? The biblical story does not have a conclusion with a vague and fruitless hope residing in a future, younger generation.

Didn't God have all His desired elements in place at the beginning? This is a real story emerging from real facts concerning God's involvement in history. The beginning of creation's story and its meaning can now be understood in the very life, death, and resurrection of Jesus Christ, the One Who leads the dance for all ages.

Just because God is omniscient and is our omnipotent Lord doesn't mean that what He won in Jesus didn't come at considerable cost to Himself. God became vulnerable for us. Latter days have proven a Camelot hope to be naive and fruitless. But in God's one story, the zeal of the Lord Almighty has accomplished this (Isa. 9:7). God has secured and restored His eternal victory of reconciliation in Jesus Christ (Phil. 2:6-8, 10-11; 2 Cor. 5:19).

Satan, the spiritual source of perversity in the old order, is now destined to spend all eternity in the company of other spiritual creatures;

they share his self-perverted and ego-centered nature. What an indescribable hell that must be! Satan has lost his place in heaven (Rev. 12:7-9) and, because he is *a spirit being*, is destined to spend all eternity, or part of it, in that spiritual condition of eternal torment (Rev. 20:10).

After embracing the vision of God's holiness, His majesty, and His awesome presence, was it possible for Isaiah to say no to the Almighty One? Undoubtedly, he could have responded negatively, or else there would not have been a need for the question to be posed (Isa. 6:8). However, what we learn from this encounter is that, in community, the closer we abide in the Light of God's glory, the less likely is the desire to make self-centered decisions.

Otherness is of the essential nature of humanity, inbreathed with the very nature of the Trinitarian God. In the new creation, the man Christ Jesus forever points to the awesome, holy, and majestic presence of God's Light and glory. Indeed, I suspect that, being privileged to encounter the awe-filled and ineffable holiness of God, my soul-searching questions will seem trivial and unimportant. That's what happened to Job, and he was only privy to the wonders of the old order!

We have seen clearly that *freedom of choice is at the very heart of kingdom life.* It is a vital principle of life in a creation dominated by the power of love. There can be no love where there is no freedom. There can be no freedom where there is no choice.

The tree that represented the knowledge of good and evil no longer appears in the new creation of Revelation. *But this doesn't mean that the ability to make choices has gone.* True and loving relationships must entail the freedom to choose. Surely, without this ability, an important principle of creation would be abolished. If Satan has lost his place in the new creation, does that mean its citizens are no longer tempted?

Choices now arise from a redeemed and restored nature. Out of freedom, Eden's citizens choose to serve one another. Having once seen the horrendous consequences of self-focused decision, this restored citizenship of memory would most surely desire the superiority of love's enormous power. Jesus, the real Adam, still challenges His community: "If you love me you will keep my commandments" (John 14:15). Like the king of the old Israel, Jesus sits at the gate to mediate differences that may result in disharmony. (2Sam.19:8)

Obeying the command of the King is still a matter of choice. Having been redeemed and restored in Jesus, and now tasting the unimpeachable joy of essential relationships, we will *eternally remember* the awesome penalty and futility of resisting the astounding power of God's loving commands.

While we are in this present time, all people are invited to *choose Christ* in response to His finished work. Clearly, we understand that there are consequences associated with the choices we make. If the church is truly to be a prophetic voice and a light to the nations, then at every opportunity *the primary apostolic invitation must be extended.* But, in the new order of restoration, we realize that God's purposes for His creation have been secured in Jesus, the Lamb of God.

The Lord's sovereign purposes have been accomplished. The wolf lies down with the lamb (Isa. 65:25). God's reborn creatures feed off new creation's eternal banquet of innocence, The celebration of Holy Communion had formerly been a foretaste and sign of the eternal and heavenly banquet. All creation is once more in a perfect state of *harmonious relationships* under the Lordship of the real Adam. No longer are citizens of the new order separated by the barriers of language. The calamities of Eden have been reversed in the finished work of Christ. And, as the Light of God's glory was the manifest sign on the first day of creation, so it is the everlasting Light on the *endless first day* of restoration.

There will be a profound reality of a continuing priesthood operating in the ministry of worship and praise. The right number has been gathered in. All of the redeemed are eternally free to make *creative choices* under the loving lordship of Christ.

We have not been called to be mindless, moronic robots. Here is an astounding paradox: when our hearts are primarily set on love for the Lord and the glory of His kingdom, questions concerning our trust for God are subsumed in the astounding truth that *God really trusts us!*

Yes, at the present, inferior decisions may be made; prideful motivations may surface; sin will surely creep in. But the Lord Jesus is always with us (Matt. 28:20). By the power of the Holy Spirit, it really is possible for God's community to live in signature of life in the new Eden.

Love is Life, and Life is Love; and the greatest of all is love (1 Cor. 13:10, 13).

Love is the overriding force that permeates everything associated with the *perfect*—that is, the new creation under the headship of Jesus (1 Cor. 13:10).

The one story of creation, redemption, and restoration has been presented in the analogy of a collage. An impressionistic Picasso may have left us with a story that was vague and open to an infinite variety of interpretations. This one story may have appeared too elusive to discern very clearly. A Constable may have left us passively with so much detail that little room is left for questions, untidiness, personal choices, or meaningful involvement.

Some people may prefer that easier and stifling approach. But what we see in God is the Creator who doesn't offer Abraham a blueprint. He offers a Way, a Direction, and a presence (see also Ex.33:13-14, Jn.14:6). The fact is, the story of a pilgrim people was often very untidy and wayward, but the prophetic sign of God's original direction was always apparent before them. Just as there was need for a Good Friday in order to experience Easter Sunday, the corollary was that the path of the Way had to be walked by faith in order for the full picture to appear.

The idea of putting together the pieces of a collage reminds us much more of the picture into which Christ came. Sometimes there are bits that don't contribute to making sense of the one story. How do we know how to extricate those bits from the panoramic arrangement?

In this book, I have pointed out very strongly that the criterion for evaluating each piece of the picture is what it contributes to declaring Jesus Christ to be *the meaning and focus of all history*. He is the beginning and the end (Rev. 1:8, 17). He is, therefore, truly our Savior, Lord, and King. He is the way, the truth, and the life. If any pieces do not contribute to the development of this picture, then they don't fit God's one biblical story at all.

With questions on their minds and with faith in their hearts, martyrs of old died in the belief that God, *in Christ alone*, made sense of history. They died with the word *Maranatha* on their lips. It was not a whimpering cry of defeat. It was a triumphant affirmation of hope in the ultimate meeting with Christ, the Lord of new creation. "Maranatha, come quickly Lord Jesus," was the summary statement of lives offered in thanksgiving for God's salvation. It was also a cry of thanksgiving because creation's meaning had been restored in the Alpha and the Omega of life (Rev. 22:13).

Paradoxically, the garden in which we presently walk is both tragic and beautiful. On the one hand, it is racked with the ravages of death and decay. It groans in pain and travail while it also pants in the memory, yet glorious anticipation, of new creation. Although signs of glorious light seem to be fast diminishing in a return to darkness and chaos, there still remain magnificent icons of God's sustaining love and glory.

We have not yet arrived at the point where we cry in desperation for the mountains to fall on us (Luke 23:30). But the signs are ominously near. As servants of the Lord Jesus, we have yet much to offer God through the glorious freedom of loving and joyous stewardship. In the process of trusting that the sovereign God is victor, with martyrs and confessors of every age we are given the assurance that "we are more than conquerors through him who loved us" (Rom. 8:37).

Our goal, our prize, and our joy, will be God Himself; God alone!

Harmoniously and in faith, we resonate with all creation in a benedicite of praise, "O all ye works of the Lord, bless the Lord. Praise Him and magnify Him forever."[1]

"The Spirit and the bride say, 'Come.' And let everyone who hears say, 'Come.' And let everyone who is thirsty come. Let any one who wishes take the water of life as a gift" (Rev. 22:17).

And so, in this eternal outburst of praise, we who are alive and remain join with all creation in our longing for the Sovereign One, who says: "'Surely I am coming soon.' Amen. Come, Lord Jesus" (Rev. 22:20).

"God saw everything that he had made, and indeed, it was very good" (Gen. 1:31).

Like the poor man who was invited to stand at Abraham's side (Luke 16:23), we are called to live in the glorious promises given to all of Abraham's descendants (Gen. 12:3; Isa. 27:6; Gal. 3:29).

By God's grace, through Jesus, we are invited to enter into the glorious Light of the first and eternal day! (Rev. 21:23)

An Invitation to Accept Jesus Christ as Savior and Lord

*P*lease read the following and, when you can make these words your own prayer of commitment, offer it to God. This, or a similar prayer, is one of dedication that you will repeat many times in your relationship with God.

Heavenly Father, I thank you for loving me. Thank you for sending your Son so that I may enter a new life of eternal relationships. Lord Jesus, I come to your cross, to the place where I may begin again. I ask you to forgive me for all the sin of the past, and for all that has offended you and hurt others. Please forgive me, and set me free from the pain of broken relationships. Thank you for your forgiveness. I ask you to come into my life to be my Savior and my Lord, now and forever. Thank you, Lord Jesus, because you are now in my life. By the power of the Holy Spirit and through your church, enable me to be conformed to the image of Christ, to follow and serve you all the days of my life. Amen

ASSURANCE

The following verses of the Bible are *assurances* that God has heard and answered your prayer:

1 John 1:9
Revelation 3:20
John 15:14
Acts 2:38

I urge you to join a church where the authority of the Bible is held high, and where a home-group-based congregation provides an avenue for a life of growth in discipleship and in your priestly service to almighty God.

3. Robinson, J.A.T. *In The End God*, pp.91-92.

(1) Most Greek texts, including the Nestle-Aland 1983 edition, use the word, sunestaeken. It's important to note that this verb is used in the perfect tense which would mean that the meaning of a past event is still effective for today. Molton's Analytical Greek Lexicon translates its root to mean, 'to place together,' but in its specific use for this text, 'to have been permanently framed.'

v1. "Destroy this temple, and in three days I will raise it up . . . But he was speaking of the temple of his body." (John 2:19,21) Note, Jesus said this in the context of His cleansing the old temple, which He correctly predicted would be destroyed. In John 11, after the raising of Lazarus, Jesus connected the new temple, in his body, with the resurrection. From that time on, the religious establishment "planned to put him to death." (v.53) In Rev. 21:22 there is no temple in the vision of restoration. ". . . for its temple is the Lord God the Almighty and the Lamb." The Temple doesn't *contain* the glory; the Temple (Jesus) *is* the glory!

v11. The author's book, There Must Be Another Way, now revised as, The Church I Couldn't Find, is a call to Reformation in practice. It speaks of how churches may make disciples for a 21st century world. Published by Westbow Press, Bloomington, IN, 2013

v111. The Greek preposition, eis, is sometimes translated to mean 'one.' The KJV translates this as, 'one blood,' meaning that, through Christ, we are all descended from the stock of Adam-Eve relationships, i.e., "Sons and Daughters of God."

1x. There have been a number of attempts that try to show that Jesus never really died. They range from recorded accounts in Matthew 28:11-15 to Hugh J. Schonfield's,

The Conspiracy of the Empty Tomb
x. In the Book of Revelation this raising from the dead is for the purpose of a second death. (Rev. 20:14)

x1. See courses by Charles Alexander; click "Resources" www.timothyministry.ca

x11. One such effective course, produced by the Timothy Institute of Ministry, is entitled, "Growing in Christ." Click on Resources at: www.timothyministry.ca

Resources by Charles Alexander
For congregational resources in developing effective disciples, and for useful aids in developing church-planting congregations, please see the author's Web page at www.timothyministry.ca.

Other books by Charles Alexander
Published by Essence-Guardian Books, Canada
Books may be obtained on Amazon/Kindle, or at local Christian bookstores.
Angels Don't Wear Shoes: A very light and humorous apologetic concerning Jesus—the focus of the entire spiritual quest.
The Church I Couldn't Find: It's so hard to find a church that actually operates on New Testament principles.

PREVIEW

*F*ormerly titled *Embracing the Dance of Eden,* much of this book is now revised and enlarged. A modern treatment of time clarifies remarkable second-reformation revelations regarding its meaning in relation to the one biblical story. Surprising interpretations emerge when this story is viewed from perspectives of God's "eternal nowness" and creation's unchanging principles. Some questions that emerge:

Predestination: Did the reformers get stuck in one place?

A place called hell: Does it really exist?

Chances of post-death repentance: Can a Hindu get to heaven?

How did Jesus descend into Hell?

Why are there no chances for a post-death repentance?

Immortality: Is it for everyone?

Miracles: How may ordinary people walk on real water?

One miracle: Why is the resurrection the key to life's meaning?

First-day Light and new creation: Who gets it?

Heaven: Did those people really see it, or was it a near-death experience?

Judgment: It's a lot sooner than you think.

Latter days: Is it reasonable to suggest that we are in them?

"My spirit goes to heaven": Why is that wrong?

Creation principles: Why mainline churches are in a mess because we don't know them.

Modern issues: Can an old book, like the Bible, speak to them today?

The biblical paradigm of Old and New Testaments: Isn't there a better one?

Time and the Bible: How does a modern view affect biblical interpretation?

ENDNOTES

Introduction

[1]   Hugh Ross, *Creation and Time* (Colorado Springs, CO: NavPress, 1994), 130.

[2]   Mark W, Worthing, *God, Creation, and Contemporary Physics* (Minneapolis, MN: Augsburg Fortress, 1996), 4.

[3]   Worthing, *God, Creation, and Contemporary Physics,* 5.

[4]   Hans Kung, *The Beginning of All Things,* trans. J. Bowden (Grand Rapids, MI: Eerdmans, 2007), 1.

Chapter 1: Getting on the Same Page

[1]   Peter C. Craigie, *The Old Testament* (Nashville, TN: Abingdon Press, 1986), 216.

[2]   Craigie, *The Old Testament,* 302.

[3]   John Meyendorff, *St. Gregory Palamas and Orthodox Spirituality* (New York: St. Vladimir's

[4]   Seminary Press, 1974) 109.

[5]   Ira Rifkin, *Spiritual Perspectives on Globalization* (Woodstock, VT, 05091: Skylight Paths Publishing, 2003), 44.

[6]   Richard Kennedy, *The International Dictionary of Religion* (New York: Crossroad, 1984), 48-49.

[7]   John R. W. Stott, *Understanding the Bible,* (Grand Rapids, MI: Zondervan, 1959), 221.

Chapter 2: It's About Time

1   Stephen Hawking, *A Brief History of Time* (New York: Bantam Books, 1990), 33.

2   Hawking, *A Brief History of Time*, 33.

✓3   Kung, *The Beginning of All Things*, 15.

4   Gregory E. Ganssle, ed. *God & Time-Four Views* (Downers Grove, IL: IVP Press, 2001), 23.

5   John Polkinghorne, *The Faith of a Physicist* (Minneapolis, MN: Fortress Press, 1996), 59-60.

6   Polkinghorne, *The Faith of a Physicist*, 81.

7   Bernard Haisch, *The Purpose-Guided Universe* (Franklin Lakes, NJ: Career Press, 2010), 20

8   John Macquarrie, *Twentieth Century Religious Thought* (London: SCM Press, 1983), 28.

9   Hugh Ross, *Beyond the Cosmos* (Colorado Springs, CO: NavPress, 1999), 46.

10   Clark H. Pinnock, *Most Moved Mover: A Theology of God's Openness* (Grand Rapids, MI: Baker Academic, 2001), 3.

11   Pinnock, *Most Moved Mover*, 32.

12   Hugh Ross, *The Creator and the Cosmos*, (Colorado Springs, CO: NavPress, 2001), 97.

✓13   Ross, *The Creator and the Cosmos*, 102.

14   Martin Gorst, *Measuring Eternity* (New York: Random House, 2001), 4.

15   Gorst, *Measuring Eternity*, 6.

✓16   Gorst, *Measuring Eternity*, 34.

17   Gorst, *Measuring Eternity*, 283.

18   Michael Green, *The Empty Cross of Jesus* (Downer's Grove, IL: Inter-Varsity Press, 1984), 62.

Chapter 3: Creation: When Time Was a Friend

1   Jack Finegan, *Myth and Mystery* (Grand Rapids, MI: Baker Book House, 1989), 34.

2   Kenneth Kramer, *World Scriptures* (Maywah, NJ: Paulist Press, 1986), 26.

3   Paul S. Davies, *God and The New Physics* (New York: Simon and Schuster, 1983), 223.

4   Ross, *Creation and Time*, 129.

5   Francis S. Collins, *The Language of God* (New York: Free Press, 2006), 206.

6   Kallistos Ware, *The Orthodox Way* (New York: SVS Press, 1986), 34.

7   Vladimir Lossky, *Orthodox Theology* (New York: St. Vladimir's Seminary Press, 1978), 52.

8   Frank Wilczek, *The Lightness of Being* (New York: Basic Books, 2008), 6.

9   Ross, *The Creator and the Cosmos*, 63, 95.

10 Denyse O'Leary, *By Design or by Chance* (Kitchener, ON: Castle Quay Books, 2004), 35.

11 Basil the Great, *On the Holy Spirit* (New York: St. Vladimir's Press, 1980), 38.

12 Ross, *Creation and Time*, 76.

13 Austin Farrer, *The One Genius* (London: S.P.C.K., 1987), 2.

14 Rick Warren, *The Purpose Driven Life* (Grand Rapids, MI: Zondervan Press, 2000), 22-23.

15 Hexham, Irving, Pocket Dictionary of New Religious Movements. IVP, Downers Grove, IL 2002, p.51

16 Wilczek, *The Lightness of Being*, 186.

17 Ross, *Creation and Time*, 139.

18 F. L. Cross and E. A. Livingstone, eds. *The Oxford Dictionary of the Christian Church*, rev. ed. F.L. Cross and E.A Livingstone, Published in the United States by Oxford University Press, New York, 1983), 129.

19 Lee Strobel, *The Case for a Creator* (Grand Rapids, MI: Zondervan, 2004), 191.

20 Collins, *The Language of God*, 106-107.

Chapter 4: First-Day Light on a Glorious Priesthood

1   Hawking, *A Brief History of Time*, 9.

2   Ware, *The Orthodox Way*, 64.

3   Lossky, Vladimir, The Mystical Theology of the Eastern Church, SVS Press, New York 10707, 1976, p.134

4   Early Modern Homo sapiens, BBC webpage: http://anthro.palomar.edu/homo2/mod_homo_4.htm

5   Kung, *The Beginning of All Things*, 164

6   Kung, *The Beginning of All Things*, 164.

7   Kung, *The Beginning of All Things*, 165.

8   Strobel, *The Case for a Creator*, 23, 44, 45, 238.

9   O'Leary, *By Design or by Chance*, 238-240.

10 Collins, *The Language of God*, 187.

11 Thomas Smaille, *The Forgotten Father* (London: Hodder and Stoughton, 1980), 12.

12 Collins, *The Language of God*, 260.

13 John T. Robinson, *In the End God* (London: Fontana Books, 1968), 89.

14 As quoted in Michael Marshall, *The Restless Heart* (Grand Rapids, MI: Eerdmans, 1987), 78.

Chapter 5: How Did Time Become an Enemy?

1 Kenneth Latourette, *A History of Christianity*, rev. ed. Volume 1 (New York: Harper and Row, 1975) 1:8.

2 Lossky, *Orthodox Theology*, 79.

3 The concept of there being two gods is based in Dualism. This idea took different directions and was conceived in different philosophies. For example, not only were there two "first causes," but these forces represent, on one hand, the idea of pure spirit being good, while on the other hand there was matter, which was essentially evil; mind and matter are both distinctly and unconnectedly real and opposite in nature.

4 Robert R. Capon, *The Third Peacock* (Garden City, NY: Doubleday & Co., 1972), 41.

5 Capon, *The Third Peacock*, 19.

6 C. S. Lewis, *The Problem of Pain* (London: Fontana Books, 1961), 122.

7 Peter C. Wagner, *Warfare Prayer* (Ventura, CA: Regal Books, 1992), 92.

8 Geerharder Vos, *Biblical Theology* (Grand Rapids, MI: Eerdmans, 1948), 44.

9 Gnosticism has many ramifications. Basically, it attempts to deal with questions of evil by separating pure existence (pure spirit) from matter, which is evil. *Gnosis*, or knowledge, is the key that liberates the soul on the path of perfection. Mind and matter are distinct entities. This knowledge is not commonly possessed, but is secret and passed on through ritual and secret ceremonies. And, in the belief that the soul is immortal, universalism holds the idea that the love of God is ultimately irresistible to everyone. Some even assert that Satan will also be won over by God's love-eventually!

10 Robinson, *In the End God*, 108.

11 Cross and Livingstone, *The Oxford Dictionary of the Christian Church*, 109.

12 John Calvin, who in some things was heavily influenced by Augustine, developed the thought that humanity was totally depraved, and therefore not capable of responding to good moral choices apart from the prevailing

grace of God. This thinking led to a theory of predestination, whereby he held that there were certain individuals who were "elected" to salvation. Of course this led to serious questions regarding humanity's capacity to exercise free will. However, many of his followers went further by developing a theory that if some were destined to be counted among the elect, then others were not (double predestination). Jacobus Arminius, another Dutch Reformer, reacted "against the deterministic logic of Calvinism." "The Arminians insisted that the Divine sovereignty was compatible with a real free-will in man; that Jesus Christ died for all men and not only for the elect." (Quotations from Cross and Livingstone, *The Oxford Dictionary of the Christian Church*, 90.) In this book, I have stressed that predestination is not so much about individual salvation, but the call of God upon His community.

13   Lewis, *The Problem of Pain*, 25, 27.

Chapter 6: First-Day Light on the Mountains of Israel

1   Graham Hancock, *Fingerprints of the Gods* (Toronto: McCelland Bantam, 1996), 208.

2   Ian Wilson, *Before the Flood* (London: Orion Books, 2001), 25.

3   Wilson, *Before the Flood*, 32.

4   Matthew Fox, *Original Blessings* (Santa Fe, NM: Bear & Company, 1983), 22.

5   John H. Marks, *The Interpreter's One Volume Commentary of the Bible: Genesis* (Nashville, TN 37202, Abingdon Press, 1989), 14.

6   Craigie, *The Old Testament*, 288.

Chapter 7: Who Is This Jesus?

1   Gardiner Day, *The Apostles Creed* (New York: Scribners, 1963), 58.

2   Meyendorff, *St. Gregory Palamas*, 38.

3   Vladimir Lossky, *The Mystical Theology of the Eastern Church* (New York: St. Vladimir's Press, 1976), 134.

4   Meyendorff, *St. Gregory Palamas*, 40.

5   N. T. Wright, *Who Was Jesus?* (Grand Rapids, MI: Eerdmans, 1992) 84.

6   Albert Schweitzer, *The Quest Of The Historical Jesus* (New York: MacMillan, 1968), 7.

7   Schweitzer, *The Quest Of The Historical Jesus*, 7.

8   Rudolph Bultman, *Jesus Christ and Mythology* (New York: Charles Scribner's Sons, 1958), 43.

9   Brown E. Raymond and John P. Meier, Antioch and Rome, Paulist Press, New York, 1983, 98

10   Meyendorff, *St. Gregory Palamas*, 123.

11   D. M. Baillie, *God Was In Christ* (London: Faber and Faber, 1961), 63-64.

12   Ross, *Beyond the Cosmos*, 119.

13   Raymond E. Brown, *An Introduction to the Gospel of John*, ed. Francis J. Maloney (New York: Doubleday of Random House, 2003), 47.

14   Robert M. Grant, *Historical Introduction to the New Testament* (New York: Harper and Rowe, 1963), 160.

15   D. Moody Smith, *John Among the Gospels* (Minneapolis, MN: Fortress Press, 1992), 75.

16   John A. T. Robinson, *Redating the New Testament* (London: SCM Press, 1984), 275.

17   Though the people of Islam, rather strangely, refer to Christians as "people of the book," we see that early Christian experience was not common on the basis of a book, but on the basis of a Person: Jesus Christ. Note that Islam also describes the Jews as "people of the book."

Chapter 8: Is He the Real Adam of God?

1   Kenneth Leach, *True Prayer* (Toronto: Anglican Book Centre, 1980), 6.

Chapter 9: When Is Redemption's Story Complete?

1   E. Shillibeeckx, Jesus (New York: The Crossroad Publishing Co., 1986), 296.

2   Shillibeeckx, Jesus, 297-298.

3   John A. T. Robinson, *Can We Trust The New Testament?* (Oxford: A. R. Mowbray, 1977), 114.

4   W. H. Vanstone, *The Stature of Waiting* (New York: Seabury Press, 1983), 17.

5   Vanstone, *The Stature of Waiting*, 21.

6   Vanstone, *The Stature of Waiting*, 5, 7.

7   Cross and Livingstone, *The Oxford Dictionary of the Christian Church*, 3.

8   William Temple, *Readings in John*, (Wilton, CT: Morehouse-Barlow Co., 1985), *Introduction*

9   Green, *The Empty Cross of Jesus*, 62.

10   Baillie, *God Was In Christ*, 185-186.

11   J. W. Stott, *The Cross of Christ* (Downer's Grove, IL: Inter-Varsity Press, 1986), 101.

12   Stott, *The Cross of Christ*, 123.

13   Elizabeth O'Connor, *The New Community* (New York: Harper & Row, 1976), 58.

14   For more, please read *The Church I Couldn't Find*, by Charles Alexander.

15   Bill Kaufmann, "Chronicle of Shame," *The Calgary Sun* (February 7, 2005), 15.

16   David Watson, *I Believe In Evangelism* (Grand Rapids, MI: Eerdmans, 1977), 12-13.

17   Donald C. Posterski, *Reinventing Evangelism* (Downer's Grove, IL: Inter-Varsity Press, 1989), 27-28).

18   George R. Hunsberger and Craig Van Gelder, *Church Between Gospel and Culture* (Grand Rapids, MI: Eerdmans, 1996), 23.

Chapter 10: The Time Road from Calvary to Hell

1   Anthony Bloom, *Meditations on A Theme* (London: Mowbrays, 1972), 118.

2   Bloom, *Meditations on A Theme*, 116.

3   Ross, *Beyond the Cosmos*, 126.

Chapter 11: Eternal Life: Is It for Everyone?

1   Hancock, *Fingerprints of the Gods*, 310-333.

2   John Blanchard, *Whatever Happened to Hell?* (Wheaton, IL: Crossway Books, 1995), 37.

3   Hancock, *Fingerprints of the Gods*, 417.

4   Sherman Netland, *The Unexplained: Immortality* (A&E Network, air date March 6, 1997),

5   Anita Bartholomew, "Life After Life," *Reader's Digest* (Canada) (October 2003), 144.

6   Strobel, *The Case for a Creator*, 249.

7   Strobel, *The Case for a Creator*, 257, 263.

8   Polkinghorne, *The Faith of a Physicist*, 21.

9   Polkinghorne, *The Faith of a Physicist*, 21.

10   Cross and Livingstone, *The Oxford Dictionary of the Christian Church*, 1144.

11   Cross and Livingstone, *The Oxford Dictionary of the Christian Church*, 1415.

12   Robinson, *In The End God*, 91-92.

13   Tom Wright, *Luke for Everyone* (London: SPCK, Westminster John Knox Press, 2001), 284.

14   Randy Alcorn, *Heaven* (Carol Stream, IL): Tyndale House, 2004), 41-76.

15   Clark H. Pinnock and Delwin Brown, *Theological Crossfire: An Evangelical/ Liberal Dialogue* (Grand Rapids, MI: Zondervan, 1991), 226.

16   Ross, *Beyond the Cosmos*, 209-211.

17   Ross, *Beyond the Cosmos*, 211-213.

18   St. Cyril of Jerusalem, *Lectures on the Christian Sacraments*, F. L. Cross, ed. (London: SPCK Press, 1977), 62.

19   J. I. Packer, *Crux*: "The Problem of Eternal Punishment," Crux, no. 3 (September 1990): 19

20   Blanchard, *Whatever Happened to Hell?* 56-57.

21   The following represents some concerns of others who oppose the view of annihilation. "For the annihilationist, there is no possibility of perfect justice or the rightings of wrongs. Good will remain unrewarded and evil unpunished. The serial murderer and the tiny child, the rapist and the kindly old lady, the ruthless dictator and the gentle nurse, everything they are and everything they have been and done will be wiped out of existence." Blanchard, *Whatever Happened to Hell?* 67.

22   Ross, *Beyond the Cosmos*, 208.

23   J. Stott and D. L. Edwards, *Evangelical Essentials* (Downer's Grove, IL: InterVarsity Press, 1988), 320.

24   Stott and Edwards, *Evangelical Essentials*, 314.

25   Stott and Edwards, *Evangelical Essentials*, 318-319.

Chapter 12: The Mystery of Time Restored

1   Rogers, Cleon L, *The Topical Josephus* (Grand Rapids. MI: Zondervan, 1992), 65.

2   Wright, *Who Was Jesus?* 74.

3   John Hick, ed. *The Myth Of God Incarnate* (London: S.C.M. Press, 1977), 59-60.

4   Basil The Great, *On The Holy Spirit*, 58.

5   Lossky, *The Mystical Theology of The Eastern Church*, 137.

6   Lossky, *Orthodox Theology*, 62.

7   Ross, *The Creator and the Cosmos*, 111.

8   Bloom, *Meditations On a Theme*, 119.

Chapter 13: Pentecost: An Awesome Moment of Light

1. Morton T, Kelsey, *Tongue Speaking* (Garden City, NY: Doubleday & Co., 1964), 35.

2. C. K. Barrett, *Peakes Commentary on the Bible: The Gospel of John*, ed. Matthew Black and H. H. Rowley (London: Thomas Nelson and Sons, 1964), 867.

3. Stott and Edwards, *Evangelical Essentials*, 26.

4. Sam Wellman, *Wesley* (Philadelphia: Chelsea House Publishers, 1999), 107.

5. Richard F. Lovelace, *Dynamics of Spiritual Life* (Downers Grove, IL: Inter-Varsity Press, 1979), 125.

6. St. Cyril of Jerusalem, *Lectures on the Christian Sacraments*, 50.

7. George Maloney, *Simeon the New Theologian, The Discourses (Introduction)*, (New York: Paulist Press, 1980), 16.

8. George Maloney, *The Mystic of Fire and Light* (Denville, NJ, Dimension Books, 1975), 12.

9. Ronald A. N. Kydd, *Charismatic Gifts in The Early Church* (Peabody, MA: Hendrickson Publishers, 1984), 9.

10. Kydd, *Charismatic Gifts in the Early Church*, 17.

11. Kydd, *Charismatic Gifts in the Early Church*, 44.

12. George Williams and Edith Waldvogel, *The Charismatic Movement* (Grand Rapids, MI: Eerdmans, 1975), 66.

13. Williams and Waldvogel, *The Charismatic Movement*, 83.

14. Kelsey, *Tongue Speaking*, 46.

15. Kelsey, *Tongue Speaking*, 168.

16. Ware, *The Orthodox Way*, 134.

17. Maloney, *The Mystic of Fire and Light*, 82

18. L. J. Suenens (Cardinal), *A New Pentecost* (New York: Seabury Press, 1975) 34, 35.

19. Robert E. Webber, *The Younger Evangelicals*, 3rd ed. (Grand Rapids, MI: Baker Books, 2003), 109.

20. A. M. Allchin, *The Kingdom of Love and Knowledge* (New York: Seabury Press, 1982), 38.

Chapter 14: From Latter Days to the New Eden

1. Hans Kung, *Why I Am Still a Christian?* (New York:Bloomsbury Academic, 2005), 28.

2. George E. Ladd, *A Commentary on the Revelation of John* (Grand Rapids, MI: Eerdmans, 1972), 14.

3   Ladd, *A Commentary on the Revelation of John*, 11.

4   Ladd, *A Commentary on the Revelation of John*, 11.

✓ 5 Robinson, *In The End God*, 105.

6   Ladd, *A Commentary on the Revelation of John*, 7.

7   Merrill C. Tenney, *New Testament Times* (Grand Rapids, MI: Eerdmans, 1965), 368.

✓ 8 8 Olsen, Ted, *"Go Figure,"* Christianity Today, (Web page: www.christianitytoday.com/ct/2011/april/gofigure-apr11.html 3/20/2013- originally posted 3/28/2011).

✓ 9 Margaret Munro, "Escaping methane adds to Arctic's climate worries," *The Times Columnist* (March 8, 2006), A2.

✓ 10 *Water, Water: The Water Apocalypse* (The Discovery Channel, air date April 14, 2006. Host: Mark de Villiers).

11   Reuven Doron, *One New Man* (Cedar Rapids, IA: Embrace, 1993), 31.

12   Norma Archbold, *The Mountains Of Israel*, 3rd ed. (Atlanta, GA: A Phoebe's Song Publication, 1993), 25.

13   Charles Ryrie, *Dispensationalism* (Chicago: Moody Press, 1966), 39.

14   Ryrie, *Dispensationalism*, 212.

15   Ross, Hugh, *The Creator and the Cosmos*, 198-199.

Conclusion: Eternity in First-Day Light

1   General Synod of the Anglican Church of Canada, *The Book of Common Prayer*, First Edition, Toronto, General Synod of the Anglican Church of Canada. 1962), 26.

CPSIA information can be obtained at www.ICGtesting.com
Printed in the USA
LVOW12s1944240813

349392LV00003B/9/P